The Case
Against Israel

MICHAEL NEUMANN

CounterPunch

The Case Against Israel

Michael Neumann

CounterPunch
PETROLIA

PRESS

First published by
CounterPunch and AK Press 2005
© CounterPunch 2005
All rights reserved

CounterPunch
PO Box 228 Petrolia, California, 95558

AK Press
674A 23rd St, Oakland, California 94612-1163

AK Press UK
PO Box 12766, Edinburgh, Scotland EH8 9YE

ISBN 1-904859-46-1

ISBN-13 9781904859468

Library of Congress Control Number: 2005935384

A catalog record for this book is available from the
Library of Congress

Typeset in *Tyfa*, designed by Frantisek Storm for The
Storm Type Foundry, and *Stainless*, designed by Cyrus
Highsmith for The Font Bureau, Inc. Cover and Title
Page also use *Amplitude*, designed by Christian
Schwartz for The Font Bureau, Inc.

Printed and bound in Canada.

Design and typography by Tiffany Wardle.

Cover Design by Tiffany Wardle.

Contents

Preface **1**

Introduction **3**

Part I: Zionism and the Birth of Israel

The Zionist Project **11**

Consequences of Zionism **41**

A Verdict on Zionism **67**

Part II: The Current Situation

The Occupation **93**

The Settlements **107**

Palestinian and Israeli Alternatives **129**

Palestinian Attitudes and Strategies **143**

Terror **155**

Other Reasons for Supporting Israel? **171**

Afterword **193**

Sources **195**

Endnotes **199**

Index **215**

Preface

I T IS CUSTOMARY FOR WRITERS ON TOUCHY SUBJECTS TO LAY OUT THEIR biases before proceeding. Mine are pro-Israel and pro-Jewish.

My parents were German Jews, and my family on both sides —three sides, counting my German Jewish stepfather—suffered greatly under the Nazis. Some of my relatives sought refuge in Palestine in the early 1930s; some of their descendants are Israeli citizens. So naturally I was initially well disposed towards Israel, which promised never to let the horrors of the past repeat themselves. I also felt no sympathy for the Palestinians: losing their land seemed a trifle compared to the sufferings of Jews, Gypsies, and others in Europe. Though a leftist in the sixties, I never joined the fashion for applauding Palestinian terrorism at that time.

Readers can judge for themselves whether my prejudices have induced me to let Israel off too lightly. In any case, I use no material from Palestinian sources. Reports based on Palestinian testimony are included only if they come (a) from neutral non-Palestinian individuals or organizations such as Human Rights Watch and Amnesty International, and (b) from Israeli or Jewish sources.

One more thing about bias: I find that Israel and Zionism were unequivocally in the wrong throughout its history. I find the faults of the Palestinians minor by comparison. Does this mean that I am biased in favor of the Palestinians?

No doubt a biased pro-Palestinian view of the conflict would arrive at the same conclusions. No doubt it is possible that, despite my claim to the contrary, I am biased in favor of the Palestinians. But to suppose that my conclusions themselves constitute proof of, or even strong evidence for such bias would be moronic. If you've robbed my house, and the judge correctly finds that you did so, his judgment may or may not be biased, but the finding itself is no evidence of bias at all. Maybe the judge was simply right. Maybe Israel is simply guilty. To show that I am biased would require more than showing that I invariably criticize Israel and not the Palestinians. It would require showing that I do in fact have pro-Palestinian interests or motives, or that I evaluate the evidence unfairly. Even that, of course, would not show that I am wrong.

Many people were immensely helpful in the preparation of this text. One person was invaluable. In today's climate, to acknowledge them by name would only expose them to persecution.

Finally, this book presents the case against Israel, not Israelis. Some Israelis are responsible for the present situation; some are not. Just as the existence of many decent Israelis does nothing to justify Israel's policies, so the wrongness of those policies cannot condemn its entire population.

Introduction

THIS ESSAY SEEKS TO LAY OUT A COMPREHENSIVE CASE AGAINST Israel; that is, to argue that Israel is, generally speaking, in the wrong in its conflict with Palestinians. The Palestinians, I will claim, are generally speaking in the right. There are grey areas in this black-and-white landscape: no doubt the Zionists at times did something right, and the Palestinians something wrong. But it is definitely the Palestinians, not Israel, who deserve the world's support.

Thousands of people have written on this topic: why me? Some write, not because they have any particular expertise, but because they have strong convictions gathered from a variety of sources. There is nothing at all wrong with this. A non-expert can make good use of expert sources, and I hope this is also true in my own case.

Other authors do have some particular and relevant expertise. They are historians, political scientists, Arabists, and so on. I am none of these, but the question I—and most others—address is not historical or a matter for political scientists. Nor is it a question about the nature of the Middle East. It is not about what happened, or about political structures, or about culture. It is about what *ought* to happen: what *ought* to occur in Palestine? What solution to the conflict *should* be adopted? While the expertise of historians, political scientists and Arabists is extremely valuable in coming up with the answer, it is not sufficient, and here I might have some contribution of my own to make.

I am a moral and political philosopher: if I have an expertise, it is in moral and political argument. Examining the work of other writers, on my own side as well as on the Zionist side, I find much of what is said has far less relevance to the question of what *ought* to happen than is generally supposed. But in the end, this is what we want to know. I hope to show this and to show that, when the real question is kept firmly in mind, the Israel/Palestine conflict is not so complex as it has been made out to be.

Assumptions

As much as possible, my factual assumptions are not particularly controversial. They are supported by the writings of respectable historians and journalists, mostly Jewish. This is not to say that their work has gone unchallenged by Zionists, but rather that it has not been refuted or severely criticized by non-Zionists. In most cases, the historical claims are also consistent with the work of Zionist historian Benny Morris. Where he and they disagree—for example, where Norman Finkelstein criticizes Morris' reading of Zionist intentions in 1948—I have not needed to rely on his critics' material. As for the attacks on Morris by Zionist historians such as Efraim Karsh, they center on the details of the 1948 fighting and on the question of when, if ever, the Zionist leadership had a full-blown policy of transfer. My arguments do not depend on such matters.

Where morals are concerned, I have attempted to argue only from similarly uncontroversial principles. I assume, for instance, that there is some basic right of self-defense that on occasion permits a violent response. I assume that one group can't normally acquire the power of life and death over another without their consent. I also make assumptions that are not quite so innocuous, especially that the rightness or wrongness of an action is to a large extent a matter of its consequences rather than of the intentions that motivate it. Another assumption is that one is responsible for the foreseeable consequences of one's action, even if those consequences depend on the reactions of others to what you do. These, however, are mainstream views in moral philosophy, contested but also very widely accepted. They are entirely independent of more extreme consequentialist doctrines such as utilitarianism. I myself believe that ethical judgments may well report *some* sort of facts, and that they are objective in the limited sense that they do not merely express the sentiments of the one making the judgment. These beliefs have little bearing on the arguments I offer below.

What is not discussed

There are irrelevancies and irrelevancies. A couple of topics are so tangential to the Israel/Palestine conflict that I will use this space to explain just that—rather than discuss them in the body of the text.

Anti-Semitism

The claim that opposition to Israel is anti-Semitic is unworthy of discussion for two reasons. First, it is patently false. Since not all Jews are Israelis or supporters of Israel, to be against all Israelis or Israel is not to be against all Jews. Second, opposition to Israel is almost always opposition to Israeli policies, not to the existence of Israel, and it is often held that such policies are in fact harmful to Israel, Israelis and Jews. These claims can hardly be considered anti-Semitic. Indeed the accusation can hardly be made in good faith.

No doubt many anti-Semites oppose Israel, and do so for anti-Semitic reasons, and conceal their motives. None of this is relevant to whether or not Israel is in fact in the wrong. No doubt many people opposed Japanese fascism for racist reasons. It does not follow that such opposition was mistaken.

The Case Against Israel

Legal niceties

I follow the judgment of responsible organizations such as Human Rights Watch and Amnesty International in their claims that Israel commits human rights violations and war crimes. Beyond this, I do not discuss whether Israel violates international law or convention, for three reasons. First, if these are taken as serious legal claims, then the matter must rest with the experts. But, second, it is hard to take international law very seriously. It has no central authority to enforce it. The UN, an obvious candidate, is unavailable because the most powerful countries can veto any sanction they dislike, whether against themselves, their clients, or their friends. There is also no authoritative source of interpretation. International tribunals are not universally accepted as unimpeachable arbiters of the law, and their standards of evidence are, to say the least, relaxed compared to the criminal law of many nations. In these circumstances, it is always possible to quibble and get into tangled legalistic—not legal—arguments. This would be true of pretty much any accusation brought against pretty much anyone.

The third reason I do not discuss legal issues is the simplest and most important: sometimes the law is wrong. There is absolutely no ground for supposing that merely because a practice (apparently) contravenes international law, it is therefore wrong: one could well imagine, for example, urgent interventions to prevent gross cruelties that violated the privileges of the sovereign state that was perpetrating them. I, therefore, confine my attention to moral and political argument, not legal disputation. Any reference to the legitimacy of Israeli actions or of the state of Israel itself should be understood in this spirit.

For similar reasons, I say virtually nothing about UN resolutions or the Balfour Declaration. Resolutions, like laws, might enjoin what is right or what is wrong, might rest on true or false premises. The exclusion of UN resolutions turns out to be even-handed: it means that the UN was not in a position to legitimate the foundation of the state of Israel, but also that I do not rely on its numerous resolutions condemning Israeli actions. As for the Balfour Declaration, what on earth—other than some quaintly medieval "right of conquest"—would give England the right to determine the destinies of the Middle East? England itself, with American coaxing, implicitly rejected such a right when it went along with Woodrow Wilson's Fourteen Points after the First World War. In any case, England's stab at redrawing the maps of its conquests has resulted in multiple catastrophes, and one might well think that the Declaration—a source of unending micro-interpretation—belongs to the same class of bumbling, well-meaning but arrogant misdeeds.

A sketch of the main argument

WHAT I WILL SEEK TO ESTABLISH IS THE FOLLOWING:

The Zionist project, as conceived and executed in the 19th and early 20th century, was entirely unjustified and could reasonably be regarded by the inhabitants of Palestine as a very serious threat, the total domination by one ethnic group of all others in the region. Some form of violent resistance was, therefore, justified. That Zionists Jews, and Jews generally, may later have acquired pressing reasons for wanting a Jewish state does not change this. The illegitimacy of the Zionist project was the major cause of all the terror and warfare that it aroused.

Sometime in the late 1970s or early 1980s, there was a fundamental change in the situation that is reflected in the organization of this essay. Israel's existence became as secure as any state has a right to expect. Its settlement policy was not defensive but a form of ethnic warfare, and, therefore, outrageously wrong. The Palestinians were justified in claiming that once again some sort of violent response was not only permissible, but necessary. Moreover, all this holds regardless of whether the previous arguments hold: regardless of whether the Zionist project was justified.

Though these arguments are easy to sketch, to fill them out takes much time and space. This is because so many irrelevant issues are raised, on every occasion, when the Israel/Palestine conflict is discussed. It is essential to show that these issues are indeed irrelevant. I will do so by addressing a quite large number of specific questions. The answers will both reduce the discussion to relevant points and justify the premises of the main argument.

The essay has two main parts. The first discusses Israel's foundation and the issues it raised. The second discusses the current situation.

Part 1:
Zionism and the Birth of Israel

The Zionist Project

To some, Zionism conjures up an image of fresh-faced pioneers in short pants, turning the desert to green. To others, it means a Merkava tank running over a wheelchair-bound civilian.[1] For now, Zionism will be taken to imply that there is a people, the Jews, who have a right, one they should exercise, to a homeland in the Land of Zion, that is, in Palestine.

The legitimacy of "Zionism" in this sense is almost a dead issue. It is not directly relevant to the most pressing issue in the Israel/Palestine conflict: whether or not Israel should withdraw from the Occupied Territories. If the Jews have a right to a homeland in Palestine, they might still have no right to the Occupied Territories. Conversely, Israel could have a right to the Occupied Territories even if the Jews did not have a right to a homeland in Palestine. For example, some argue that Israel's right to the Occupied Territories rests on the entitlements of any state to its own defense; these entitlements don't depend on the legitimacy of Zionism. On the Palestinian side, the Palestinians could have a right to the Occupied Territories even if the Jews had a right to a homeland in Palestine, or no right even if the Jews had no right to those territories either.

But the legitimacy of Zionism has considerable *indirect* relevance to the current Israel/Palestine conflict. In part this is because few consider solutions to that conflict from a purely practical standpoint. Most commentators don't simply ask what division of land and sovereignty will bring peace. They also want to know to what extent each party is in the right. The legitimacy of Zionism looms large in this area. It has much bearing on such issues as whether the "Arabs" have been unreasonable and paranoid, whether they are violent and warmongering, whether they are willing to make peace, whether they are willing to keep it. (I will argue later that such willingness is in fact inessential to a solution, but most people do not and will not share my point of view.) And, of course, similar questions arise with respect to the Israeli government as a standard-bearer of Zionism. If Zionism is or was a legitimate project, then there will be a much stronger case for solutions that maximize Israel's strength, preserve it as a *Jewish* state, and advance the Zionist cause.

Zionism is, in important respects, far from unique, and its defenders use this. Why, they say, shouldn't the Jews have a right to a homeland? Doesn't every people have this right?

Self-Determination

The question cuts both ways. If no people have this right, neither do the Jews. (They might have a right to Palestine for some other reason, but not this one.) I will argue that, in the sense relevant to the Israel/Palestine conflict, no people have this right. Each individual person certainly has a right to live somewhere, but an ethnic group has no right to live somewhere together. From a narrow point of view, this should not be very controversial: no one seems to think that all Italians, all over the world, have a right to live in one huge nation, excluding all others. If they all want to go back to Italy, fine, but certainly they expel others to make room in their "homeland," or expand that homeland to fulfill the project of reversing their Diaspora. And if all Italians were to travel to some distant planet, they might have a right to it. But that right would rest on the fact that they got there first, not on some right to all live in the same place, just because they were all Italian. If twenty Italians got there first, they might own the whole planet and could determine who lived there. They would not have to admit all Italians on the basis of some right of all Italians to live together in one place.

But these objections take the right of a people to its homeland too literally. What is really meant, when such a right is proposed, is that peoples have a right to determine their own future, their own affairs. This alleged right was given international standing at the Versailles peace conference in 1919. Woodrow Wilson, speaking in support of this agreement, referred to

> the sacredness of the right of self determination, the sacredness of the right of any body of people to say that they would not continue to live under the Government they were then living under, and under article eleven of the Covenant they are given a place to say whether they will live under it or not.[2]

and in his famous Fourteen Points he had this:

> An evident principle runs through the whole program I have outlined. It is the principle of justice to all peoples and nationalities, and their right to live on equal terms of liberty and safety with one another, whether they be strong or weak.[3]

Though his statements are less than entirely explicit, it is generally supposed that "Woodrow Wilson made self-determination an inalienable right for disenfranchised peoples around the world."[4] The UN Charter states that one of the purposes of the United Nations is "To develop friendly relations among nations based on respect for the principle of equal rights and self-determination of peoples."[5]

But neither international approval nor the United Nations' Charter are sufficient to bring rights into existence: If the UN said that people had a right to eat their children, would that make it so? There is no right of self-determination of peoples. The whole idea is a bad one.

The ideal known as "the self-determination of peoples" is built on myths of unanimity. Its models include:

THE AMERICAN FANTASY Soberly determined merchants team up with rangy, sharp-shooting settlers to throw off the British yoke and found a nation. Women sew flags.

THE ENGLISH FANTASY Sturdy yeomen and Protestant martyrs throw off popery and foppish tyranny to found a nation.

THE GENERIC EUROPEAN FANTASY Stocky peasants and wavy-haired intellectuals yearn to achieve their destiny, recorded in long, mercifully un-translated Romantic epics. They are suppressed by nasty bureaucratic monarchies or Ottoman Turks.

THE REST-OF-THE-WORLD FANTASY Clumsy, naïve intellectuals with heavy accents and peasants in relatively colorful dress have caught the fever. They band together to found a nation.

Despite the fact that many popular nation-building movements don't center on the ballot box, self-determination is typically identified with democracy. Real-life historical events such as the French or Russian revolutions, where the masses gravitate towards dictatorship, don't get counted. Bloody class warfare, even if it seems to involve a people determining its destiny, is not on the menu. The bloodless English revolution of 1688 is part of self-determination, but not the nasty civil war, a few decades earlier that made 1688 possible. The Cuban and Chinese revolutions also fail to make the grade.

These exclusions protect a Wilsonian daydream from far uglier realities. One can understand why: it's such a nice dream. Taken as a mere ideal, there is absolutely nothing wrong with at least some forms of self-determination. Nothing else considered, it's great if peoples determine themselves.

In exactly the same sense, there is nothing wrong with the ideal of what might be called "racial liberation." There are imaginary cases, which make the liberation of one race from another sound very attractive. What *if* race A does everything in its power to dominate everyone in general, and race B in particular? Race A might spare no opportunity to control the economy of country B (the homeland of race B), to destroy race B's culture, and to instill race B with habits damaging to its prosperity and its future. In fact, race A might be out to enslave race B and eliminate any of its members who resist. Nothing else considered, it would be great if race B liberated itself, even if that required using violence. Taken as a mere ideal, there is absolutely nothing wrong with "racial liberation."

But "racial liberation" is, of course, very close to Nazi ideology.[6] There is a great deal wrong with pretending this ideal applies to the world, with propagating such an ideal, and with attempting to implement it. This is because the ideal does not in fact apply to the world. Even granting that there are such things as races, they don't, as a matter of fact, act collectively, much less act collectively to wipe out other races. And there *is* no race A out to do such dire things to race B. There are only racist individuals, perhaps belonging to some race A, who sometimes try to do these things. It is these individuals who must be constrained, not race A. Moreover, spreading such an ideal invites its misapplication, with terrible results. Attempting to implement the ideal will lead to disaster. Much the same can be said of the Wilsonian ideal of self-determination.

Perhaps at some points in world history there have actually been peoples who had to be free to determine their destiny. Perhaps this could be done without creating innocent victims. One can imagine that, in the distant past, there were two tribes, each homogeneous and unanimous in their interests as well as their desires. Geography and other circumstances allowed each to establish an independent homeland, and to do so without harming one another. But if so, history has not provided any authoritative account as opposed to pleasant myths—of such doings.

Instead, circumstances arise—if not inevitably, all too frequently—that are concealed by a fatal ambiguity in the word "people." Suppose someone speaks, for instance, of the self-determination of the German people. There is a sense in which self-determination might be a legitimate goal for Germans: the sense of "people" where "German" simply means inhabitant of Germany. But this is typically *not* the sense of people used when self-determination is at issue. There are, as German nationalists said, Germans living in Poland, Austria, Russia, and other parts of Europe, just as there are Mexicans living in the United States of America.

There are certainly countries that *already exist* in which "people" has a civic rather than an ethnic significance. "Canadians" or "Americans" often has a civic meaning, and democracy is considered to respect the right of these "peoples" to determine themselves. But when one speaks of *creating* a country, or adjusting its borders, the "self-determination of peoples" has a sinister undertone. It amounts to advocating the assignment of territory and political power according to ethnicity, as close to race as makes no difference. When someone says that a people's sovereign territory is too small, or that they should have such a territory, you can bet the people are an ethnic group, not merely the inhabitants of certain districts. The self-determination of the Croatians was not understood to include that of the Serbs within what was traditionally considered Croatia, and the self-determination of the Sudeten Germans was not considered to include that of the ethnically non-German inhabitants of Sudentenland. The self-determination of several Eastern European peoples was considered quite compatible with the continued persecution of gypsies who had long inhabited the same region. When people speak so innocently of the right of self-determination of the Xians, they ought to realize that they are advocating the political supremacy of an ethnic group.

If ever a road to hell was paved with good intentions, this is it. Here history itself speaks loudly enough to require no additional argument. If Wilson did not see this in 1919, there is no excuse for not seeing it after 1939. No greater monument to human stupidity and ignorance can be conceived than the frequent and blithe espousal of ethnic nationalism today.

Even if there were something right with the self-determination of ethnic groups—that is, with granting political supremacy to such groups in certain regions—noble theory would be defeated by ignoble practice. The state of Yugoslavia was proclaimed in 1919 by the Yugoslav National Council. The Western powers recognized this product of self-determination and for many years it seemed that there was a Yugoslav people. Today the use of such a phrase would be a rather good but bitter joke. Algeria was liberated for the Algerians, but who were they? The exclusion of the colonial *pieds-noir* is one thing; the bitter conflict between Berbers and those considering themselves Arabs is quite another. The self-determination of the Americans notoriously excluded slaves and native Americans; the self-determination of the Indian subcontinent was a blood-drenched discovery that this was not, after all, one people. These were all cases where self-determination began as an inclusive, multiethnic affair; they ended displaying all the worst features of ethnic nationalism. Where self-determination has from the beginning a predominantly ethnic character, the results are often so bad that we do not call them by their true name. But the emergence of a truly Turkish state in the 1920s or the attempts to form a truly Hutu state in the 1990s, despite huge ethnic massacres, were as much an example of a people's self-determination as anything Wilson sponsored. These cases are not exceptions; they are the rule. At best, the self-determination of peoples has been a smokescreen for bitter religious or class warfare, as it was during the English and French revolutions. The world has long since progressed beyond a patchwork of isolated, "racially pure" enclaves. With this progression, the self-determination of peoples has not and cannot avoid its share of horror. The propagation of an ideal with such a baleful influence on reality cannot be a bright idea.

When Zionism is seen as the self-determination of a people, it is plain that people is used in its worst, most clearly ethnic sense. Zionism has never been a movement for the defense of the Jewish religion; on the contrary, many of the most religious Jews abhor it. It was never even a movement in defense of some cultural entity: when the Zionist movement began, Jews had no common language and their traditions were in many cases wildly dissimilar or simply abandoned altogether. Zionism was a movement that advocated not so much the defense of an ethnic group, as the formation of such a group in Palestine, where those who thought to fit a certain semi-racial category were to find refuge. It was a lovely dream where all Jews would live happily together and, with typical Wilsonian obliviousness, no one seemed to notice that those who did not pass ethnic muster had no place in this fantasy. If they were to be tolerated, welcomed, even loved, it was to be at the good pleasure of the Jews. Of that there could be no mistake. This is exactly the sort of vulnerable subordination that Jews, quite understandably, were trying to escape. "Trust us, we'll be nice" is not a promise endorsed by the historical record.

Zionists respond with fury when their movement is identified with racism. Many ethnic supremacists do. They protest that they do not advocate their own superiority, but simply want a land or culture or country of their own. But that is of necessity a land in which one race is guaranteed supremacy: whether or not this is on grounds of intrinsic superiority hardly matters. And that such movements and attitudes gain respectability is not the fault of the Zionists, much less of the Jews, but of an idiotically false tolerance of ethnic nationalism.

When some members of a group claim to be fighting for the self-determination of their people, ignorant outsiders rush in with their stamp of approval. Since in these cases it is precisely an ethnic state that is lacking, the community leaders or representatives are nothing of the sort: they represent only a particular faction with a particular agenda. Thus, the membership of what are considered mainstream Jewish organizations doesn't greatly exceed the membership of dissident Jewish groups.[7] Similarly, the European ethnic nationalists of the 1930s were bitterly opposed by millions belonging to their respective ethnic groups; white nationalists certainly don't represent the white race, and African nationalists often stand for ethnic warfare rather than for their people. The self-determination of peoples is not a reality but a smokescreen for extremists who may sometimes be a majority but who certainly have no right to portray themselves as the treasurers of some rich heritage to be projected into some future cultural and political renaissance.

There are cases where what may be *perceived* as the self-determination of peoples is a legitimate enterprise. For many, the Cuban or Algerian revolutions, or the Vietnamese war against colonial and American occupiers were so perceived. But their justifications rest on non-ethnic rights—the rights, for instance, of those who happened to inhabit these countries—not on a supposed right of a supposed ethnic or cultural entity to determine its destiny.

We are taught to laugh indulgently when the invariably anxious, invariably worldly-wise ethnic mother or grandmother bemoans the very thought of her darling child marrying an ethnic outsider. We are taught to sympathize with the desire to keep a culture intact. But—also invariably—the culture is not intact: in the modern world, there are important class differences, subcultural differences, religious differences. Above all, the cultures or peoples are by now impure, and there are always battles within a people about this. Invariably, the culture that ethnic nationalists seek to preserve is not a live natural phenomenon but something whipped up from a faded, largely falsified past to serve a suspect political agenda. Granny is a nasty racist; she should be treated as such. Other grannies—certainly many other Jewish grannies—deplore her attitudes.

Were cultures ever so pure, ever so intact, it would make little difference. The world has not given us the luxury of separate playgrounds. We have to live together, and a division of culturally or ethnically distinct states could be sustained only by continued purification campaigns and the suppression of ethnic minorities. To this we certainly have no right. Peoples do not, for this reason, have the right even to decide whether or not to maintain their ethnic purity: it is only individuals who may decide to do this. Zionism can, therefore, not be justified according to some right of self-determination of peoples.

Jews and Palestinians as peoples

Before leaving the general area of self-determination, it is necessary to look at a question that continually surfaces in the Israel/Palestine conflict—to what end, I am unsure. It is often said that the Palestinians were not a people. The most notorious example of this vague ploy is a 1969 remark by the then Prime Minister of Israel, Golda Meir:

> It was not as though there was a Palestinian people and we came and threw them out and took their country away from them. They did not exist.[8]

This might be a good time to remind non-Jewish readers that the Yiddish term "chutzpah" does not, as sometimes supposed, mean something like "endearing insolence"; it just means "insolence". That's what we have here. The need to debate Meir's contention is obviated by, among many other sources, the impressive work of Baruch Kimmerling and Joel S. Migdal, *The Palestinian People: A History.* They provide authoritative and utterly convincing evidence that yes, there was indeed a Palestinian people. Even without opening the book, one might wonder how there could be a Palestine—the term appears throughout Zionist literature—without Palestinians, or what possessed the British to refer to "representatives of the Palestinian people" in 1939.[9] But the persistence of Meir's type of argument suggests that we should consider whether it is even worth debating these matters.

When it is said that the Palestinians are not a people, or were not a people when the Zionists settled in Palestine, there are limits to how much the words can wash away. This much seems beyond dispute: before the Zionists came, there was a bunch of people who lived in the area. Whether they were called Palestinians, whether the area was called Palestine, whether the people in this area considered themselves a people, Palestinian or otherwise, are all questions without the slightest importance when assessing Zionism. There was no United States of America before the American revolution, so, of course, no one could consider himself an American in the sense of being a citizen of a place called the United States of America. No one suggests that, for this reason, these revolutionaries somehow had less legitimacy for not being identifiable in this fashion. No one suggests they were any less entitled to reject subjugation by the British. What people are called, whether there is a name for the area in which they make their home, whether they have some sort of national self-consciousness—none of this has any bearing on whether they must accept, not merely settlers in the general vicinity, not merely settlers who intend to become predominant in the region, but settlers who propose to install themselves as sovereigns over that area. And today the identity of Palestine or the Palestinians has absolutely no bearing on whether Israelis should control the territory they occupy or the people within it.

Suppose, for example, that there exist four peoples with different ethnic designations in four adjacent areas designated A, B, C, D. These peoples have no common identity, no common culture or history, and have never formed a sovereign state. In fact, not even these four areas have such identity, culture, history, or political autonomy. Suppose that some other group of people seeks to form a nation by taking a chunk from each of the four areas. We could describe this region as *A-chunk-B-chunk-C-chunk-D-chunk*. The region as a whole has no name. Its inhabitants belong to no single ethnic group. Suppose that the occupying group excludes from sovereignty the actual inhabitants of this region. There is nothing in this story that excludes the right of the inhabitants to resist this project, because no one should be forced to submit to another's sovereignty in such circumstances. Having a project to inhabit a certain region in no way entitles you to wield the power of life and death over its current inhabitants, or for that matter to give them a choice of submission or departure. Since your project is illegitimate, it may be resisted just as fiercely as any other project that gives someone, illegitimately, the power of life and death over your existence.

Before leaving this topic it might be useful to note that the Jews, too, might not be a people. It would not be enough to be co-religionists, like the Catholics, who are also not "a people." But of course the Jews are not all co-religionists because some are not religious, and this was certainly the case even in the 19th century. (Besides, what of all the diaspora Jews who became Christian? Would they too have a right to a homeland in Palestine?) When Zionism got started, the Jews did not have a common language—modern Hebrew did not exist. They still have no common language, since millions of Jews speak not a word of Hebrew. Jews did not have a common culture: Moroccan, Russian, and English Jews lived in worlds apart. They did not have a common history: for some, persecution was a bitter reality and for others, full citizens of their countries, a distant memory. They not only lacked a national state, but the desire for such a state: that was the project of a few European upper-middle-class activists.[10] Many Jews were fervent nationalists or patriots for the countries they inhabited; others were fervent internationalists; most were not interested in such matters. And, of course, they did not live in one geographical area.

There is a big difference between a minority wanting to be a people and actually being one. Most of these differences have increased rather than diminished with the evolution of Israel. That most North American Jews are fervent supporters of Israel does not trump the fact that Jews are, for the most part, members of other peoples: American Jews are Americans; Mexican Jews are Mexicans, and so on. They have rights of citizenship in their respective countries; they speak the language of those countries (most don't speak Hebrew or Yiddish); they are increasingly secular and, therefore, lack whatever bond religion might impart. They have no collective institutions, either political or cultural. They have no leaders. The rise of Israel has created not a Jewish people, but an ethnically diverse Israeli people, of whom 20 percent are non-Jewish. So, perhaps Zionists should not be too upset if one does not accept a politically viable right of the self-determination of peoples.

The Zionist Project

As an exercise in self-determination, it seems that the Zionist project was illegitimate simply because all such projects are. But perhaps Zionism can be seen in other ways. Certainly, there are Zionists such as Noam Chomsky who believe that some socialist variety of Zionism was justified. Is that so? The answer requires a closer look at what Zionism is and must be.

The definition of "Zionism" and the characterization of the Zionist project have been, almost from the beginning, a highly politicized affair. To some extent, some Zionists have always wanted to soft-pedal or even conceal their true objectives. This is not particularly nefarious; it is a standard political tactic. Today, interestingly enough, it is the Merriam-Webster dictionary rather than some Zionist source that preserves the caginess of the old days:

> Zionism: an international movement orig. for the establishment of a Jewish national or religious community in Palestine and later for the support of modern Israel.[11]

The question here is the nature of the community envisaged. North America is dotted with little religious communities of Mennonites, Buddhists, and other sects. But this could hardly be what Zionists had in mind because such communities were nothing new in 19th century Palestine. Not only various Christians but orthodox Jews had established themselves there, some recently, some centuries earlier. (These communities may have predated Islam but not necessarily the ancestors of the now mostly-Islamic Palestinians.) Zionism portrayed itself as a something new, not as a mere continuation of this very low-key, small-scale, and intermittent process. So, we are left with the notion of a *national* community. What might this be? Very often we hear of a homeland for Jews in Palestine. Thus the *American Heritage Dictionary:*

> A Jewish movement that arose in the late 19th century in response to growing anti-Semitism and sought to reestablish a Jewish homeland in Palestine. Modern Zionism is concerned with the support and development of the state of Israel.[12]

Of course, the character of Zionism changed once there was a state of Israel to "support and develop," but could pre-Israel Zionism be understood as the quest for a homeland as *opposed* to a state? Was this to be a scattering of Jewish homes and farms, or a Jewish country with its own army, police, and government?

The complex story of the Zionist tactical decision to keep this question open is recounted in many histories.[13] Its intricacies need not detain us. Since neither the British nor the French were prepared to establish anything more than a semi-autonomous

Jewish district in Palestine under colonial administration, of course the Zionists initially pretended that they would settle for such an arrangement.[14] David Hirst, commenting on the vagueness of the Balfour Declaration,[15] says that

> The document bears Balfour's name, but in reality it was the Zionists themselves who, in very large measure, both inspired the Declaration and framed its text. It must be reckoned the finest flower of Zionist diplomacy at its most sophisticatedly ambivalent. ...suffice it to say here... that the Zionists who framed the declaration saw in it the charter of a future Jewish state...[16]

What can hardly be open to dispute is that, throughout their existence, the main Zionist organizations always worked for a Jewish homeland in the sense of a Jewish state, what we could call a "Jewish country." Though the Zionists occasionally tried to convince the British, French, and Palestinians otherwise, their intentions were scarcely secret. The founder of Zionism, Theodore Herzl, had already in 1896 written an essay called "Der Judenstaat." In it, he said:

> The Idea which I have developed in this pamphlet is a very old one: it is the restoration of the Jewish State. ... Let the sovereignty be granted us over a portion of the globe large enough to satisfy the rightful requirements of a nation, the rest we shall manage for ourselves.[17]

A mere community within Palestine was not going to be enough. In Tom Segev's words, "The final draft of the [Balfour] declaration did not give the Zionists everything they wanted: the British government stopped short of designating Palestine a Jewish state."[18] But the Zionists never lost sight of that goal.

That they made efforts to conceal this goal is also not open to dispute. Max Nordau, Herzl's vice-president at early Zionist congresses, wrote in 1920 that:

> I did my best to persuade the claimants of the Jewish state in
> Palestine that we might find a circumlocution that would say all
> we meant, but would say it in a way that would avoid provoking
> the Turkish rulers of the coveted land. I suggested "Heimstätte"
> as a synonym for state... It was equivocal but we all understood
> what it meant... to us it signified *Judenstaat* and it signifies the
> same now.[19]

The British were in on the half-hearted deception:

> As Lloyd George made clear, the British government, including
> himself and Balfour, always understood "a national home for
> the Jewish people" to mean a Jewish state, and that it used the
> circumlocution merely to deflect Arab opposition is clear from
> a memorandum of Herbert Young, a young Foreign Office offi-
> cial, in 1921: the problem of coping with Palestinian opposition
> "is one of tactics, not strategy, the general strategic idea... being
> the gradual immigration of Jews into Palestine until that
> country becomes a predominantly Jewish state. ...But it is ques-
> tionable whether we are in a position to tell the Arabs what our
> policy really means."[20]

The world—and the Palestinians—knew what was contemplated. Chaim Weizmann himself, the most cautious of the
Zionist leaders, let the cat out of the bag in 1919 when he told a
London audience that "I trust to God that a Jewish state will
come about; but it will come about not through political declarations but by the sweat and blood of the Jewish people."[21]
Looking back in 1949, he took pains to make clear that Zionists
always sought a Jewish state. Speaking of the controversies that
ruffled early Zionist meetings, he says:

> Yet it should be understood that we fought these problems out
> internally, on the floor of the Zionist Congresses. For we always
> recognized that the Congress had come to stay; we, not less than
> Herzl, regarded it as the Jewish State in the making, and what-

ever our differences with the "head of the State," we were forever strengthening the "State" itself, that is, the Zionist Organization and its parliament.[22]

So whatever others may have at various times wanted to believe, the homeland in question was to be a sovereign state. In fact, current historical debate is divided far less on this question (or on the question of whether Zionists saw a need to transfer of the Arab population out of Palestine[23]) than on the question of whether such a transfer was settled Zionist policy in 1947–48.[24] Benny Morris, even after his disenchantment with anti-Zionist historiography, says this of the Balfour Declaration:

> The key term, "national home," was clearly a euphemism for "commonwealth" or "state."[25]

For now all that matters is that from the beginning, when mainstream Zionists said they wanted a Jewish homeland, what they really wanted and what was clearly wanted, was Jewish sovereignty. Ben-Gurion was explicit in attributing this sovereignty even to the supposedly hesitant and moderate Weizmann:

> Weizmann's vision was linked wholly with Israel and there was about it a realism and more than one level. It was basically realistic because it saw that the ancient homeland of the Jews was the only land in which Jewish sovereignty could and must be revived, and that it was the only land for which the Jews would make the required effort.[26]

This comment comes from 1964, but was hardly a revelation. In the words of a textbook describing the situation at the time of the Balfour Declaration,

> Active Zionists were confident that with work and time a Jewish national state having all the rights and appurtenances of a typical European national state would be created. They worked toward that goal; many acclaimed it openly.[27]

The American Jewish philosopher Morris Cohen, writing on Zionism in 1919, took its objective of a Jewish state as common knowledge:

> Though most of the leaders of Zionism in America are sincerely and profoundly convinced of the compatibility of Zionism and Americanism, they are nonetheless profoundly mistaken. Nationalistic Zionism demands not complete individual liberty for the Jew, but group autonomy. ...A national Jewish Palestine must necessarily mean a state founded on a peculiar race, a tribal religion, and a mystic belief in a peculiar soil...[28]

Cohen's reference to "nationalistic" Zionism might lead one to think he recognizes some non-nationalist form of Zionism, but this is not the case:

> ...Zionism is not merely a philanthropic movement to help the homeless. It claims to be a solution to the Jewish problem; and its emphasis on Palestine rests on a nationalist philosophy which is a direct challenge to all those who still believe in liberalism.[29]

Zionism's very choice of Palestine presupposes, for Cohen, the intention to found a Jewish state.

A year later, in 1920, Lord Curzon wrote in a Foreign Office minute that "The Zionists are after a Jewish state with the Arabs as hewers of wood and drawers of water."[30] And indeed, the Zionists did "acclaim it openly": a British Commission of Enquiry cited with alarm a 1921 article in the *Jewish Chronicle*, which stated:

> ...the real key to the Palestine situation is to be found in giving to Jews as such, those rights and privileges in Palestine which shall enable Jews to make it as Jewish as England is English, or as Canada is Canadian.[31]

Remember that in 1921 England and Canada were seen as racially and culturally homogeneous sovereignties; a Jewish Palestine would be the same. Nor was the Commission seizing on some unimportant or unrepresentative outburst. Two years earlier, Weizmann had made clear, in a public and official statement, just what lay behind this phraseology. Here is Walter Laqueur's account:

> When a Zionist delegation appeared on 27 February 1919 before the Supreme Allied Council, Weizmann was asked by Lansing, the American secretary of state, what exactly was meant by the phrase "a Jewish national home." Weizmann replied that for *the moment* [my italics] an autonomous Jewish government was not wanted, but that he expected that seventy to eighty thousand Jews would emigrate to Palestine annually. Gradually a nation would emerge which would be as Jewish as the French nation was French and the British nation British. Later, when the Jews formed the large majority, they would establish such a government as would answer to the state of the development of the country and to their ideals.[32]

In other words, in time the Jews would, on their own, establish a state to their liking. Much is sometimes made of the difference between Weizmann and more assertive Zionists, but this passage indicates that the difference was between gradualism and more radical strategies. Except at the very fringes of the Zionist movement, the ultimate objective was never in dispute. When in 1939 the British stated that "it was not part of their policy that Palestine should become a Jewish state," the Chief Rabbi of Jerusalem tore up the announcement, the Zionists proclaimed a general strike, and there were demonstrations in which a British policeman was shot. Days later, several Palestinians were killed in terror attacks.[33]

It is, therefore, entirely reasonable to define Zionism as Zionists themselves define it today. (There may be other definitions, but the concern here is with politically relevant concepts rather than lexicographic niceties.) The Jewish Virtual Library says that:

> Zionism, the national movement for the return of the Jewish people to their homeland and the resumption of Jewish sovereignty in the Land of Israel, advocated, from its inception, tangible as well as spiritual aims. Jews of all persuasions, left and right, religious and secular, joined to form the Zionist movement and worked together toward these goals. Disagreements led to rifts, but ultimately, the common goal of a Jewish state in its ancient homeland was attained.[34]

For everyone who mattered, the homeland was always to be a state. And the essential element of this proposal is correctly and succinctly voiced by the Israeli Ministry of Foreign Affairs:

> Zionism is the national movement espousing repatriation of Jews to their homeland—the Land of Israel—and the resumption of sovereign Jewish life there.[35]

The ministry's statement echoes the 1948 "Declaration of the Establishment of the State of Israel," which said that:

> ...recognition by the United Nations of the right of the Jewish people to establish their State is irrevocable.
>
> This right is the natural right of the Jewish people to be masters of their own fate, like all other nations, in their own sovereign State.[36]

In these pronouncements lies the very heart of the Zionist project. It is implicitly understood by most writers on the Israel/Palestine conflict, but implicit understanding is not enough. *The central fact of the conflict is that Zionists sought sovereignty in Palestine.* From this, all else follows: the Arab response and all that came after it.

Demanding a state

If the importance of this fact has been ignored, it is probably because reassuring claptrap from our politicians down the decades has obscured what it is to live in a sovereign state. Academic sociology and political theory are much more hard-headed about this than "real-world" political rhetoric.

Here is what one academic says about the state, what we might call an independent and sovereign country:

> The concentration of all physical force in the hands of the central authority is the primary function of the state and its decisive characteristic.[17]

There's nothing here about standing for values, voicing the will of the people, advancing their interests, democracy, truth, beauty, justice or human rights. This is not an assertion of some cynical *Realpolitik*. The author does not suggest that we shouldn't judge states according to some high standard. He attempts to describe what we consider the minimum condition of being a genuinely independent country. He echoes the seminal work of Max Weber, who said:

> "Every state is founded on force," said Trotsky at Brest-Litovsk. That is indeed right. If no social institutions existed which knew the use of violence, then the concept of "state" would be eliminated, and a condition would emerge that could be designated as "anarchy," in the specific sense of this word. Of course, force is certainly not the normal or the only means of the state—nobody says that—but force is a means specific to the state. Today the relation between the state and violence is an especially intimate one. In the past, the most varied institutions—beginning with the sib [clan]—have known the use of physical force as quite normal. Today, however, we have to say that a state is a human community that (successfully) claims the monopoly of the legitimate use of physical force within a given

territory. Note that "territory" is one of the characteristics of the state. Specifically, at the present time, the right to use physical force is ascribed to other institutions or to individuals only to the extent to which the state permits it. The state is considered the sole source of the "right" to use violence. Hence, "politics" for us means striving to share power, either among states or among groups within a state.[38]

Do not be misled by Weber's references to legitimacy. He does not require that a state be legitimate. It need not have the right to use force; a "right" will do fine. People must acknowledge the authority of the state but that authority need not have any moral or constitutional basis. It is enough that there is general agreement: these institutions, these guys, are the boss. It is the successful *claim* of legitimacy, not its validity, that matters.

Weber believes that perceptions of legitimacy result from respect for tradition, the charisma of a leader, or a belief that the régime is legal. But whatever is sufficient to produce the perception also suffices to sustain a state. It may be that the population of the area simply thinks there is nothing to gain, and much to lose, from defying the powers that be. If in addition people feel that defiance would be foolish, irrational, then the state is perceived to be legitimate in the sense that rational prudence recommends obeying its commands. An invader who rules without laws or institutions, whose violence is so capricious and anarchic as to create chaos rather than government, heads no state. But suppose a hated dictator is considered by his subjects to be a usurper and to have no moral right to govern. As long as he rules through law and government, as long as his subjects acknowledge that they must submit because it would be crazy to do otherwise, he has got himself a state. A state requires the successful maintenance of law and order, and it requires *some* sort of *perception* of legitimacy. The minimal sort is a consensus that, for reasons of rational prudence, the ruler ought to be obeyed. It is not necessary for anyone to think he has a *right* to be obeyed. As long as people have beliefs that sustain "the concentration of all physical force in the hands of the central authority," there is a state.

So if Zionism attempted to establish a Jewish state in Palestine, it attempted to establish a Jewish monopoly on violence in Palestine. One might think this comes too quickly, or represents no threat: aren't many states constitutional, democratic, respecters of human rights? Why mightn't a Jewish state be like that?

It might, but not too much can be made of this. The constitutional or other guarantees offered by any state are revocable at any time—at least if, following Weber, we see the state as a human community rather than the realization of some idealized model. If the United States of America is necessarily something that conforms to its founding ideals, to what is described in its constitution, then without the Bill of Rights it ceases to exist. In fact, since the Bill of Rights is frequently violated, it may not exist right now. But that's an awfully idealized view of the United States. Normally we don't see a state as defined by its ideals. We'd admit that America, the country and the human community, could fall far short of its constitution and the high-minded values it embodies. From that less exalted standpoint, there is no state whose protections cannot vanish, and there never will be. That's why we cannot simply take it on faith that the citizens of a state—much less the non-citizens or second-class citizens within its borders—will always enjoy the protections they're supposed to be guaranteed.

There's always a way around your rights if enough people, or the right people, want to violate them. Americans or Canadians or the English could always decide to revoke their constitution and draw up a new one, perhaps specifying that redheads born on Tuesdays should be executed. If their constitution said no such law could ever be enacted, the Americans or Canadians or

English could decide that they wanted to change that provision. If the constitution specified that it could not be changed or abrogated, these would be empty words: sure it could. And, in practice, virtually any state—country—already has some recognized process whereby its constitution can be changed in fundamental ways. In the U.S. there are amendment procedures, and a later amendment can nullify a former: anything in the constitution can be changed, so no rights are really fixed. In Canada, if constitutional assemblies in every province turned homicidal towards certain redheads, nothing would prevent the Canadian constitution from be altered to accommodate this sentiment. So in some ways the whole notion of constitutional protections is an illusion. The *government*—the particular administrators of state power—may be constrained by the constitution of the state. But the *state itself*—the human community—is, everywhere in the world, an absolute dictator bound neither by morality nor by law. Even in the most impeccable democracy, there are ways to institute anything humans can do to one another. Frequently, as in the case of the democratic Weimar Republic of Germany, just invoking emergency legislation is quite enough to open the gates of hell.

A Jewish state

For the Zionists to demand a state, any state, was therefore no small thing for anyone—like the Palestinians—falling within its proposed boundaries. But what the Zionists demanded was a *Jewish* state. Whether this was racism is not of any immediate concern. For one thing, to say that something is racist is not, for many people, immediately to say that it is unjustified: there are those, for instance, who accept affirmative action as "reverse" racism yet still defend it. For another, the project might have begun as racist yet outgrown its racism by instituting sufficient protections for non-Jews. Or it might not have outgrown it altogether, but exhibited a form of racism that, though reprehensible, was not particularly virulent.[39] It, therefore, does not seem particularly fruitful to examine whether Zionism was racism.

What matters for an understanding of the Israel/Palestine conflict is rather what the expression "a Jewish state" would mean to any reasonable person. What, in particular, could the Palestinians reasonably expect when they heard that such a state was to be established in Palestine?

When a state is described in relation to the territory it controls, its ethnic character is open. The French state is not necessarily a state for some ethnic group called Frenchmen, just as the Belgian or Yugoslav or Jamaican state weren't states for ethnic groups of that name. But a Catholic state would be a state run by Catholics; a black state would be a state run by blacks; a heterosexual state would be run by heterosexuals. This could hardly be clearer: what would be Catholic or black or heterosexual about a state not run by at least some members of those groups? When, as in the post-World-War-I era, the ideology of self-determination added to the picture, the expectation develops further. Now it is that ethnic states would be run, not just by *members* of their ethnic groups, but in some sense by those ethnic groups *themselves*. At the very least, such states would be governed in the name of those group members in the area. This would amount to something more than a formality. Thus, an Armenian state would be not simply have Armenian rulers. These rulers would truly govern in the name of Armenians. They would not just *claim* to act for their Armenian subjects or citizens, but would genuinely rule on their behalf, that is, for their benefit. The Armenian inhabitants might—and from Wilson's standpoint, would—be governed democratically, by themselves. If not, one would hope and expect that they would be governed *for* themselves, or *for*, in the interests of, Armenians as a whole.

A Jewish state would therefore be a state run by and *for* Jews. In such a state, Jews would be sovereign. The state would be run in their interests.

For non-Jews to expect as much was and is, therefore, entirely reasonable. Only a consistent, ongoing, highly public campaign to explain that this was certainly not going to happen would be sufficient to dispel this expectation. Nothing remotely like that occurred. So, it is worth reviewing what living under Jewish sovereignty must mean.

It means that Jews have a monopoly on violence in the areas they control. The perceived legitimacy of this monopoly need go no further than a settled expectation familiar to Star Trek fans: resistance is futile. A Jewish state is simply a state where Jews are firmly in control and where that much is recognized. Within its borders, Jews hold the power of life and death over Jews and non-Jews alike. That is the true meaning of the Zionist project.

If that's what the project is and was, there are a lot of things it wasn't. The Jews who came to Palestine as individuals and in small groups had various motives. But the overall direction of the Zionist movement, the ultimate goal to which all these individuals and groups would be directed and the one which it would in fact achieve, is something else again. Most accounts of the settlement do not focus on this ultimate purpose, and are therefore misleading. The Zionists and their camp followers did not come simply to settle. They did not come simply to "find a homeland," certainly not in the sense that Flanders is the homeland of the Flemish, or Lappland of the Lapps. They did not come simply to "make a life in Palestine." They did not come simply to find a refuge from persecution. They did not come to "redeem a people." All this could have been done elsewhere, as was pointed out at the time, and much of it was being done elsewhere by individual Jewish immigrants to America and other countries.[40] The Zionists, and therefore all who settled under their auspices, came to found a sovereign Jewish state.

In this state, however tolerant, however easygoing, however joyful, however liberal, Jews would always have the final say, on everything. Affairs would be run in the interests of whatever its rulers or inhabitants considered the interests of the Jewish people. Within that state, the final decision on how much force was to be used to advance those interests was entirely in the hands of its Jewish occupants. This does not have to mean that non-Jews had no representation, no say at all. It does not mean that non-Jews had no civil rights, or that their human rights would necessarily be violated. But it does mean that—since it is the essence of a Zionist state to be Jewish, run by and for Jews— things would always be arranged so that sovereignty remained in Jewish hands. This might be by law or it might be by political manipulation; it might be *de jure* or *de facto*. So it would be for Jews alone to decide whether non-Jews had civil rights, whether their human rights would be honored, indeed whether they would live or die. The purpose of establishing a sovereign Jewish state may or may not have been domination; that doesn't matter. That would certainly be the effect of its establishment.

What then of the claims that Zionism wasn't necessarily the demand for a sovereign Jewish state? Certainly, there were people who called themselves Zionists and who demanded something else, though what it was always remained obscure. There was talk of a "state;" its mechanisms never clearly defined. There was talk of a homeland guaranteed by international powers, or simply a homeland. It would be correct to say that not all Jewish settlers demanded a Jewish state, and that some of these settlers considered themselves Zionists. It would be incorrect to say that the Zionist project or enterprise was anything less than an attempt to establish a Jewish State.

In the first place, we have seen that a Jewish state was the objective of the Zionist leadership and the mainstream Zionist movement.[41] Second, by the time "nonexclusive" Zionism had become visible, in the 1920s, its notions of cooperation with the Palestinians had already become unworkable. Too much blood had been shed: the 1921 Jaffa riots had taken 200 Jewish and 120 Palestinian lives, followed in 1929 by the killing of 207 Jews and

181 Palestinians in Hebron. A contemporary Jewish comment on the first serious anti-Jewish riots, in 1920, already asserts that in Palestine there was a general understanding that Zionism would mean a Jewish state, and that this understanding ushered in bloodshed:

> ...we all know how the [Balfour] Declaration was interpreted at the time of its publication, and how much exaggeration many of our workers and writers have tried to introduce into it from that day to this. The Jewish people listened, and believed that the end of the *galush* [exile] had indeed come, and that in a short time there would be a "Jewish state." The Arab people too... listened, and believed that the Jews were coming to expropriate its land and do with it what they liked. All this inevitably led to friction and bitterness on both sides, and contributed to the state of things which was revealed in all its ugliness in the events at Jerusalem last April [1920].[42]

The British showed as little capacity or indeed inclination to curb the ethnic violence as they were to show in India and many other possessions. I know of no case in which cooperation between ethnic communities followed anytime soon on massacres of this scale. Third, even most "nonexclusive" Zionists were not distinguished by an explicit renunciation of a Jewish state, but rather by a commitment to partition Palestine rather than go for the whole thing. By then, the Palestinians correctly saw that the main tendency of Zionism was to create a Jewish state in Palestine, the intentions of a tiny nonexclusive minority with nebulous plans for some implausibly cooperative two-people government had no point of contact with the political realities.[43] This is probably why the "nonexclusives" remained, in the words of Norman Finkelstein, "numerically weak and politically marginal."[44]

This certainly was the opinion of the British. *The Palestine Royal Commission Report* of 1937 speaks of the bi-nationalists with indulgent sympathy. It refers to two "minority groups" (the second being the extreme nationalists):

> One of these is a group of intellectuals centered at the Hebrew University, who hold that the only solution to the problem of Palestine is for the Jews to show themselves not "like other nations" in the quality and temper of their nationalism, to subordinate political ambitions to cultural and spiritual ends, to acquiesce in such a limitation of their numbers as would make them a permanent minority in Palestine, even in the last resort to submit to Arab rule. The moral courage of that school of thought must command respect; but it enlists no effective support in the National Home.

If this was the conclusion at which the British arrived, it must be supposed that thoughtful Palestinians concluded the same thing. Bi-nationalism was never a serious alternative to Zionism, and everyone but the "political" bi-nationalists realized this.

This dogged lack of realism reflects on the bi-nationalists themselves. Their vague ideas were not policies or platforms but mere attempts at self-deception, at believing that they could have their cake of a homeland in Palestine without eating the conflict that such ambitions inevitably produce. They could see for themselves that, in contrast to their own ineffectual moderation, the most extreme forms of Zionism were on the rise. The bi-nationalists were a testimony, not to the possibility of a "decent Zionism," but only to the prevalence of idle, wishful thinking among a few Zionists. To say that Zionism wasn't necessarily a project to establish a Jewish state is like saying that, because a few guys buy *Playboy* only for the articles, *Playboy* isn't essentially a soft-core porn mag.

Many Zionists could not or would not face the facts of their own objectives. Some came in a fog of blithe enthusiasm that painted the Palestinians into a backdrop for charming experiments in collective living. These settlers, we would now say, were in denial: they simply refused to imagine that there could be some real clash of interests between the Palestinians and themselves. Indeed, at times they simply refused to imagine the Palestinians at all: children's books of the era often reduced the Palestinian population to a few picturesque shepherds. Other Zionists, notably Ben-Gurion, may have deliberately created a fog: he sometimes suggested that a Jewish state would not imply Jewish domination,[45] but could he have believed it? It isn't complicated: were or weren't the Zionists going to accept a state in which, perhaps on matters of life and death, it was possible for the citizens to decide against the Jews? To this very day, many Zionists, Israeli Jews, and Jewish "socialists" refuse to ask this question. There is no doubt, however, how they would respond if they had to give a straight answer. In their fantasies, push might never come to shove. But if it did, it would be the Jews who shoved the non-Jews. The whole point of Zionism was to ensure this outcome, and it could not be ensured without Jewish sovereignty.

The point here is not that the Zionists or Jewish settlers were racist, colonialist, or generally unpleasant. Most likely some were, some weren't, and some held within themselves a mass of contradictory or willfully indistinct attitudes. It would have made no difference even if the Zionists had passionately loved the Palestinians and wanted nothing more than peace and harmony. As long as the goal of a Jewish state remained central to Zionism, as long as the evidence of this objective was there for all who cared to look and listen, the course of future events was all but set.

Consequences of Zionism

Reactions

PALESTINIAN TENANT FARMERS, AS FAR BACK AS THE 1880s, reacted violently to Zionist attempts to supplant them on land purchased from absentee Ottoman landlords. By the 1890s, dismay and resistance were no longer confined to the peasantry, though at this stage there was little fighting. In 1899, the Mayor of Jerusalem, Yusuf Zia al-Khalidi, wrote the chief rabbi of France, imploring him to hold Zionists in check: "In the name of God, leave Palestine in peace."[46] The Zionists continued to obtain property from large landowners and their settlements continued to provoke both fear and resentment. Whether the settlers behaved well or badly is not our concern here. What matters is that well before the Balfour Declaration, Arab political leaders were fully aware of Zionist intentions. According to the recollections of one early Palestinian nationalist, Herzl's *Der Judenstaat* was translated and appeared in an Arabic newspaper.[47] Around 1915, one of the most moderate and conciliatory Palestinian activists said, "I am sure that if we do nothing to affect the status quo the Zionists will attain their object in a few years (in Palestine) where they will found a Jewish state..."[48] After the declaration, Palestinian notables saw the British occupation as "a transparent ruse to hand the country over to the Zionists."[49] So, there is no doubt whatever that the Palestinians knew and understood that they were confronting the prospect of a Jewish state in Palestine.

Consider just what they realized. They realized that many thousands of people, with whom they had had no contact and to whom they had done no wrong, had come and were coming from thousands of miles away to establish a state of *their own* in as much of Palestine as they could get. The state would be run by and for those people. The current inhabitants of Palestine might be able to leave: for most of them, who lived in great poverty, this was not a live option. Those who could not would have to submit to the new state. Because they were not Jewish, they would not partake of sovereignty in this state: whatever its constitution, things would be arranged so that Jews had the deciding say, at the very least in all matters the Jews decided were of vital importance. Ultimately, "the Jews" would hold the power of life and death over the Palestinians.

Was this so alarming? Didn't the Ottomans, and then the British, already hold exactly that power over the Palestinians? What did it matter if now the Zionists were to rule?

In the first place, perhaps the Palestinians took Anglo-American values to heart. These values include a principle already mentioned: that no one need submit to sovereignty without consent. And the Palestinians did not submit. In 1834, they had revolted against Mohammed Ali, the viceroy of Egypt, when he took over Palestine. The revolt was suppressed: about 10,000 Palestinian peasants were shipped to Egypt. This was not all:

> Sections of entire towns, including the Muslim quarter of Bethlehem, were destroyed, and their inhabitants expelled or killed. And, in a measure that struck very hard, even given all the other atrocities those in Palestine faced, the Egyptians disarmed the population...[50]

If the Palestinians did not rise up against the Ottomans when they regained control, that testifies more to lack of means than of desire to resist.

In the second place, Ottoman rule was nothing like what could be reasonably expected from Zionist sovereignty. Initially the Ottomans, as elsewhere, were content to rule through local potentates, leaving the countries they conquered almost untouched. Even when they made feeble, ineffectual efforts to impose direct rule, as they did in Palestine after the Egyptian occupation, their presence was minimal. There was never any question of settling the area with Turks—the idea would never have crossed the Ottomans' mind—nor was there any thought of ruling in the interests of some Turkish ethnicity: the Ottomans were Muslims first and Turks a far-distant second. So, the realities of Ottoman rule were hardly comparable to the prospect of Zionist rule, which involved not only the settlement of a large new population in the area, but imposing a monopoly of force in the interests of that population.

Third, the Jewish state, unlike the Ottoman Empire, would be entirely new. It would not be "the devil you know," a long-established institution whose ways might be predictable and, therefore, might afford some security beyond whatever paper guarantees its constitution conferred. (Even today, Israel does not have a constitution.) The stability and character of the new state, as opposed to its mere blueprint, could not be foreseen. Not that even long-established institutions are to be trusted, as the American Japanese learned in the Second World War. But new states, even new democracies, are perhaps particularly unpredictable: that was the lesson to German Jews who put their trust in the Weimar Republic. The Palestinians were faced not even with a new state, but with a mere proposal. Given their recent experiences and the talk of extreme Zionists, "let's trust them!" would not have been a rational response.

Given the increasing tide of Jewish immigration, the project of an ethnically Jewish state and of re-establishing the ancient kingdom of Israel might well involve the transfer, perhaps accompanied by large-scale massacres. Israel Zangwill, an early

Zionist, had spoken of "a land without people, waiting for a people without land." What would happen when the immigrants found there were people after all? No Zionist in those days, to the best of my knowledge, ever contemplated extermination of the Palestinians, though many spoke among themselves of compulsory transfer backed by armed force.[51] Transfer itself might well be a death sentence in a region that, whatever its ultimate capacities, was no stranger to ethnic conflict: the Palestinians had in 1860 seen massacres of up to 20,000 people in the struggles between Maronite Christians and Druze around Mount Lebanon.

The Zionists had often portrayed themselves as the leaders of one "people," the Jews, who wanted Palestine for themselves. They might, when politically useful, provide reassurances about their intentions. But clearly, they could not very well have Palestine for themselves without ridding it of its present inhabitants. The Palestinians, therefore, had good reason to fear an ethnic conflict in which extermination became far from unimaginable. And this is in fact how sentiments have evolved. Today, extremists identify the Palestinians with Amalekites whom God commanded to be wiped out.[52] The prospect of an ethnically Jewish sovereign state, equipped and motivated to conduct ethnic warfare, was not comparable to the position of Palestinians at the time—rule by a sometimes dangerous but remote and generally inert, decaying empire.

A rational person takes even a small risk of great disasters seriously: drivers rightly insure themselves against physically injuring other drivers even though the actual probabilities of this happening are tiny. The Palestinians were in no position to measure probabilities, but they were right to suppose, as did the founder of Zionism, that they might very well find themselves at war with the Jews coming to their area. Their military resources were virtually nonexistent. Given British support for Zionism and the growing support for that same cause within the Jewish community, time was not on their side. Moreover, if Zionism was out to establish a Jewish state, which was and appeared to be the case, there was no room for compromise. In as much of Palestine as the Zionists controlled—and, as we will see, they were out to control as much as possible—either the Jews were to be sovereign or they were not. Because in any functioning state some institution must be able to resolve disputes, there is no such thing as partial sovereignty, and, by definition, in a "Jewish state" the supreme institution must be in Jewish hands.

Certainly it was possible that the Zionists would settle for less than all of Palestine. It was possible they would not forcibly transfer the indigenous population; it was just barely possible that, somehow, Zionism would be abandoned altogether. But there was no basis for supposing any of these outcomes likely. Nor could it be assumed that even a territorial compromise could be attained without catastrophe: many, like those of the Thirty Years War, were reached only after great slaughter, and brought no lasting peace. Indeed, the Palestinians could look at all of modern European history from the 17th century religious wars to the year of the Balfour Declaration as a record of failed territorial compromises.

When settlers move into an inhabited area, territorial compromises are all too often mere pauses in a savage process of dispossession. This was apparent at the time. The rise of Zionism coincided with the last bloody stages of just such a process in the American West. Significantly, the American settlers' progressive and very violent displacement of the native inhabitants was not some grand scheme thought out in advance. At many points in the story, the settlers seemed to have got all they wanted. But successful settlement and increasing immigration brought new usurpations. Enough was never, it seemed, enough. Even if the Zionists had never dreamed of taking all of Palestine from the Palestinians, it would have been foolish to suppose that they would not come to do so, bit by bit.

The prospect of a Jewish state, therefore, posed a mortal threat to the Palestinians, a prospect of ethnic subjugation and very likely of what is now called ethnic cleansing. They would have been irrational not to resist Zionism as fiercely and effectively as possible. In similar cases, for example the case of native peoples all over North America, no one today thinks a violent response inappropriate. If the same judgment has not been brought down in the case of the Palestinians, it is largely because Zionists, then and now, concealed or obscured their goal of a Jewish state, and because the true significance of that goal has been buried in an avalanche of sentimental nonsense about homelands, redemption, refuge, settlement, and so on. Somehow all this has covered up the elementary truth that an ethnic state is one in which those outside the dominant ethnic group are, for all political purposes, enslaved, that is, at the mercy of their rulers.

The Palestinians' right to resist did not rest on some doctrine of ethnic nationalism, on idealizing the "self-determination of peoples." They could appeal, not to rights of ethnic self-determination, but to rights of self-government within a sovereign geographic area. When the Ottoman empire crumbled, there were important and difficult questions about what sovereign states should emerge from it: for example, was there to be one state comprising contemporary Syria, Lebanon, and Palestine, or several smaller states? But these questions are not to be confused with the question of whether outsiders had a right to draw those boundaries, or rule over those populations, or establish how they were to be ruled in the future. No such right exists, and anyone in those areas has a right to reject and resist such projects. Any population may defend itself against the threat of an externally imposed sovereignty.

Not that the Palestinians' first resort was violence. The peasant attacks at the end of the 19th century were few and minor. For the most part, the Palestinians reacted with pleas and verbal protests until 1920, some three years after the Balfour Declaration. Their pleadings were consistently ignored or rebuffed by the Zionists, the British government, and the Versailles conference. But to assess the response of the Palestinians, it is necessary to consider another possibility that, sometime after the Balfour Declaration, the Zionists should have abandoned Zionism; that they might have accepted less than a Jewish state. If so, perhaps the Palestinians should have been more peaceful, more conciliatory, and more patient.

Room for compromise?

Though bi-nationalism as a movement was, as we have already noted, politically insignificant, the Jewish leadership did occasionally, in the early 1930s, indicate willingness to consider various schemes for a bi-national state. Ben-Gurion, for instance, reports conveying an offer to London on behalf of Chaim Weizmann: Arabs and Jews would have political parity, regardless of the size of their populations.[53] Presumably this would involve something like the contemporary Lebanese constitution, which would guarantee "communal" rights, representation, and a balance of power in crucial government positions. What's wrong with that? Shouldn't the Palestinians have jumped at it, rather than resorting to violence?

In the first place, they were never offered any such thing. The proposal was made to a sympathetic British official, who rejected it as too generous: the Jews should have primacy rather than parity.[54] (Such proposals also made it into the "labor Zionist" Mapai party discussions; see below.) The ironies of the response should not divert one from asking: so what? Couldn't the Zionists have made such an offer directly to the Arabs? When it came to direct discussions, Kimmerling and Migdal report something quite different:

> Ben-Gurion's proposal was for an exchange of Jewish agree-
> ment to a pan-Arab federation linked to Palestine in exchange
> for Arab agreement to unrestricted Jewish immigration into
> Palestine and Transjordan, leading to an independent state with
> a Jewish majority. ...the idea of an Arab federation linked to a
> *Jewish state* [my italics] did not get far.[55]

But suppose Ben-Gurion might have been persuaded by the
Palestinians to offer something more like what he discussed with
the British and with party members. Chomsky suggests that historians who belittle bi-nationalism are concerned with the *sincerity* of Ben-Gurion's statements,[56] but far more important was
their *credibility*. Regardless of Ben-Gurion's state of mind, what
have given the Palestinians grounds for supposing that bi-nationalism was a live option?

To ask the question is to uncover a great divide that has
escaped Chomsky and others who take the bi-nationalist option
seriously. There is a difference between the discussion of theo-
retically possible proposals and the authoritative offer of a politically viable solution. The Palestinians *could* not have considered
the bi-nationalist option unless it was seriously proposed. But to
be seriously proposed would mean that it was proposed on
behalf of the entire or at least the definitively preponderant
segment of the Zionist movement. This would involve, in effect,
the converse of Arafat's famous acknowledgment that Israel had
a right to exist: the Zionists would have had to say, in effect, that
Israel, the future Jewish state, had *no* right to exist; that this was
no longer their objective. And Israel's dismissive reaction to
Arafat's pronouncement is a measure of what it would take to
make such an acknowledgment convincingly.

In fact, a bi-national state was never proposed by *any* significant segment of the Zionist movement. The closest to such a
proposal was a 1930 document called "Premises for the Determination of a Government in Palestine," which Ben-Gurion pre-

sented to his *Mapai* party. Aharon Cohen comments on the proposal:

> ...these tendencies in the *Mapai* party to formulate a program for Arab-Jewish accord on the basis of bi-national parity were never fully worked out. According to the "Premises" of Ben-Gurion, the time for self-government on the basis of political equality between the two peoples in Palestine would come upon our completing the construction of the Jewish national home...the party never took a definitive practical stand on bi-national parity.[57]

This indicates how far bi-nationalism was from entering the Zionist mainstream.

Chomsky points out that "the Zionist movement was not officially committed to a Jewish state until 1942."[58] Well yes. No doubt, Hitler was officially committed to world peace until 1939, and the Soviet Union was officially committed to democracy—one has only to read its constitution—throughout its history. No doubt, many Republican philanderers are officially committed to family values. What matters more is that the British government, the ruling power in Palestine, was officially opposed to a Jewish state throughout the relevant period. Since the Zionists had every interest in maintaining good relations with the British, who had already given them more than half a loaf in 1917, the lack of official Zionist commitments to a Jewish state could hardly be taken at face value: it was in effect a commitment not to spit in Britain's face, and one which paid off handsomely in British sympathies. It would have been one thing if there had been no *unofficial* commitment to such a state, but we have seen that such a commitment had been public knowledge since 1896. Also known by some and suspected by many,

> From [the first Zionist congress at] Basel [in 1901] it had
> become deliberate policy to deny that there was, or ever had
> been, an intention of establishing a Jewish state.[59]

Moreover, the Palestinians were not ignorant of mainstream
Zionist intentions. The British noted this with alarm, and their
Haycraft Commission report made these very concerns a public
matter:

> It is important that it should be realized that what is written on
> the subject of Zionism by Zionists and their sympathizers in
> Europe is read and discussed by Palestinian Arabs, not only in
> the towns but in the country districts.[60]

To give the Palestinians reason to get excited about Ben-
Gurion's offer, it was not enough to mention it in the chatter of
a cozy breakfast meeting at the prime ministerial estate,
Chequers. A serious offer would have to *begin* with the formal,
permanent renunciation of any intention of pursuing the goal of
a Jewish state on the part of all major Zionist organizations, and
the expulsion of all dissenters. This of course never happened.

Such a renunciation, in itself, would not have been nearly
enough, just as Arafat's renunciation was not enough for the
Israelis. It is truly an ivory-tower attitude to get excited about a
proposal to maintain constitutional parity between two ethnic
groups regardless of actual population size. Constitutions, it
seems necessary to remark, are pieces of paper. They require
enforcement and they must inspire confidence. Both requirements pose problems, which is why bi-national states tend
towards instability.

The problem of enforcement is the problem of sovereignty all
over again: some political force must be supreme so that it is possible to adjudicate disputes with authority. Someone or some
institution must be charged with upholding the constitution.
Who will control this function? If there is a perfect balance

between group A and group B, then there will be no such person—the constitution may specify such an office—but the office-holder will not have sufficient political power to accomplish the task. There will be a state only so long as both groups can get along.

This is a solution to ethnic rivalry that basically presupposes the problem has already been solved. It can work only so long as there is no really serious disagreement. In a prosperous, unstressed society like Belgium, constitutionally mandated bi-national equality can work quite well. In Lebanon, it failed to prevent a civil war in which some 175,000 died—this out of a total population of some 2.6 million. Palestine would be more like Lebanon than like Belgium: one could be certain that very serious disputes would arise. These would require a genuinely supreme, genuinely neutral power to settle them, and there could be no realistic prospect of such leadership. But if the ethnic groups are *not* perfectly balanced, then one group is in effect sovereign over the other: the equality mandated in the constitution persists at their good pleasure, nothing more. The Zionist movement, quite rightly perceiving that a bi-national state would afford the Jewish people no security, never exactly warmed to the idea. The Palestinians understood this very well.

Then there is the problem of confidence—confidence that the constitution will survive and will succeed in maintaining a society in which neither group holds power over the other. Here it is necessary to appreciate how very different it would be to establish a bi-national state in Palestine as opposed to any actual examples of such institutions. In Belgium, in Lebanon, in that bitter memory, Yugoslavia, we are speaking of essentially stable populations. Yet even in these cases, a slight population imbalance can cause great alarm and actual conflict: this is an unsurprising reaction whenever democracy is involved. But in Palestine one party was a movement passionately committed to free Jewish immigration. The Palestinians were not, despite the utterly discredited claims of Joan Peters, immigrants.[61] There were serious conflicts of interest between Palestinians and Zionist Jews; conflicts which had already produced much bloodshed, including the murder of children. In these circumstances, the Palestinians would have been fools to suppose that a binational constitution would survive an emerging Jewish majority, predominantly intent on making a homeland not *in* Palestine, but *out of* Palestine. (The next section will indicate that Zionist compromises never represented an abandonment of this goal.) And this is exactly why committed Zionists like Ben-Gurion and Weizmann could propose a bi-national state. If—a worst-case scenario—they actually got one, they could be confident of establishing a Jewish demographic predominance in Palestine that must eventually translate into political predominance. They knew that a piece of paper might delay but could not halt this process. So did the Palestinians.

But we have still not encountered the main problem with proposing a bi-national state in Palestine. The difficulties discussed so far depend to some extent on whether or not the citizens of a bi-national state do in fact consider themselves two peoples. The very constitution and organization of such a state may encourage such attitudes, but encouragement is not decisive. One may hope that, with time, citizens of a bi-national state do not find it so important that they belong to one people or another, or relegate these sentiments to cultural rather than political preoccupations: ethnic food rather than ethnic power. This happy ideal has never been realized, but there are indeed signs that it is sometimes possible. Even in Lebanon, it means quite a bit just to be Lebanese.

Zionism, however, was even more fundamentally about maintaining the collective consciousness of the Jewish people than it was about establishing a Jewish state. Moreover, this consciousness had an intensely political character: it involved above all a commitment to defend that people against its enemies. This is why bi-nationalism would have to mean something very different in Palestine from what it meant elsewhere. In the first place, we have not a pre-existing ethnic population but an immigrant group. Secondly, this is no ordinary immigrant group, because immigrant groups normally come as *individuals*. In normal circumstances, the core ugliness of anti-immigrant prejudice is precisely to attribute to those arriving a greater collective consciousness than they actually have. The Xs are coming to take our jobs is so wrong, not simply because we may in fact not want the jobs they take, or because the Xs actually create jobs, but also, and more fundamentally, because it is wrong to speak of the Xs at all as if they were some conspiratorial influx. No, they are just people, individuals and families, looking for a better life. To consider them a coordinated political force is racist paranoia. And if these are the sort of people you must deal with, why speak of a bi-national state at all? *They* don't all stick together. *They* are not a political entity. It is at most a bi-cultural state that is in the offing, and that is no threat. Indeed, this is how the fans of bi-nationalism in Palestine like to think.

But this is not how Palestinians, or any rational person, could have regarded the Jewish influx. One telling circumstance is the nature of Jewish land purchases. Ordinarily we would not think, or should not, think of individual X-ish immigrants buying land as "X-ish land purchases." Not so in Palestine:

> At the turn of the century, the Zionists had established the Jewish National Fund (JNF), whose main activity was acquiring property. The JNF was engaged in a national enterprise; the working assumption was that the land bought would not be handed over to "gentiles," that is, it would not be returned to the Arabs. Besides the JNF, other Zionist organizations allocated money for acquiring land for Jewish settlement and private buyers invested as well. The term used was "redemption" of the

land, another quasi-religious word laden with emotion and ideology.[62]

And here is how the Jewish National Fund, alive and well today, recounts its own history:

> It was the fourth day of the Fifth Zionist Congress in Basel, Switzerland in 1901. The delegates had spent the day debating a proposal for the establishment of a national fund to purchase land in Palestine, as had been suggested at the first Congress four years earlier...
>
> Herzl stood before the delegates and delivered a passionate plea for the immediate establishment of the fund: "After striving for so many years to set up the fund, we do not want to disperse again without having done anything." His speech turned the delegates around, the motion passed and the congress resolved that a fund to be called Jewish National Fund (Keren Kayemeth LeIsrael) should be established, and that "the fund shall be the property of the Jewish people as a whole."[63]

The last phrase says it all. To an overwhelming extent, Jews came to Israel under Zionist auspices *as* a people, and this was no idle pretense. To a significant extent, their movement *was* conspiratorial. Their settlement was largely a collective act, given concrete expression by collective financing and ownership. That some Jews may have wished or momentarily contemplated breaking free from this very real political identity, that bi-national proposals were advanced, that there were dreams of worthy legal documents, changes nothing of this. That this movement should have no interest in establishing Jewish sovereignty was wildly implausible.

No constitutional wand was going to wave Jewish ethnic nationalism away. It was the heart and soul of Zionism and the ineradicable determinant of a determined, organized, and increasingly fervent Jewish immigration. Indeed, reasonable

Palestinians would have demanded clear evidence that Zionism did not intend to create a *de facto* Jewish state by swamping the original population with Jews. The Zionist movement was moving Jews exclusively to Palestine; it would have had to start moving Jews from countries that persecuted them to any countries that did not. (Most other destinations had sufficiently large populations so that "swamping" would be no issue.) This would have effectively deprived Zionism of what distinguished it from other Jewish responses to persecution; there was no prospect whatever of this happening.

In these circumstances, whatever the ebbs and flows of Zionist decision-making at particular points in the run up to 1948, meaningful compromise was impossible. No realistic person could seriously believe that the fragile mechanisms of a bi-national state would survive the clash of interests between two peoples, one of which at least was determined to act as a people. By 1930, bloodshed had already reached very serious levels. The idea that the increasingly strong and confident Zionist movement[64] would declaw itself simply made no sense. A self-conceived "people" that had come as a people, determined to be no one's subordinate, to make themselves a homeland guaranteed by political power, to "redeem" what they had thought to be an "empty" land and make it a Jewish land—no one could expect such a people to happily accept the ineffectual protections and self-imposed constraints of bi-nationalism. An institutional compromise was impossible simply because the whole idea of Zionism was to have done with compromises. Ben-Gurion himself suggested as much in the late 1930s. He commented on a British proposal of partition as follows:

> The Jewish State now being offered to us is not the Zionist objective. Within this area it is not possible to solve the Jewish question. But it can serve as a decisive stage along the path to greater Zionist implementation. It will consolidate in Palestine,

> within the shortest possible time, the real Jewish force which
> will lead us to our historic goal.[65]

Somehow this does not sound like a man ready to embrace a scrupulously bi-national state whose constitution would permanently deny Jews a decisive say in national affairs. Conciliatory gestures might be sincere, but they involved settling for half a loaf only until the whole loaf could be had. From now on, according to the consistently dominant ideology within the Zionist camp, the Jews would not have to accommodate themselves to others. It was to be the other way around.

Partition?

Ben-Gurion's comment suggests that "the Zionist objective" undermined more than bi-nationalism: what applies to proposals for a bi-national state largely applies to proposals for partition as well. By the late 1930s, when these ideas came into prominence, violence had already destroyed any remnants of trust that might have made them viable. Actions and events spoke louder than the occasional moderate statements issuing from Zionist quarters: there was the founding of the hardline Zionist paramilitary organization, the Irgun, in 1931, and, in 1936, the formation of the British-led but Jewish-manned "Special Night Squads" that played a crucial role in suppressing the Palestinian revolt.[66] Why should the Zionists, who had certainly not had the worst of the fighting, abandon their long-standing desire to inhabit all the Holy Land and control all the holy places? Why would they accept the creation of a state controlled by their enemies, literally across the street from their homes? Was this an atmosphere in which moderation could be expected to prevail? Was the constant, increasingly frantic demand for increased Jewish immigration likely to favor a Zionism content with some fraction of an already tiny country? Were the growing numbers

of Zionist settlers and fighters likely to force a curtailment of
Zionist ambitions?

The Palestinians certainly asked themselves all of these questions, and rightly concluded that any partition was very likely to
be no more than a way station on the path to renewed warfare.[67]
They had no reason to think the delay would favor them. They
had no reason to suppose that the truce would hold, not least
because so many Palestinians would not accept losing their
homes. For the Palestinians to have accepted partition would
likely be to accept no more than a pause, one that would probably favor the Zionists when fighting broke out again. So while
the Zionists would derive advantages from partition—a Jewish
state and a useful breathing space—the Palestinians would derive
both the strategic disadvantages of the pause and permanent disadvantages. For many Palestinians, there would be either permanent dispossession or dangerous submission to Jewish ethnic
supremacy. Though compromise slightly favored the Zionists,
they had no reason to *stop* at a compromise solution, and the
Palestinians had no rational grounds for adopting compromise in
any form. It was, therefore, not a live option.

The most authoritative Zionist pronouncements increasingly
confirmed Palestinian expectations. Though there has been
much effort to emphasize the existence of pro-partition sentiments within the Zionist movement, Zionism as a whole and as
perceived by the Palestinians defined itself as closer to, not
farther from, its original goals. The Israeli Ministry of Foreign
affairs describes what happened very well:

> The Mandate having been wrecked by the White Paper policy,
> and far-reaching political changes being anticipated after the
> War, the Jews found it imperative to define their ultimate aims
> clearly. Owing to war-time conditions, this was done first at a
> National Conference of American Zionists in May 1942. The
> programme adopted there was subsequently accepted by

Zionist conferences and by other representative Jewish organi-
sations in various countries and finally promulgated by the first
post-war World Zionist Conference, held in London in August
1945. The programme in its original version read:

"The Conference urges that the gates of Palestine be opened—
that the Jewish Agency be vested with control of immigration
into Palestine and with the necessary authority for upbuilding
the country, including the development of its unoccupied and
uncultivated lands—and that Palestine be established as a
Jewish Commonwealth integrated in the structure of the new
democratic world." [68]

This did not exactly proclaim readiness to settle for less than
everything. Attempts to suppose that moderate intentions
somehow persisted fall flat.

Thus Benny Morris, commenting on the declaration: "the
possibility that the state should be established only in part of
Palestine was implicit." [69] But it could be implicit only if the declaration was inconsistent, because it clearly says that the state
will be established in *all* of Palestine, not part of it. If Muslim fundamentalists move into Iceland and proclaim their intention to
establish Iceland as a Muslim Commonwealth, no one is going to
think they intend to leave half of the place for people of other
religions to establish their own state! Martin Buber, keenly
involved in the politics of the time, certainly saw no compromis-
ing implications: "we went ahead," he said, "and demanded rule
over the whole country (the Biltmore program)." [70] So, too, the
textbooks: Sydney Nettleton Fisher tells us that "the Biltmore
program called for the establishment of a Jewish commonwealth
in all of Palestine." [71] The significance of these demands is not that
they prove a permanent unwillingness among all Zionists to
compromise. It is rather that the declarations gave the Palestinians every reason to expect that any compromise would mark at

most a tactical pause in the drive to establish complete Zionist control of Palestine.

In private, even a "compromiser" like Ben-Gurion did not compromise. Already in 1937 he made it very clear just what he expected from partition in a letter to his son Amos:

> I am an enthusiastic advocate of the Jewish State, even if it involves partitioning Palestine now, because I work on the assumption that a partial Jewish State will not be the end, but the beginning. When we acquire 1,000 or 10,000 dunams of land, we are happy. Because this acquisition of land is important not only for its own sake, but because through it we are increasing our strength, and every increase in our strength helps us to acquire the whole country. The formation of a State, even if it is only a partial State, will be the greatest increase of strength we could have today, and it will constitute a powerful lever in our historic effort to redeem the country in its entirety.[72]

Later in the same letter he adds: "We will be able to penetrate deeper into the country if we have a State." This was not a one-time, uncharacteristic statement. Norman Finkelstein reports that:

> The Jewish Agency Executive was ...apprised by Ben-Gurion in 1938 that, "after we become a strong force, as a result of the creation of a state, we shall abolish partition and expand to the whole of Palestine." Recall also that in his private correspondence, Ben-Gurion anticipated that the Jewish State "would have an outstanding army ...and so I am certain that we won't be constrained from settling in the rest of the country, whether out of accord and mutual understanding with Arab neighbors or otherwise."[73]

In short, the Palestinians' apprehensions concerning the real intentions of the mainstream Zionist movement were correct.

After 1945, they had even more reason to doubt the prospects for compromise. With the end of the Second World War and the discovery of the Nazi extermination camps, the Zionists, naturally, were more than ever concerned for the security of any emergent Jewish state. They were less than ever disposed to sacrifice even the slightest degree of that security to accommodate the wishes or needs of the Palestinians. On their part, the Palestinians had less reason than ever to suppose that their presence would be tolerated. They had, after all, already proven themselves a threat. Partition, therefore, could be no more than temporary: the Palestinians could not expect the Zionists to leave their bitter enemies to recoup and strengthen their forces. And indeed this extreme preoccupation with security has very likely done much to spoil any real prospect of peace ever since.

Since Zionism's project of a Jewish state represented a mortal threat to Palestinians, and since there was no realistic prospect of the Zionist movement abandoning Zionism, the only nonviolent way of stopping the institution of Jewish sovereignty was appeal to the British. But the British had already aligned themselves with the Zionists and, if they had gently rebuffed the notion of a Jewish state, they showed no sign of really putting an end to that project. In fact both Balfour and Lloyd George were Christian Zionists, on excellent terms with their Manchester Jewish constituents. Churchill, representing Manchester, also sympathized with the aspirations of its Jewish community.[74] The Zionists had well-developed political power wielded by experienced, sophisticated Europeanized leaders like Weizmann and Lord Rothschild; the other side could not hope to match this. It was not impossible that the Palestinians could defend themselves from ethnic subjugation without violence, but it was extremely improbable. In such circumstances violence is a rational course of action, regrettable but not reprehensible.

Before leaving the subject of partition and territorial compromise, it is worth glancing at some of the moralizing about this matter. Often it is suggested, with a certain indignation, that the Palestinians have repeatedly rejected compromise: "Unfortunately, the Palestinians have traditionally rejected such a [two-state] solution (1937, 1947, 1978) and in 2000 once again rejected the Barak-Clinton proposals of July–December which posited precisely such a solution."[75] Presumably the idea is that the Palestinians ought, as a matter of morality or justice, to have welcomed compromise.

If this simply means that the Palestinians should have bowed to superior might to avoid pointless bloodshed, then the issue is really tactical. Yes, Palestinians might have tried compromise in much the same spirit that many Zionists accepted it: as a means to acquire breathing space and build up one's strength to exploit future opportunities. Even in hindsight it is impossible to tell whether this move would have, in the end, avoided bloodshed. Had the Palestinians derived some advantage from tactical "compromise," the bloodshed might well have been even worse. But if the claim means that a compromise solution would have—could have—been just, this is an extraordinary point of view.

The situation created in Palestine by the Zionist influx was not typical of the cases in which territorial compromise has been achieved and welcomed. This was not like Louis XIV and the Hapsburgs, battling over the Franche-Comté. It was not like the redrawing of boundaries after the Chaco War in Latin America, nor like the compromises between two or more peoples in Belgium, Switzerland, or Yugoslavia.

These cases fall into two broad categories. One involves rather pointless political disputes between militaristic nations. This hardly fits the Israel/Palestine conflict. The other category involves two populations which have lived side by side, often for hundreds of years. Their disputes were about how to draw boundaries between territories generally recognized as "the land of" one people or another, or powers long assignable to these peoples. In short, these were compromises that resolved long-standing disputes between long-established populations whose respective claims were long recognized as perhaps exaggerated, but nonetheless possessing a certain legitimacy. No one could seriously suggest of the French and Germans, or the Walloons and Flemish, or the Slovenes, Serbs, Bosnians, and Croats, that they had no business being where they were, or desiring to run their own affairs. On the contrary, their conflicts called for balancing competing legitimacies.

Such situations have little to do with the dispute between Palestinians and Zionist Jews. Jews were indeed present in Palestine for centuries, but in small numbers. They did not spawn the Zionist movement, which originated in Europe and which, despite its pretensions, had no title to represent any Jewish population, large or small. The conflict in Palestine was between a settled population of indigenous Palestinians and not some other people, but a political movement dedicated to establishing an ethnic state in as much of Palestine as they could take. This movement did not seek to ratify the sovereignty of an ethnic group long established in Palestine: Palestinian Jews were no more likely a candidate for their own state than, say, the Greeks of Alexandria, or the Assyrians of Iraq.[76] The Zionists had a quite different objective—to implant an ethnic sovereignty in what was to them a foreign land, on the basis of a population expressly imported to secure that end. Unlike other occasions for territorial compromise, this one did not involve two existing peoples pursuing competing claims. Instead, there was a claim at whose service a people was to be created by immigration from outside the area. That claim was to be pursued against the existing inhabitants, who had never thought to advance some claim of their own against the Jewish people.

No one today suggests, I think, that the American Indians were under some moral obligation to compromise with the white settlers who came uninvited to impose a sovereignty in America: the settlers had no right to one inch of that land. No one has ever supposed that the Celts were somehow obliged to compromise with the Saxons, Angles or Jutes, or the English with the Normans, or the Chinese with the Japanese in Manchuria. Why then would such an obligation be attributed to the Palestinians? They were faced, not with a long-standing conflict between two established populations, but with an invasion conceived and executed by a political movement. No one is morally required to compromise with an invasion, whatever the limits of its ambitions.

The morality of the Palestinian response

That some form of violence seems to have been dictated to the Palestinians by their circumstances does not mean that their particular response was justified. Certainly it is not beyond criticism. In the early days, the response seems to have been unorganized mob violence and in subsequent years, until at least the revolt of 1936, there was no worked-out strategy. No doubt someone with God-like knowledge of the situation could have developed a more effective response to Zionism. Quite possibly, it would have been less directly violent: perhaps, like the Zionists, the Palestinians would have made nice, even sincere attempts at compromise, while building up their forces for an armed confrontation. Would this have been better?

If intentions are what matter most, it would have. But both commonplace morals, which tell us that the road to Hell is paved with good intentions, and modern moral theories, which assign great importance to the actual consequences of actions, suggest that intentions are not what really count. The general morality of terrorism and other questionable acts will be discussed later. For now, suffice it to say that the Palestinians don't seem to have had a lot of good options, and the ones they chose were not obviously worse than the alternatives.

The ugliness of mob violence should not deceive us into supposing that more socially acceptable responses actually do less harm. We find its low-tech attacks on individuals more distasteful than high-tech attacks, even if they are sure to harm individuals just as much. A beheading disgusts us; not so a massive air assault which will have the side effect of blowing the heads off a few children. That both the attackers and we ourselves fully expect such "collateral damage" doesn't seem to matter. This indeed is why we witness the spectacular exercise in obliviousness that sees the apostles of Western civilization berating "the Arabs" or Islam for its brutality. That Western civilization recently produced King Leopold's Congo genocide, Hiroshima, the concentration camps, and two catastrophic world wars should make us think twice before we see any particular evil in the Palestinian response.[77]

A more balanced view must ask how exactly the Palestinians, in a situation which has been shown to contain no real potential for peaceful compromise, were to react. Their situation was morally difficult because, in large measure, they were confronted with what might be called an innocent threat. Some Zionists certainly intended, from the very beginning, to crush the Palestinians. Some planned violent "transfer" or, more simply, ethnic cleansing. But very likely most Zionist settlers, and most of the Zionists to whom the Palestinians could directly respond, were less culpable. Many came in complete ignorance of their destination. Sometimes this was willful ignorance; probably more often it was the product of blithe stupidity, wishful thinking, and naïveté. These are not excuses but neither are they capital crimes. Yet not only criminals must be resisted. The philosopher Judith Jarvis Thompson, in a discussion of abortion, gives a grotesque but appropriate example of how a totally innocent person may represent a mortal danger that at least raises serious questions about the limits of self-defense:

> Suppose you find yourself trapped in a tiny house with a
> growing child. I mean a very tiny house, and a rapidly growing

child—you are already up against the wall of the house and in a few minutes you will be crushed to death. The child on the other hand won't be crushed to death: if nothing is done to stop him from growing he'll be hurt, but in the end he'll simply burst open the house and walk out a free man. Now I could well understand it if a bystander were to say, "There is nothing we can do for you. Cannot choose between your life and his, we cannot be the one to decide who is to live, we cannot intervene." But it cannot be concluded that you too can do nothing, that you cannot attack it to save your life. However innocent the child may be, you do not have to wait passively while it crushes you to death.[78]

The example is by no means an exact metaphor for the Israeli/Palestinian conflict or indeed for most cases of abortion. But the discrepancies in the comparison cut both ways. The Zionist child was not entirely innocent, and the innocents among the settler population were instruments of something not far removed from a conspiracy to subject or expel the Palestinians. The Palestinians might not be literally crushed to death by the Zionist influx, but there was a looming danger that many thousands of them would die in civil wars, forced marches, and exile. Moreover, we allow individuals and sometimes groups, especially when bereft of the protection afforded by a state to which they have consented, to defend their freedom as well as their life. If they are not free, we permit them to fight for their freedom.

The Palestinians faced a very real and serious threat. There was no realistic prospect of compromise with those who threatened them. Their resources, political and military, were very limited. Had they behaved in a "civilized" fashion, quietly building up a conventional military force of the sort that arouses our respect rather than our revulsion, no doubt their reputation would have benefited. But it is entirely possible that even more people would have suffered and died: the mobs were not efficient killing machines. Even with the full benefit of hindsight, it is far from obvious what course of action would have been morally best. The West has produced some very high-minded principles, but the actual standards by which it judges its own actions are very permissive, certainly allowing for great harm to innocent civilians when fighting for one's freedom or survival. All things considered, one need not grant blanket absolution to all Palestinians for all their sins, but there are no clear grounds for supposing their behavior deserves any special condemnation. Their response was in fact typical of ethnic conflicts everywhere, and in this case there is good reason to suppose the conflict was not their fault.

Do the Zionists deserve similar indulgence? They do not. They did not initiate the violence, which started with spontaneous peasant resistance in the 1880s. Nevertheless, the conflict *was* their fault, and we have seen why. Zionists came thousands of miles, not merely to settle or immigrate, but to erect a Jewish state. Their leaders literally conspired to dispossess or dominate the Palestinians. Though many Zionists ventured into Palestine with the ignorance and swagger of colonial adventurers, and others arrived dazzled by utopian visions, all were engaged in a project that represented a mortal threat to the indigenous inhabitants, who had done them no harm. Though some of those who constituted this threat were innocents, no adult Zionist can be said to have posed an innocent threat. They should have known better. They had a responsibility to know better. Zionism was no worse than many ethnic nationalisms nurtured by nineteenth-century European culture. But they were, all of them, a bad and dangerous idea. It was the implementation of this idea that made bloodshed in Palestine, if not inevitable, as close to it as we can expect to get. That blood is on the Zionists' hands.

A Verdict on Zionism

EVEN IF THE ZIONIST PROJECT JUSTIFIED SOME FORM OF VIOLENT response, and even if the Zionists were, therefore, responsible for that response, it is still just barely possible that the Zionist enterprise was justified as well: indeed, some Zionists have seemed willing to accept that violence was inevitable while remaining committed to Zionism.[79] There are three supposed sources of justification that must be considered before delivering a final verdict on the Zionist project. The first relates to Biblical and historical claims to Israel. The second relates to Hitler's Final Solution. The third generalizes on the second and involves the notion of Jewish self-defense.

Biblical and historical claims

Biblical and historical claims—to the effect that the past gives the Jews a right to Palestine—have been almost inextricably intertwined. Before looking very briefly at the specific historical significance of the Bible to the Zionist enterprise, it is worthwhile to assess the general status of land claims built on attention to the distant past.

Ancient history

As for ancient history, much energy has been expended on debates about who lived where in the distant past. Can this matter? Suppose yourself an inhabitant of Greece, or Turkey, or China. You can be dead sure that some people, perhaps in some cases even some individual, owned or was entitled to the land on which you exist. No one cares, and no one should care.

In the first place, it is virtually impossible to establish just who these people were: we may fit them into anthropological categories, but we can't say much more. Even if we discover some individual's title to your land, so what? Can we say that this person was truly the rightful owner, that the land was legitimately settled or acquired rather than usurped from some now nameless predecessor? And can we know whether this entitlement persisted after our discovery, that the title-holder did nothing to alienate or extinguish his claim? The pre-history and post-history of the entitlement is crucial to its application to contemporary ownership, yet that's just what's hidden from us.

In the second place, even if we could establish the true force of the original entitlement, what would we do with that? How can we relate it to anyone living today? The answer is: not closely enough. Sure, we might, with considerable luck, have found the owner's bones and determined by DNA tests that certain individuals are his contemporary descendants. But "descendants" is used here very loosely: we won't be able to tell whether these are the "rightful inheritors" of the property. What would this even mean? Are we to use the original laws of inheritance, even if they were superseded by quite different ones or simply vanished with some ancient civilization? What if our own view of inheritance is quite different: what, for instance, if we no longer want to say that property rightfully passes from father to eldest son? The idea that identifying some ancient inhabitant and somehow connecting him to some modern descendant will establish a contemporary property claim is bizarrely overconfident.

What if we decide to look, not at individuals, but peoples, e.g., at whether the Greeks, Turks, or Chinese are the rightful inhabitants of Greece, Turkey, or China? This is an even more hopeless venture. The chances that the peoples who now inhabit these areas did so without violating others' rights are minimal, but so are the chances that their predecessors were rightful occupants. And how could we ever settle on the criteria of rightful occupancy? Will we apply principles of international law to the nomadic tribes, migrations, and wars of 2000 B.C.? By what authority? Can we really even moralize about such poorly known events from such a great distance? The idea that our speculations could fix contemporary property rights is ludicrous: we have neither the facts nor the principles that would enable us to do this.

Even if the problems of knowledge were overcome, problems of right would persist. Suppose, by some miracle, we could determine that someone did indeed have an entitlement to your property, and this claim dated back to 2000 B.C. What then? It is entirely possible that you have an equally or even a more valid claim. Perhaps you acquired your property through procedures approved by your society, and the courts have validated your claim. Perhaps you have a moral claim: you knew nothing of the distant past; you worked hard to improve the land and support your family; you need the land to survive, and the other claimant does not. We are not in a position to say that you should retain your property, neither will we be in a position to say you should not.

In short, it really doesn't matter who inhabited Palestine in the distant past; it would never give us a basis for deciding who should live there in the present.

Historical claims in general

What then of the kind of historical claim that is sometimes made for Zionism, and often made for other "nationalist" movements? What if a people have had some tie to a certain area for hundreds or thousands of years? Does this entitle them to property over or sovereignty over that area?

In addressing this question it is crucial to bear in mind that ancient history already suggests: that entitlements are not an all-

or-nothing affair. Suppose, merely for the sake of argument, the "the Jews" do indeed have some claim, based on history, religion, and culture, to Palestine. In the first place, obviously, there can be the competing claims of non-Jews who inhabit the region: by their own account, the "Hebrews" came as conquerors. But equally important, this does *not* mean that there should be some sort of territorial compromise or division in which the entitlements of all parties are satisfied. All over the world, sleeping dogs are left to lie. The descendants of the ancient Saxons, Danes, Jutes, and Bohemians do not press their various historical entitlements, nor do the Persians or Turks or Egyptians or Ashanti or Bulgarians or Khmer. Even those who might see themselves as dispossessed in the remote past—like, for some areas, the Celts or Magyars or Burgundians—rarely press their territorial claims and get a cold reception when they do. Indeed, the burden of proof that such a compromise or division is appropriate typically rests on those who do *not* inhabit or control the region. In many cases existing arrangements trump historical or cultural claims.

The nature of these claims is also very much open to dispute. Do they differ from mere property claims? To what extent do they have a political dimension, and of what sort? Had the Palestinians, with the decline of the Ottoman empire, demanded their own state and insisted that "foreigners"—Jews, Turks, Syrians, Lebanese, Egyptians, Armenians—be excluded or denied sovereignty, there would have been legitimate grounds for advocating a compromise, some less drastic formula. The Palestinians, some would have said, are indeed entitled to some sort of state, to some sort of self-determination. But who counts as a Palestinian and who gets an equal voice in the emerging state is another matter. Other peoples and other individuals, one would point out, live in Palestine and have claims to self-determination too. The right of a people to a land—and we have seen reason to question the existence of such rights—does not easily translate into the right to an ethnic state, a state in which sovereignty is reserved for that people.

Even if there were such a right, it could be weak, and it could be lost. The German people had very strong claims, based on hundreds of years of history, to parts of Austria, Poland, Denmark, and probably some areas of the Baltic states and Russia. Native Americans have a very strong claim to America, but now there is the competing claim of the "Americans" to the United States. If that claim has validity, then the British also have a very strong claim to the same area, and a parallel situation exists with the Spanish and Portuguese in South America. What is the fate of these lurking entitlements?

The strength of a claim certainly decreases with discontinuous or tenuously continuous occupation. The Greeks colonized and occupied much of Asia Minor. Their presence did not cease with their assimilation into the Roman empire: the Eastern regions were substantially Greek and went on to become the independent Byzantine empire, which lasted hundreds of years and left its stamp all over the Eastern Mediterranean. When Byzantium fell to the Ottomans in 1453, a Greek presence persisted throughout that area, at least until well into the 20th Century. The parallels with "the Jews" are extensive: occupation by conquest and colonization and dispossession by the same means, save for a sort of ethnic "stub" that quietly endured. In territorial disputes, one might expect the Greeks to fare better than the Jews, because the Greeks' rule and subsequent presence were both longer and stronger. Yet if the Greeks claimed much of the Eastern Roman Empire, including Turkey, they would be suspected of insanity. And the Italians? How much of the Roman Empire is rightfully theirs? These claims, one may safely say, have been lost. So have the imperial claims of the Germans, Spanish, British, and Portuguese. Even the far, far stronger claims of the Native Americans have become little more than bids for very partial compensation. Sometimes this has to do with the conduct of the claimants; sometimes it has to do with the disastrous consequences of recognizing their partial, defeasible entitlements. But lost they are. We will not soon see the day when Germans, even future generations not responsible for Nazi crimes, can claim those parts of Poland which they inhabited for centuries.

Nor is this the end of the difficulties with historical claims: there is not only the question of their validity, but of who is entitled to make them, and how they are to be pursued. In the first place, there is always something fishy about "the Xs" demanding a free and independent Xavia. "The Xs" are typically not a state or society; otherwise they would already have a state which contains all of them and there would be no issue or controversy. And, invariably, whether it has to do with German claims or British claims or Jewish claims, there are many among "the Xs" who do not want to make them, some who deny them altogether, and many more who never considered the issue and who where never consulted. Those who pursue them vigorously are almost invariably self-appointed "representatives." We do not accept self-appointed representatives of countries, and it is not at all clear that we should accept them of "peoples." It is one thing when, for example, a nationalist leader, having mobilized tens of thousands of his supporters already inhabiting a certain area, emerges triumphant after years of struggle against a colonial master. It is quite another if a self-selected assembly of Xs outside the area proclaim an entitlement to somewhere they do not inhabit, setting out to move into that area, and establish a sovereign state. Even if there is some validity to the claim of Xs to that area, it certainly does not follow that these self-appointed leaders are the ones to pursue it.

Nor, finally, does it follow that just any sort of pursuit is acceptable. Normally, if you have some claim over my land, you aren't supposed simply to move in. Some adjudication is required, and it must be a fair procedure. The adjudication, of course, is supposed to happen before you move in, not after. It should not, like the "settlements" of 1947-1948, be designed to resolve the ongoing conflict resulting from immigration designed to bolster a claim. Such settlements are at best designed to bring peace and, therefore, as much reflect the relative strength of the combatants as their rights. And the adjudication must be undertaken by a genuinely neutral and qualified authority. In private life, such authorities may well exist; in international affairs this is rarely the case. The situation is even trickier if the area is ruled by someone—in the case of Palestine, the Turks or the British—who no one thinks has any particular entitlement to the land: how then can adjudication proceed?[80] And this is precisely why nationalist land claims are so dangerous and so rarely accommodated. When a right is of indeterminate strength, rests with a group whose composition and representation are in dispute, and lacks an authoritative forum in which it can be adjudicated, it usually lies unrealized and dissipates over time. So, even if there were some firm historical basis for a Jewish claim to Palestine, it would not follow that the claim had any considerable weight. It is time to examine whether there can be such a basis.

Biblical claims

These claims have two dimensions, historical and religious. The dubiousness of basing land claims on ancient history has already been argued. In the case of a Jewish claim to Palestine, the claims are themselves dubious. Here it is not necessary to have decided on a truth, which may elude researchers forever. It is enough to show there is serious controversy, and that is easily done. One account of recent findings can be found in *The Bible Unearthed: Archaeology's New Vision of Ancient Israel and the Origin of Its Sacred Texts*. Its authors are Israel Finkelstein, director of an archaeological institute at Tel Aviv University, and Neil Asher Silberman, director of a Belgian archaeological institute and a contributing editor to *Archaeology* magazine. These writers display no political agenda and repeat to the point of saturation their admiration and respect for the Bible. Asher and Silberman introduce their work with the claim that:

> The historical saga contained in the Bible—from Abraham's encounter with God and his journey to Canaan, to Moses' deliverance of the children of Israel from bondage, to the rise and fall of the kingdoms of Israel and Judah—was not a miraculous revelation, but a brilliant product of the human imagination.[81]

This is the authors' exceedingly polite way of saying that the Biblical accounts are sometimes nonsense, sometimes deliberate lies, exaggerations, and distortions. The status of the Biblical kingdoms is particularly relevant to Jewish claims to Palestine. One of Asher and Silberman's more devastating findings is that:

> The Biblical borders of the land of Israel as outlined in the book of Joshua had seemingly assumed a sacred inviolability ...the Bible pictures a stormy but basically continuous Israelite occupation of the land of Israel all the way to the Assyrian conquest. But a reexamination of the archaeological evidence... points to a period of a few decades [in which a strong Israel existed], between around 835–800 B.C.E. ...[82]

In other words, they find that the "great" Jewish kingdoms existed in something like their fabled extent for a tiny fraction of the period traditionally alleged. Even then, their boundaries never came close to the "Greater Israel" of contemporary Jewish fundamentalism. The rest of the time, Judah and Israel are thought to have been, for the most part, very primitive entities, devoid of literate culture or substantial administrative structure, extending to only a small, landlocked part of what is now called Palestine. The great structures of the Biblical era are, all of them, attributed to Canaanite cultures. Moreover, the inhabitants of Biblical Israel and Judah seem to have been, for most of the time and for the most part, practitioners of Canaanite religions rather than Judaism, or of various syncretic cults. These "Israelites" were not, that is, "Jewish" in one important sense of the term. The authors refer to the Biblical kingdom at its greatest extent as "a multiethnic society."[83] The idea that such a past could validate a Jewish historical claim to Palestine is simply ludicrous, even if it could be shown—which it cannot—that today's Jews are in some legal sense, heirs to the ancient Israelite kingdoms.

What then of the religiously based claims, which impressed even some Muslim Palestinians who piously took them as historical fact?[84] The mystery here is why these claims should ever be taken seriously in the first place. We no longer live in an age when one religion can demand belief from all the world. That "God gave Israel to the Jews," it must apparently be said, requires belief in the existence of the Jewish God and in the Bible as the word of God. No amount of "respect" for others' beliefs can require accepting those beliefs as true. In the case of religion, this is fortunate because religions contradict one another. The idea that the Bible or Judaism can in any way validate Zionism deserves no further discussion.

It is worth noting, however, that not even all religious Jews believe that Judaism supports Zionism.[85] Orthodox Jewish opposition to these claims is increasingly vocal. A historian of these tendencies explains that these views can also be found outside the orthodox tradition:

> The link that the Jews have with the Land of Israel is therefore contractual rather than organic. It is contingent on their loyalty to the Torah...
>
> In line with this idea of contract, the Jewish tradition attributes the exile of the Jews from the Land of Israel to their abandoning Torah commandments. The tradition does not view Jews as hapless victims, but rather as makers of their own fate. Maimonides and other classical sources indicate that the way

back to the Land of Israel is ...repentance and return to the commandments. ...the redress for exile is not and should not be sought in developing a mightier army. In fact, the Talmud (BT Ketubot, 111a) refers to oaths that the Jews were to swear prior to their second exile, in which they are enjoined not to rebel against the nations and to re-occupy the Land of Israel by force. Given this tradition, some Judaic scholars see Israel's military exploits not as a sign of impending messianic redemption but rather as a blasphemous act of rebellion.[86]

So, even if religion was a valid basis for land claims, it would not provide a valid basis for Zionism. For that to happen, the minimum credential would be a unanimity among religious authorities that does not exist.

The Final Solution

Zionism was from the start an ill-considered and menacing experiment in ethnic nationalism. Neither history nor religion could justify it. The Jews had no claim to Palestine and no right to found a state there. Their growing need for refuge may have provided some limited, inadequate, short-term moral sustenance for the Zionist project, but it could not render that project legitimate. The mere fact of later suffering cannot retroactively convert a wrong into a right: my attempt to usurp your land does not become legitimate simply because I am savagely beaten by someone else, far away, when my project is near completion. Nor did the well-founded desperation of the Jews during the Nazi era provide any justification for Zionism; at most it provided an excuse. If someone is murdering my family in Germany, that does not entitle me to your house in Boston, or my "people" to your country. All Jews fleeing Hitler were indeed entitled to some refuge. One might even suppose that it was the obligation of the whole world, including the Palestinians, to do what they could to provide such refuge. But this is not the whole story.

For one thing, those with ample means to provide refuge, and those who are responsible for the need, have by far the greater share of responsibility. The Palestinians fell into neither category. Even more important, there is an enormous difference between providing refuge and providing a sovereign state. No amount of danger or suffering requires this, and indeed it may conflict with the demand for refuge. Simply to control one's own affairs is not necessarily the safest alternative. Arguably, for instance, the Jews were safer in the United States, where they are not sovereign, than they ever were in Israel. This is not only a fact but was always a reasonable expectation, so the need for refuge is also no basis for Zionism.

There is certainly some basis for saying that, *given* the failure of the great powers to fulfill their obligations to provide refuge, the Jews had a right to find it where they could. If this meant displacing Palestinians, that too might not only be understandable but justifiable: there *is* some plausibility to the claim that I may force my way into your house to escape a lynch mob, even if others are far more responsible for helping me than you are. At the very limit of generosity, one might even make a partial case for Jewish sovereignty on similar grounds: I might have a right to commandeer your house to arrange my defenses against those seeking to kill me. But none of this can justify the Zionist project. Once the danger is past, all my rights cease to apply. At most, the Nazi menace might have justified some Jewish activities in Palestine between 1933 and 1945. After that, the Jews no longer had a right to refuge in Palestine, much less to a Jewish state. That such a state might have some questionable tendency to protect the Jews against possible recurrences of the danger is not nearly enough. I cannot retain possession of your house simply because, even after the lynch mob and its organizers have been suppressed, there is some indeterminate chance that I might somehow be exposed to such dangers again. The Final Solution does not justify the Zionist solution.

We are often told that the lesson of the Nazi era is that "Jews can only rely on themselves." It is unlikely that Jews can rely absolutely on anyone, *including* themselves: not all Jews behaved with courage or integrity during that catastrophe. Besides, a presumed need for Jews to rely only on themselves doesn't confer some right to construct an ethnic state in Palestine, or to subjugate the Palestinians. Having to rely only on yourself doesn't in any way extend your rights over others. The world is full of criminals who, from a very early age, could rely only on themselves. This might make their crimes more understandable, but it does not make them any less criminal.

No desire to make up for past wrongs, however intense, and no exhortations to remember the victims, do anything to justify support for Israel. The overwhelming majority of the victims, many of them non-Jewish, are dead. No one has the right to "remember" them by supporting a state they might very well abhor. To suppose that all the Jewish victims would have loved Israel is to "honor" them through the crudest sort of ethnic stereotyping. As for the tiny number who survive, we do not know how many of them are Zionists, and in any case it would be grotesque to conduct international politics according to their presumed wishes. If there are any great lessons of the Nazi era, they are to watch out for fascism, racism, and ethnic nationalism. Supporting Israel hardly embodies these lessons.

Finally, it is nonsense to claim that supporting Israel is somehow owed to the Jewish people. "The Jewish people" is a figure of speech, not a reality. The reality is that there are many individual Jews alive today, many of whom do not benefit from or enjoy Israel's existence. The overwhelming majority did not suffer under the Nazis. A minority had relatives who did; in general they have received compensation. Compensation certainly does not make things right again, but to augment it with the gift of an oppressive, detested state hardly improves the situation. It is even greater madness to see support for Israel as doing penance for Nazi horrors or Allied indifference. The sinners are mostly dead and certainly not offering contrition. And what sort of penance allows Zionist Jews to threaten the existence of the Palestinians? It is as if a penitent international court allowed a grieving woman, widowed by a murder in Italy, to beat up some innocent person in Spain.

Zionism as Jewish self-defense?

Zionists have always declared that only by constructing a Jewish state could the Jews find a true refuge from persecution. Today, this claim doesn't look very convincing. There are many places Jews can go to find refuge other than "their own state." Israel, though its own existence is very secure, is perhaps the most dangerous place in which large numbers of Jews live today. But without the benefit of hindsight, the claim had promise. In the early days of Zionism, the Jews certainly seemed to need sanctuary, and their fears were soon to find horrifying confirmation. This need, as has often been pointed out, did not require a Jewish state in Palestine: Uganda, which was offered, would have been further out of harm's way, and larger. In either case, the rights of indigenous populations would have been violated, and the settlement would have posed a mortal threat. But weren't the Jews fleeing a mortal threat themselves? Didn't that give them an equal right to do whatever was necessary to ward it off? Granted that other countries could have accommodated them more generously, perhaps even provided unoccupied land, but they didn't. These failures only compounded the pressure on the Jews. So, it seems as if the Zionists as well as the Palestinians could plead self-defense, and that the situation was a tragedy in which two rights made a wrong.

The argument is specious. The threat was all too real, and the Jews certainly had every right to defend themselves, but Zionism did not offer them a defense. At the time, it rarely even claimed to do so.

Appeals to self-defense require more than the apprehension of some future mortal threat. They require an imminent one, something that any reasonable person would agree is definitely about to happen. (Country A can't attack Country B just because Country B is hostile and building up its army; it must at the least have mobilized and moved its forces towards the border.) Even then, the appeal justifies only what is necessary to meet that threat. While no moral agent can be expected to explore all the possible alternatives, their actions must at least appear to be a necessary response to the threat: I cannot build a fort on your property when I could just as well lock my doors. More than that, it must be reasonable to suppose that these actions are the only practical course of action: I cannot run you over to escape an attacker if I could just as well have gone in another direction.

Zionism never passed these tests. In fact, it was precisely the Zionist component of the Zionists' response that had nothing to do with Jewish self-defense. When they protected Jews against an imminent threat, Zionists were not acting as Zionists. When they acted as Zionists, they weren't protecting Jews against an imminent threat.

Let's agree that Jews faced something like an imminent and mortal threat more than once during the early days of Zionism: there were pogroms in Russia and Ukraine; there was the rise of Hitler. In these areas, the Jews really had only one practical response to their persecution—to leave. Leaving for Palestine was justified because leaving for *anywhere* was justified—that was pretty much all the Jews could do to save their lives. But leaving for anywhere was the Jewish response, not the Zionist one. The Zionist response was to insist that Jews leave specifically for Palestine and build a state there. Was this response—this insistence—a justified act of self-defense?

It is hard to see how self-defense required an obsessive focus on Palestine. There was no need for all the Jews who left to go to the same place. Zionists held that Jews could protect themselves in Palestine by building a powerful state of their own. But fleeing to a single destination could hardly conjure up some automatically strong state; this would take, as everyone agreed, decades. So, the immediate result of fleeing to a single destination would be quite the opposite of what the Zionists wanted: there would be a large population at the mercy of some non-Jewish sovereign. This was in fact the situation of the Jews in Palestine throughout the time when Jews were most in need of protection.

So, while the generically Jewish response of seeking refuge wherever they could was genuine self-defense, the specifically Zionist response of insisting on emigration to Palestine was not. It amounted to choosing a single escape route, not because that strategy saved the most lives, but because it promoted Jewish sovereignty. Ben-Gurion himself made this brutally clear at the time, saying that:

> If I knew that it was possible to save all the children in Germany by transporting them to England, but only half of them by transporting them to Palestine, I would choose the second—because we face not only the reckoning of these children, but the historical reckoning of the Jewish people.[87]

This seems a rather vague reason for leaving children to die. In simpler terms, Ben-Gurion was far more committed to Jewish sovereignty than to saving Jews from what came to be called a holocaust. Already in 1933, the Jewish Agency and the Nazis had signed the *"haavara"* (transfer) agreement that allowed Jews to emigrate with 1,000 pounds—but only for Palestine, where the British required that sum for admission.[88] Segev comments that this agreement "effectively isolated the *yishuv* [the Jewish community in Palestine] from the dominant current of world Jewish response to the rise of the Nazis."[89]

So much for Zionist immigration politics that were, unsurprisingly, Zionist rather than defensive. What then of Zionism's fight for a state in Palestine? Was this a justifiably defensive act?

We have already seen that, in the short run, a Jewish state in Palestine wasn't an option at all: no one supposed that the Zionists could, in a few months, construct a state capable of protecting its citizens. If it wasn't an option, it couldn't be a defensive option. So in the short run, there was nothing defensive about a state-building project which, all agreed, would not be complete in time to counter the threats Jews actually faced at the time. Even if Palestine had been considered the one ideal destination, this still would not have called for building a Jewish state: more Jews could have entered Palestine had the Zionists clearly renounced and abandoned all intentions of building a state there. Zionists did help Jews by getting them out of Europe, but helping them get out of Europe wasn't Zionism. Attaching Zionist strings to this rescue only made things more difficult.

Well, does the drive to build a Jewish state in Palestine seem like justifiable self-defense when we look at the bigger picture? Here we might want to relax our requirements. Perhaps self-defense at the level of ethnic groups or nations doesn't require an imminent threat. Perhaps it is enough if the course of action chosen can plausibly be represented as the only possible response to a more distant threat. One can imagine such cases. Suppose an asteroid, some years from now, is virtually sure to hit my country, and your country has the only point from which I can launch an interceptor missile, which is my only chance of avoiding disaster. Maybe then I am justified in invading your country to launch the missile. If the launch requires elaborate constructions and long preparation, maybe I can even take over your country. But was Zionism the only plausible response to some long-term threat?

In the long run, a strong Jewish state might indeed provide better protection than any alternative. But a strong Jewish state was not the alternative available; it was rather a drive to *build* such a state. Was that the only plausible way for Jews to defend themselves?

The first question should perhaps be, against what? In the long run—some decades in the future, which was when the drive to build a state was expected to bear fruit—what would be the situation of the Jews? The Zionists had no specific threat in mind, like the asteroid. Their strategy was, therefore, not a response to any specific threat; it was hardly even a strategy. As a program for helping the Jews, Zionism was little more than a *theory* about how future threats could be countered. It held that sometime, somewhere, some sort of new threats to the Jewish people would emerge, and the state of Israel would provide safe haven against them. The point bears repeating: the Zionists never even claimed that Israel, an independent, sovereign Jewish state, would rise as a bulwark to save the Jews from some predicted pogrom or holocaust. Their program was not like Hadrian's Wall, designed to repel known invaders who had been attacking for years and who clearly would attack again. The idea was rather that the *next* time, some decades in the future, whatever dangers might materialize, Zionists would be ready to save the day.

This theory provided no justification for anything at all. There was a well-established, widely believed competing theory that emigration, dispersion, and perhaps assimilation offered the best hope of survival. Both theories tended to overlook the obvious: that what mattered most was to be *aware* of impending threats. Given such awareness—and unfortunately no one was sufficiently aware, early enough, of the Nazi threat—both theories had something going for them. The Zionist theory offered an ironclad solution, except that its implementation was terribly uncertain: no one could be sure that the Jews could establish an independent state, that the state would be strong enough to ward off any impending threats, or that there would *be* such threats. (And, in fact, since the foundation of the state of Israel there haven't been.) The solution, moreover, required that all threat ened Jews reside in Israel already, or have no trouble getting there in time of need: was this plausible?

On the other hand, the competing theory—"just leave"—was compellingly simple. What mattered, according to this theory, was to find safe haven anywhere possible, as soon as possible, in response to threats. Assimilation might provide further protection. The case of Germany was to show that such protection was anything but a guarantee, but the theory did not require that. It would be enough if Jews did not become complacent anywhere, but were ready to leave when danger loomed. To this end, Jewish organizations were set up to provide warnings and facilitate such moves. The "just get out" theory was at least as plausible as Zionism, and probably had more claim to be counted as a strategy. It had all the advantages of a common-sense, unambitious solution; one that had in fact saved many thousands of Eastern Jews from a terrible fate. In this it contrasted well with the picky, narrow refugee policies of the Zionists. The "just get out" idea, unlike the Zionist idea, was tried and true. When getting out was impossible, nothing would work. When it was possible, it worked as well as anything else.

The Zionist theory had competition, not only from the "just leave" theory, but from non-Zionist "Jewish state" theories, most notably the Uganda option. Where would be the right place for a future state? There could be no certainty about this, but to plunk a Jewish state in the middle of an "Arab" world was not, obviously, the best choice. Perhaps Uganda would be a good idea after all: the British were in control of the whole area, which was remote from known sources of persecution. Perhaps, some better accommodation with the existing population could be achieved. These issues were debated, and the debates had all the hallmarks of a contest between theories rather than strategies: they concerned a cloudy future where both the nature of the threats and the viability of the responses were quite incalculable. The theories were hardly testable, so the discussion was terminally speculative. Even today, the answers are quite unknown. It is still unknown whether there will be another great threat to Jews, and whether Israel or "just getting out" will prove the better option. It is almost as if we are back to the beginning, when people wondered whether getting all the world's Jews packed into one small territory was such a good idea. It certainly makes a convenient target.

Zionism cannot, therefore, represent itself as self-defense. It is not like the asteroid case. It is more like the case where a country thinks it *might* be hit by an asteroid sometime in the future, and that your country *might* provide the best launch point, and that a takeover of your country *might* be necessary. Even if all these claims were as plausible as those of several competing theories, they would certainly not entitle you to take over my country. This is fortunate, because people and nations see potential threats anywhere and everywhere contemplate vaguely plausible aggressive responses: to take these as sufficient reason to act would ensure catastrophe. To the frightening realities that endangered Jews in the early days of Zionism, Zionism provided no specifically Zionist response: all the Zionists could do was help people leave for destinations not in Jewish control. But as a response to possible threats in the more distant future, Zionism offered only one of several plausible responses. It was by no means the only response nor was there a consensus that it was the most plausible one, nor could anyone discern any specific threat in that more distant future.

This cannot be sufficient reason to subjugate or displace an entire people who were no threat at all, especially when this plan made first the Palestinians and then the British far more hostile to providing refuge for Jews in Palestine. The British decision (in 1939) to restrict immigration into Palestine did not arise from some simple wish to stop the influx of Jews: it came from the known intention of Zionists to create a Jewish state. We have seen that this specifically anti-Zionist reaction was apparent to

Jewish observers as early as 1920. Zionism was a non-response to a real threat, and the implementation of a theory about how to respond to yet-unperceived, possible future threats. That does not add up to an acceptable self-defense case for taking over Palestine. Zionists were making difficult decisions in difficult circumstances and, perhaps, they were not to blame for their actions, but that doesn't make those actions any less wrong.

The situation of the Zionists was nothing like that of the Palestinians. The Palestinians faced an immediate, concrete mortal threat: the Zionists were there, among them, growing stronger daily, inviting them to submit to Jewish sovereignty or depart. Moreover, they had good reason to believe that the Zionists wanted to dispossess them entirely, over the whole of Palestine. A Palestinian appeal to self-defense does not license a Zionist appeal—not because Jews had no right to self-defense, but because the Zionist appeal was an illegitimate invocation of that right.

Zionism and the establishment of Israel

Zionism always was, despite strategically motivated denials to the contrary and brief flirtations with other objectives, an attempt to establish Jewish sovereignty over Palestine. This project was illegitimate. Neither history nor religion, nor the sufferings of Jews in the Nazi era, sufficed to justify it. It posed a mortal threat to the Palestinians, and it left no room for meaningful compromise. Given that the Palestinians had no way to overcome Zionism peacefully, it also justified some form of violent resistance.

The illegitimacy of Zionism has important implications for the legitimacy of Israel itself and for the early history of that state. It was wrong to pursue the Zionist project and wrong to achieve it. For that reason, how it was pursued and achieved has little bearing on the fundamental rights and wrongs of the Israel/Palestine conflict. This means that many huge controversies simply don't matter. These include some which have all but been settled by the work of Zionist historian Benny Morris, who concedes, for example, that the Zionists did intend, at least as some point, forcible transfer of the Palestinians, that the Palestinians did not leave because "Arab broadcasts" encouraged them to do so, that the Israeli forces did indeed commit massacres during the war of independence, and so on. Had the goal of a Jewish state been justified, some Zionist violence would have been justified, some criminal, but this would reflect only on the conduct of the Zionists themselves, not on the legitimacy of their project or of the Jewish state.

On the other hand, since the Zionist project never was legitimate, much that is said in its defense, and in Israel's defense, whether sound or unsound, is irrelevant. It does not matter if the Zionists wanted peace: of course they did! Who wouldn't want to rob someone's land and dominate their very existence without having to fight for that objective? It does not matter if some of the land was obtained by purchase; it would not matter if every square inch of it had been so obtained. The Israel/Palestine conflict is not about mere land ownership but about its use to establish the sovereignty of one ethnic group over another: that this unacceptable objective is achieved by purchase or by other means does not make it any less wrong. It does not matter if the Zionists achieved wonderful things or "turned the desert green." That I do wonderful things while acquiring the power of life and death over you hardly legitimates my venture. It does not matter if Palestine was or wasn't a poor, neglected area; this could not possibly give anyone supreme power over its inhabitants. And it does not matter if the Palestinians ever made genuine attempts to achieve peace, because peace was never a live option except by submission to Jewish sovereignty. That was never something to which the Palestinians ought to have consented.

Little or nothing that occurred from the 1920s until the late 1960s matters either. That, in its various wars, Israel was or wasn't the aggressor makes no difference. In the first place, the actions of the Arab states were not that of the Palestinians and could not affect their right to freedom from Jewish sovereignty. In the second, Israel was always defending an illegitimate project: that it did so aggressively or defensively, brutally or gently, cleverly or stupidly, in an equal or an unequal struggle, none of this makes its defense justifiable. It may have been justified to try and save the lives of Jewish refugees, but that never justified the state of Israel or the intention to establish it. Had the Zionists not been Zionists, had they asked for nothing more than the right to seek refuge in a land rather than rule it, matters might have been different, but they weren't.

That many thousands of Jews fled Arab countries after 1948 also doesn't matter. Whether the treatment of these Jews was to any extent justified doesn't matter. An excessive reaction to a wrong act doesn't make the act any righter. If the Allies overreacted by mistreating Germans or Japanese during or after the Second World War, that has no tendency whatever to justify the German or Japanese actions preceding the reaction.

What is incontestable is that Zionism set in motion all the terrible sequence of events that followed. It did not do so as a catalyst for already existing animosities, nor did it initiate a process whose character changed unpredictably as a result of forces far beyond the scope of the Zionists' control. That an attempt to establish Jewish sovereignty over the Palestinians should be met with fury, violence, and implacable hostility was anything but unforeseeable. That other people and states in the region should take the side of the Palestinians, perhaps even fight for them, was hardly not to be expected. That Jews in these regions should be victimized was all too likely. That millions of Palestinians should be forced into a squalid, dangerous exile, which bred further hatred and violence, should not have been any surprise.

Moreover, Zionists did at various times have the alternative of abandoning Zionism in a more or less convincing manner. They could have dropped not only calls for a Jewish state, but for a Jewish homeland; they could have repudiated the dangerously vague goals endorsed in the Balfour Declaration. They could, in other words, have stated that they wanted no more than a certain level of Jewish immigration, dropping all demands for collective ethnic representation or power. Whether these measures would have brought peace before 1948 is unclear: the Palestinians had ample reason for distrusting such gestures. After 1948, opportunities expanded: an offer to abolish the state of Israel in favor of a bi-national state under UN supervision would certainly have had more credibility. All in all, Zionism initiated a process whose evolution was foreseeable and understandable. Zionism and the Zionists are, therefore, to an unusual degree responsible for the consequences of that fateful step. Their project was not like raising a child who, unexpectedly, turns psychotic, but like releasing a homicidal maniac—a child of ethnic nationalism—into the world. This is why the blame for the conflict falls so heavily on Zionist and so lightly on Palestinian shoulders.

Does all this mean that Israel has no right to exist? Yes and no

Israel has no legitimate foundation. If Israel collapsed simply because it lost external and internal support, nothing wrong would have happened. Nor would it be wrong to destroy Israel as a political entity *if* its continued existence would have even worse consequences: limited violence might be acceptable, but not genocidal warfare. Israel has no right to exist in the sense that *some* means of putting an end to its existence may be justified. But in another sense, Israel does have a right to exist. Given today's political realities, no one ought to try and wipe Israel off the face of the earth.

In some ways, the more cynical Zionists are right: Israel's foundations, even if every single allegation of ethnic cleansing is completely accurate, are no worse than those of most other states. Virtually no state has legitimate foundations, and in that sense virtually no state has a right to exist. In theory, therefore, everyone has a right to interfere with the existence of those states. In practice, however, such "interference" is almost never justified. The mere fact that, say, the United States is founded on genocide, massacre, and exploitation is not sufficient reason to destroy the United States. This is because the cure of destruction is in practice worse than the disease of illegitimate existence. In practice, wiping out a powerful state such as the U.S. or Israel would cause even more suffering than letting it survive. More important, attacks on these states would almost certainly be unsuccessful and merely add to the evil of illegitimate existence the much more serious evil of catastrophic warfare. So Israel, like any other illegitimate state, does for all practical purposes have the right to exist. It would be wrong to try to destroy these states, not because it would be wrong if they vanished, but because the attempt would, in fact, have dreadful consequences. Israel's existence is tainted, not sacred, but it is protected by the same useful international conventions that allow others, in the name of peace, to retain their ill-gotten gains. Israel's right to exist, as Yohoshafat Harkabi points out, can be distinguished from any right "to be born" or to come into existence.[90]

These conclusions mark a fundamental divide in the assessment of the Israel/Palestine conflict. Israel's existence is to all appearances an indelibly accomplished fact. Debates about its right to exist are pointless. Debates about the legitimacy of Zionism now matter only so far as they affect new issues generated by Israel's occupation of the West Bank and the Gaza strip after the 1967 war. These issues will occupy the second part of this essay.

Part II: The Current Situation

The Occupation

WERE THIS A HISTORY OF ISRAEL, MOST OF IT WOULD PROBABLY cover a period running from the late 1930s to the early 1970s. For our purposes, the momentous events of this period—the failure of partition, the 1948 war, Suez, the Six Day War, and the Yom Kippur War—are also very important, but require no discussion: if they did not resolve the main issue discussed above, they eliminated it.

Zionism raised the question of the legitimacy of the Jewish state. Israel's wars assured that such a state *will* exist. From a political standpoint, that puts an end to the discussion of whether it ought to exist: to debate this now is to engage in fruitless moralizing. If a case must be made against Israel today, it is because the 1970s saw the emergence of a new issue: Israel's continued occupation of the West Bank and the Gaza strip or, more importantly, its settlement of those areas. This issue is just as pressing as its predecessor. Assessing it requires an appreciation of Israel's position when the settlement policy was instituted and when it matured. Were the settlements and/or the occupation some sort of strategic necessity? Are they now? And *was* Israel's existence really all that secure?

Israel's strategic position

Shortly after the Yom Kippur war in October 1973, it was apparent that Israel's existence as a state was, barring a world apocalypse, secure. Although Egypt had done well in that war and caused Israel considerable anxiety, several factors indicated that Israel's strategic position was actually very strong.

First, Israel did successfully repel the threat. Though the war provoked much soul-searching and deflated Israeli egos, it has justly been called "a victory perceived as a defeat."[91] Enemy troops never got inside its 1948 borders. Emergency U.S. aid may have been an essential prerequisite in this success. But, second, it became clear that U.S. aid or, failing that, the pacifying influence of the main international powers, could be relied on.

After 1973, there was a fundamental change in U.S. policy: "As a direct result of the war, the United States quadrupled its foreign aid to Israel and replaced France as Israel's largest arms supplier. In fact, the doctrine of maintaining Israel's 'qualitative edge' over its neighbors was born in the war's aftermath."[92] Though Israel had soundly defeated the forces on its northern and western fronts, encircled the Egyptian 3rd army, and got within sixty-five miles of Cairo, though it was now unlikely to repeat the carelessness that led to the Arab forces' initial success, it now in addition had gained an immense strategic advantage in the firm, open-ended, and extremely generous support of the United States. Egypt, on the other hand, had already expelled its Soviet military experts before the war, in July 1972, and the Soviets had at that time counseled against attacking Israel.[93]

Had there been any doubt about the strength of U.S. commitments to Israel—and there wasn't—Israel could still be confident that the world would not allow Arab states a military victory over Israel. This is because Israel, with its nuclear capacity, now could force the world to prevent any war from seriously threatening Israel's existence. Israel's leverage here was called "the Sampson option": Israel would use nuclear weapons, even at the risk of self-destruction, if its neighbors seemed on the brink of victory. Perhaps this is why those neighbors never again showed any sign of making war on Israel, either singly or in alliance.

In addition, the Yom Kippur war was followed by a marked improvement in the diplomatic situation. This involved more than the rapprochement between Israel and the U.S. Egypt's Sadat took his "victory" as a launch pad for a peace initiative, starting with a resumption of relations with the United States a month after the war. This initiative culminated with the Camp David accords of 1978: Israel was now at peace with what had been by far its strongest opponent. In fact, Egypt had shown its lack of belligerence a year earlier: when a Likud government was elected on a "Greater Israel" platform, Sadat responded with his pledge to go anywhere, even to the Knesset, in the cause of peace.[94]

It was not only in regard to Egypt that Israel's security situation had much improved. Syria was still an enemy of some consequence, but Israel had in the Golan Heights, occupied during the Six Day War of 1967, a significant buffer against Syrian attacks. Jordan had entered the 1973 war only reluctantly; it was clear the Jordanians were no threat. On the contrary, they had done Israel a great service in 1970 by decimating Israel's most committed opponent, the Palestinians, who had suffered great losses in the "Black September" fighting that had resulted in their expulsion from Jordan. Outside Israel, Palestinians now had both numbers and (very weak) forces only in Lebanon, where they were hated by the Christian population and could never be expected to pose a serious threat. In short, Israel had only one, much weaker enemy on its post-1967 borders, and that enemy was in no position to pose a threat to Israel proper.

Syria was—with the exception of strains over Lebanon in the mid-1970s—closely supported by the Soviet Union, but this was no net disadvantage to Israel. Syria, unlike Egypt, has extensive borders with a major oil producer, Iraq, and relatively easy access to the Gulf states. For the U.S. and its allies, an Israeli victory over Syria would eliminate its only powerful and fixed enemy in the region. So, quite apart from any Zionist sympathies, for the

U.S. the decisive ascendancy of a Soviet client in the region would have been unthinkable. The Israelis could, therefore, count on the U.S. to prevent such a victory. Indeed, in the words of one observer,

> ...the United States and the Soviet Union had [by 1970] accepted their mutual status of parity. This meant that the United States and the Soviet Union could not act in the region without incurring counter-action by the other superpower. Israel was not inhibited in this way and could strike at will with only the tacit approval of the United States Government to support her.[95]

On top of all this, though it is customary to see Israel as standing alone against its regional allies, the same could be said of its neighbors. Only some factions within Lebanon ever considered their Syrian neighbor a friend; for the others it was a menace. Syria made an enemy of Jordan by sending 200 tanks to aid the Palestinians during the 1970 Black September conflict. Jordanian-Egyptian relations were cool because the Hashemite Monarchy under King Hussein felt threatened by Nasser's aggressive, socialistic brand of "Arab nationalism." Since the late sixties, with a very brief interlude in the late 1970s, relations between Syria and Iraq have been very bad: the two countries almost went to war over water in 1978, and Syria (like Lybia) supported Iran during the Iran-Iraq war. Syria and Egypt had mistrusted one another ever since the breakup of the United Arab Republic in 1961. Saudi Arabia and most of the Gulf States despised Syria and Egypt for their "Arab socialism." The following has been said of King Feisal:

> For him, Nasser rather than Israel was the devil incarnate and the Egyptian leader's revolutionary creed as sinister a carrier of the Marxist plague as Zionism, and extraordinary identification and obsessive conviction that Feisal had first given public expression to in 1962...[96]

Speaking of the 1967 war, Feisal told an Arab diplomat: "If someone throws stones at a neighbor's windows he should not be surprised or complain if the owner comes out and beats him with a stick."[97] Nor was Feisal likely to warm to Sadat, who had advised Nasser to support a Marxist régime in Yemen that opened the way to a five-year military confrontation between Egypt and Saudi Arabia.[98] In 1969, revolutions in the Sudan and Lybia brought an estrangement between Feisal and those countries.[99] As for Jordan, its Hashemite rulers were traditional rivals, not friends, of the Saudi royal house. When the Iraqi régime was Hashemite, it was despised by Syria and Egypt. When the régime was replaced by militant Baathists in 1968, they fell out with their Syrian counterparts and appalled both Jordan and Saudi Arabia. In short, Israel's friendlessness was not the regional exception but the rule.

None of this is to say that Israel had no strategic concerns in the mid-1970s or even after 1990, when the fall of the Soviet Union meant that no superpower backed its enemies. It is rather to say that the threats to Israel's existence and territorial integrity were much like those menacing the United States and the Soviet Union. If, by some slim chance, Israel should be faced with nuclear destruction, its rivals would be at least as vulnerable. If, by some slim chance, Israel should be faced with defeat in a conventional attack, its rivals would be faced with nuclear destruction. Moreover, it is very difficult to imagine circumstances in which Israel would not be in a position to devastate the cities of any attacker by conventional means. The idea that anyone could overrun Israel or destroy its cities without consequences suicidal for the attacker has long been a non-starter.

What holds for Israel within its post-1967 borders, also holds for Israel within its pre-1967 borders. Much has been made of how easily Israel, within those borders, could be cut in half. This is simply false, a stand-in for what is simply true: that, other things being equal, it is far easier to advance a short distance than a long one. Certainly Israel is very narrow near its North–South midline, and certainly troops advancing along that line would not have far to go. But in the 1967 war, Israel's pre-emptive air strikes made it quite clear that Israel would not let hostile forces get into a position to make any such advance. Like other countries, Israel has and always can set virtual tripwires, announced or unannounced, for what it considers an act of war. Among these, naturally, would be moving troops towards Israel's narrowest point. Though it is arguable that Israel needs buffers, nothing requires that these buffers need lie within its borders, and indeed official buffer zones have sometimes been delineated outside them.[100] It cannot be wholly unimportant that Israel's greatest victory was when it lived within its old borders, and its greatest setback when it lived beyond them.

There is at least one other factor that should enter into a security assessment. Israelis have an option that Israel does not have: they can leave. In that sense, for Israel to be threatened is not like, say, Chad being threatened. Perhaps no population in history has, since the 1960s, had such easy emigration options: their numbers are relatively small; there are many countries who would receive them, and many Jewish communities are very willing and able to help. This option is normally not mentioned because it is considered not only difficult but improper to ask people to leave their own country. However, Israel is a very young and illegitimate country built on immigration. Its victims are not shrouded in history but living in camps. In these circumstances, the emigration option looks quite a lot better than it would elsewhere.

If this assessment of Israel's security seems far too complacent, it may be because two notorious factors have been omitted. First, there is Israel's exposure, not to military threats, but to small-scale terrorism. Second, and closely related, there is a notion cherished by Zionists the world over: that Israel is up against implacable fanatics with whom there can be no peace and no compromise: no concessions, we are told, will satisfy these people, and will simply be taken as signs of weakness. Faced with the suicidal hatred of millions, Israel can never have peace or security: sooner of later, these people will always get through. Evidence for this view, it is said, can be found in the Palestinians' rejection of peace offers, the viciousness of their terrorism, and expressions of hatred throughout the Arab and/or Muslim world.

A moderate expression of this outlook is voiced by Walter Reich, who was removed as director of the U.S. Holocaust Museum for refusing to escort Yasser Arafat on a tour of the exhibits. His warm review of David Horovitz' *Israel in the Age of Terrorism* states that:

> Critics of Israel have insisted that it's the Jewish settlements and the Israeli occupation of the West Bank and Gaza that have provoked and sustained the terror of the intifada. But the deal the Israelis offered at Camp David would have ended the occupation and dismantled the vast majority of the settlements. Rather, as Horovitz documents, the intifada was started as a strategy to achieve a political end—the demoralization of Israel; the mobilization of international sympathy for the Palestinian cause when Israel tried to defend itself against suicide bombings; and an agreement that would militarily exhaust, psychologically devastate, demographically overwhelm and ultimately destroy Israel.[101]

Benny Morris also sees in the Arabs nothing but irreconcilable hostility:

> The whole Arab world, with the Palestinians in the vanguard, continues to insist on Israel's illegitimacy and to hope for its disappearance. The dispatch of droves of suicide bombers into Israeli cities, by the fundamentalist organizations and by

> Arafat's own "secular" Fatah, is merely the concrete manifesta-
> tion, in microcosm, of this outlook.[102]

Taken together, these claims seem to imply that, short of eliminating at least the Palestinians, Israel can never be secure. They
also suggest that Israel should never be less aggressive or violent
than it is now, because moderation would simply encourage "the
terrorists." Never mind Morris' hysterical nonsense about "the
whole Arab world": so the Egyptians "continue to insist on
Israel's illegitimacy and to hope for its disappearance?" To evaluate this assessment, it is necessary to look at Israel's occupation, its settlements, and its alternatives. The evolving character
of the occupation determines the extent to which the present situation is in Israel's control and, therefore, the extent to which it
is Israel's responsibility.

The occupation

Some claim that the Six Day War was not thrust upon Israel,
but engineered by Israel.[103] Either way, no one seems to think that
Israel's spectacular success and its control of the Occupied
Territories had been foreseen. The war and the occupation raise
questions of political legitimacy that reappear through the subsequent course of events.

Arguably, since the Zionist state was illegitimate, so was its
defense, and, therefore, all of Israel's military exploits. There are
at least two reasons to reject such arguments.

First, as an established if illegitimate state, Israel now had a
large population that, left undefended, might well suffer great
loss. Much of this population was innocent of Zionist wrongdoing, either because of age, or because they were Palestinian, or
because they came to Israel as desperate refugees who could not
pick and choose their destination. Someone had to protect this
population against the consequences of Zionist adventures, and
only Israel was available to fill this role.

Second, there is the notion that one cannot easily lose one's right to self-defense. Thomas Hobbes thought that wrongdoing tended to cement rather than erode this right:

> ...in case a great many men together, have already resisted the Soveraign Power unjustly, or committed some Capitall crime, for which every one of them expecteth death, whether have they not the Liberty then to joyn together, and assist, and defend one another? Certainly they have: For they but defend their lives, which the Guilty may as well do, as the Innocent.[104]

The more your actions, right or wrong, put your life in danger, the more you are justified in defending yourself. On this account, the very injustice of Israel's establishment and the bitterness it rightly provoked legitimized Israel's military preoccupations and their tendency to favor pre-emptive strikes. Self-defense of an unjust cause is, thinks Hobbes, no further injustice.

With admirable consistency, Hobbes held that the right of self-defense extended even to criminals resisting arrest:

> ...if a man be held in prison, or bonds, or is not trusted with the libertie of his bodie; he cannot be understood to be bound by Covenant to subjection; and therefore may, if he can, make his escape by any means whatsoever.[105]

No political movement has ever demanded such a right and no nation has ever offered it. A less extreme versions of Hobbes' proposal come closer to contemporary political ideas on self-defense. Robbers, we seem to think, have no right to defend themselves against bank guards, and an invading aggressor army does not have a right to defend itself against the defenders: in defending themselves, the Wehrmacht and Saddam Hussein's forces in Kuwait did commit a further injustice.[106] On the other hand, a nation may defend its boundaries: the Iraqi and German forces, even if they represented a criminal state, were not wrong to resist invasion. In this case, there is not really a right of self-defense but what is in some legal theory called a privilege, a situation where neither party involved does an injustice: the invaders were not wrong to invade, and the defenders not wrong to resist. Such a "right" or privilege would mean that the Arab states were not wrong to plan—if this was the case—an attack on Israel, nor would they have been wrong to initiate one. But Israel cannot be faulted for parrying such an attack, even with a pre-emptive strike.

For similar reasons, the "occupation" itself, in the narrowest sense of that word, was no great crime. Israel was at war with its neighbors. Even if it was not innocent in precipitating that war, it was not trying, as far as we can tell, to acquire more territory. That it should want a buffer against ground attack and a more defensible border was understandable: Israel did not yet have the crushing military superiority it later developed; Egypt had not yet made peace or broken with the Soviets; Jordan was not yet in armed conflict with the Palestinians. If Israel did not *need* the territory for security purposes, it nevertheless was, in straightening out its frontier, making very normal defensive moves. But to say that Israel, at this point, squandered opportunities for peace would be a comical understatement. Soon after 1967, Israel worked hard at becoming the pariah it is today. The more it came to be in a position to resolve the situation, the more it committed itself, for the most contemptible of reasons, to unending and depraved racial warfare. The catalysts for this appalling process were the settlements.

The start of the settlements

Those who claim that the Palestinians refused peace before the settlements started forget, or would have us forget, how different things were in 1967 from how they are today. Jon Kimche, a moderate Zionist, well-connected to Israeli government circles, describes the situation immediately following Israel's victory:

> Dayan and his military advisers, especially Schlomo Gazit, rec-
> ognized the potentiality of a settlement with the Palestinians on
> the West Bank immediately after the war when the Palestinians
> still felt that they had *been liberated rather than conquered by the
> Israelis.* [my italics]
>
> The Palestinian leaders "telephoned" their desire for an
> immediate settlement. About 40 of the West Bank notables and
> radicals put their names to a call for a provisional Palestinian
> Assembly. But there was no reply.[107]

They regarded the Israelis as liberators because they hoped
for an independent state, free from the rule of King Hussein.
Kimche goes on to quote a letter to him from a senior adviser to
the Israel's Prime Minister, explaining why the initiative failed:

> The Arabs have been quick to sense a change in the mood of the
> Israeli authorities and they have adjusted their own attitudes
> accordingly. No one in fact talks about an independent state at
> all. For the word has been passed round that, by agreement with
> the Israelis, King Hussein is coming back to the West Bank.
> This means for the West Bank Arabs that they must avoid
> making statements which would be considered as traitorous by
> the Hashemite authorities [because to advocate a West Bank
> Palestinian state would be to advocate the breakup of Jordan].[108]

Kimche comments:

> There was one real chance of a settlement on the morrow of
> victory; it was lost when the Israel Government turned to
> Hussein instead of inviting the Palestinians to come home and
> take over their rightful heritage as of right and not on suffer-
> ance, to enable the Palestinians to do what they had been unable
> to do under Ottoman rule, under British rule and under
> Jordanian rule—to establish their own National Home in
> Palestine alongside the Jews.[109]

No one can be sure that the chances for peace were quite as good as Kimche seems to think. Perhaps Hussein would have torpedoed any deal; perhaps the Palestinians themselves would change their minds. Two things, however, *are* certain. The first is that Israel was now in a much better position to resolve the "Palestinian problem;" a position which improved steadily over the next fifteen or twenty years. The second is that the settlements represented a decisive rejection of peace.

Israel was, in 1967, wavering between sponsoring a Palestinian state and giving the Occupied Territories back to Jordan. This is probably a measure of how little, immediately after the war, the Israelis wanted to hang onto what they had captured. Though policy was murky at the time, it may be that the very first settlements where thought of merely as military affairs, designed to stave off small-scale attacks such as the Palestinians mounted against northern Israel. Such a defensive measure would have been questionable but not outrageous. Very quickly, however, the settlement movement and the settlement policy began to take shape.

According to Chomsky,

> Settlements in the Occupied Territories began immediately after the war, sometimes without government authorization, though this regularly came later. ...by December 1969, the Meir government had established as one of its "essential goals" the "acceleration of the installation of military settlements and permanent agricultural and urban settlements in the territory of the homeland" (the official wording).[110]

The reference to "permanent agricultural settlements" is chilling. By this time, the damage had been done: there would be no Palestinian homeland nor even any attempt to work out some arrangement between the Palestinians and King Hussein. But the government's policy was hardly more than a response to unofficial initiatives at the most influential levels of Israeli society. In

1968, Moshe Dayan, defense minister and the hero of the war, said that:

> We are doomed to live in a constant state of war with the Arabs and there is no escape from sacrifice and bloodshed... If we are to proceed with our work against the wishes of the Arabs we shall have to expect such sacrifices.

What work? Dayan is addressing the Kibbutz Youth Federation on the Golan Heights, and he continues:

> This is what used to be called "Jew after Jew"... It meant expansion, more Jews, more villages, more settlements . Twenty years ago we were 600,000; today we are near three million. There should be no Jew who says "that's enough," no one who says "we are nearing the end of the road." ...It is the same with the land. ...there will be complaints against you if you come and say: "up to here." Your duty is not to stop; it is to keep your sword unsheathed, to have faith, to keep the flag flying. You must not call a halt—heaven forbid—and say "that's all; up there, up to Degania, to Musfalllasim, to Nahal Oz!" For that is not all.[111]

One need not think of Zionism as Nazism to find irresistible the comparison with fascist ideologies of "blood and soil." This sleazy enthusiasm has nothing to do with Israel's security needs and, as we shall soon see, actually militates against them. The urban counterpart of this expansion was already well underway by the time Dayan spoke: the formal annexation of East Jerusalem had already been effected on June 28, 1967, with a degree that extended the boundaries of the Israeli municipality. The next day,

> ...the Assistant Military Commander of Jerusalem had "the honor to inform" the Mayor of East Jerusalem, Ruhi Khatib, that his municipal council was dissolved. Municipal property and

records were seized, and all government departments were brought under Israeli jurisdiction.[112]

These facts on the ground were what mattered, not the much-discussed interpretation of UN resolution 242 and its successors. Whatever their words, by their actions the Israelis had declared unequivocally their studied lack of interest in a Palestinian state or indeed of any accommodation with the Palestinians.

Israel's rejection of a Palestinian state was not in itself a commitment to racial warfare. Israel might have continued the occupation or even annexed the territories yet left the Palestinians with something remotely resembling a secure and tolerable existence. This was not to be. With the development of the settler movement and the policies that sheltered it, Israel was to go beyond the normal transgressions that go with the founding of most states. Even as it cherished its own fantasies of persecution, it was to menace another ethnic group in a manner that the Western powers it aped had just, one hopes, outgrown. This extraordinary development deserves a closer look.

The Settlements

From outposts to ethnic cleansing

SOME ISRAELIS MAY HAVE SEEN THE FIRST POST-1967 SETTLE-ments as outposts, advance warning stations guarding the new frontiers against possible attack. This never made a lot of sense: why not just have *real* advance warning stations, military positions, instead? No one has ever explained why a sprawl of civilian subdivisions and enclaves was required when, to all appearances, a few purely military outposts would have fulfilled any defensive functions at least as well, and at far less cost to both Israelis and Palestinians. Dayan himself stated that "from the point of view of the security of the State, the establishment of the settlements has no great importance."[113] Other officials shared his assessment:

> We have to use the *pretext* [my italics] of security needs and the authority of the military governor as there is no way of driving out the Arabs from their land as long as they refuse to go and accept our compensation.[114]

In 1969, moreover, Dayan had emphasized that the settlements were eternal: "the settlements established in the territories are there forever, and the future frontiers will include these settlements as part of Israel."[115] In private, he had already in 1967 made it quite clear how the Palestinians were not, in fact, to have a secure and tolerable existence: "there is no solution," he said, "and you shall continue to live like dogs, and whoever prefers—shall leave..."[116]

Dayan's bite was pretty bad, but not quite as bad as his bark. His flirtations with neo-fascism did not completely determine his policies or actions. If he was not prepared to compromise with the Palestinians, he also did not seem intent on making their life unbearable.[117] Things would change. By the mid-1970s, both the settler movement and the settlements themselves had become increasingly terrifying forces.

The settler movement's messianic notions of racial destiny have been amply documented.[118] Yehoshafat Harkabi, a former Major General and intelligence chief in the Israeli Defense Forces, describes how they interpret the *"halakha*—the body of religious laws designed to encode a unique and binding lifestyle."[119] Harkabi, like others, considers Rabbi Zvi Yehudah Kook to be the mentor of the *Gush Emunim* settler movement and cites him as saying at a public meeting that:

> I tell you explicitly that the Torah forbids us to surrender even one inch of our liberated land. There are no conquests here and we are not occupying foreign lands; we are returning to our home, to the inheritance of our ancestors. There is no Arab land here, only the inheritance of our God—and the more the world gets used to this thought the better it will be for them and for all of us (*Year by Year*, 1968).[120]

This strongly suggests that the Palestinians should expect to lose every inch of their land. The strong suggestion quickly becomes a certainty with sinister implications. Harkabi (whom I cite extensively because of his unimpeachable authority) continues:

> Rabbi Shlomo Aviner, the former rabbi of Bet El (the Jewish settlement established in Samaria on a site of religious significance)... explained this as follows:

"Let me draw you an analogy. It's as if a man goes into his neighbor's house without permission and stays there for many years. When the original owner returns, the invader claims: "It's my house, I've been living here for years!" All of these years he's been nothing but a thief! Now he should make himself scarce and pay rent on top of it. Some people might say that there's a difference between living in a place for thirty years and living in a place for 2,000 years. Let us ask them: Is there a statute of limitations that gives a thief the right to his plunder? ...Everyone who settled here knew very well that he was living in a land that belongs to the people of Israel, so the ethnic group that settled in this place has no title to the land. Perhaps an Arab who was born here doesn't know this, but nevertheless the fact that a man settles on land does not make it his. Under the law, possession serves only as proof of a claim of ownership; it does not create ownership. The Arabs' possession of the land is therefore a possession that asserts no rights. It is the possession of territory when it is absolutely clear that they are not its legal owners, and this possession has no juridical or moral validity." (Artzi, p. 10)

For Rabbi Aviner and his followers then, the first Arabs to settle in the Holy Land were thieves, and the crime has been bequeathed from father to son down to the present generation.[121]

Rabbi Kook himself agrees:

We find ourselves here by virtue of the legacy of our ancestors, the basis of the Bible and history, and no one can change this fact. What does it resemble? A man left his house and others came and invaded it. This is exactly what happened to us. Some argue that there are Arab lands here. It is all a lie and a fraud! There are absolutely no Arab lands here.[122]

This lack of Arab entitlement implies, for many, expulsion. Harkabi quotes the well-known Israeli rabbi and former paratrooper Yisrael Ariel:

> ...there is a commandment to settle Eretz Yisrael, defined by our sages also as the commandment of "inheritance and residence"—a commandment mentioned many times in the Torah. Even the new student understands that "inheritance and residence" means conquering and settling the land. The Torah repeats the commandment—"You shall dispossess all the inhabitants of the land"—many times, and Rashi explains that this means to expel them. [123]

For others, expulsion may not be enough:

> Some nationalistic religious extremists frequently identify the Arabs with Amalek, whom the Jews are commanded to annihilate totally (Deuteronomy 25: 17-19). As children, we were taught that this was a relic of a bygone and primitive era, a commandment that had lapsed because Sennacherib the Assyrian king had mixed up all the nations so it was no longer possible to know who comes of the seed of Amalek. Yet some rabbis insist on injecting a contemporary significance into the commandment to blot out Amalek.
>
> Rabbi Yisrael Hess, formerly the campus rabbi of Bar-Ilan University, published an article in the student newspaper, *Bat Koll* (February 26, 1988), entitled "The Commandment of Genocide in the Torah," which ended as follows: "The day will yet come when we will all be called to fulfill the commandment of the divinely ordained war to destroy Amalek." Knesset member Ammon Rubinstein, citing this article, adds: "Rabbi Hess explains the commandment to blot out the memory of Amalek and says that there is no mercy in this commandment: the commandment is to kill and destroy even children and

infants. Amalek is whoever declares war against the people of God."[124]

Sometimes it is made clear that this "seed of Amalek," like other non-Jews, are racially inferior:

> A reasoned analysis of the status of non-Jews in a Jewish state can be found in an article entitled "A New Approach to Israeli-Arab Peace" published in *Kivvunim* 24 (August 1984), an official publication of the World Zionist Organization. The author is Mordechai Nisan, a lecturer on the Middle East at Hebrew University in Jerusalem. According to Dr. Nisan, Jews are permitted to discriminate against foreigners in a way that Jews would angrily denounce were it done to them. What is permissible to us is forbidden to others:
>
>> While it is true that the Jews are a particular people, they nonetheless are designated as a "light unto the nations." This function is imposed on the Jews who strive to be a living aristocracy among the nations, a nation that has deeper historical roots, greater spiritual obligations, higher moral standards, and more powerful intellectual capacities than others. This vision, which diverges from the widely accepted egalitarian approach, is not at all based on an arbitrary hostility towards non-Jews, but rather on a fundamental existential understanding of the quality of Jewish peoplehood.
>
> Thus the concept of the "Chosen People" as an aristocracy provides sanction for the unequal and discriminatory treatment of non-Jews, who are inferior. Nisan does not consider the possibility that other nations might also claim aristocratic status for themselves.[125]

Another rabbi, a backer of the settlers, gave racial supremacism the trappings of science in an interview with *Jewish Week*, April 26, 1996:

"If every simple cell in a Jewish body entails divinity, is a part of God, then every strand of DNA is part of God. Therefore, something is special about Jewish DNA." Later, Rabbi Ginsburgh asked rhetorically: "If a Jew needs a liver, can you take the liver of an innocent non-Jew passing by to save him? The Torah would probably permit that. Jewish life has an infinite value," he explained. "There is something infinitely more holy and unique about Jewish life than non-Jewish life."[126]

Are these a few wild men? Harkabi denies it: "...the nationalistic religious extremists are by no means a lunatic fringe; many are respected men whose words are widely heeded. Their demand that halakha direct policy is shared with different emphases by many religious circles."[127] Because Israel's voting system allocates seats purely on the basis of national votes for a party, not by district, extremist parties have substantial influence, especially since minority government in Israel is the norm rather than the exception. Moreover, extremists have had an important presence with the large Likud party. Just as there is no doubt that extremists do not represent the majority of Israelis, there is no doubt that they do much, directly and indirectly, to shape Israeli policy. An Israeli commentator describes the current situation as follows:

It is not difficult to imagine what the settlers' lobby means in a country with notoriously narrow parliamentary majorities. Though 70 percent of Israeli voters say in the polls that they support abandoning some of the settlements, 400,000 settlers and their right-wing and Orthodox supporters within Israel proper now control at least half the national vote. They pose a constant threat of civil war if their interests are not fully respected. At their core is a group of fanatical nationalists and religious fundamentalists who believe they know exactly what God and Abraham said to each other in the Bronze Age.[128]

Unfortunately, Israel is at least a democracy for its citizens, and this tends to place responsibility for the situation on their shoulders.

The growth of the settler movement soon left its mark on the public face of Israel. On this question, one can do no better than cite the verdict of Benny Morris:

> Through the 1980s, the Arabs picked up the signals that Israel ultimately intended to evict them—not merely from extremists such as the Moedet Party Rehav'am Ze'evi, the former IDF general who preached voluntary transfer "in air-conditioned busses," but from mainstream politicians as well. In July 1987 Deputy Defense Minister Michael Dekel, who was close to Prime Minister Shamir, publicly called for the transfer of Palestinians to Jordan. Cabinet minister Mordechai Zippori, not at all a hard-liner, in 1982 told Jewish settlers near Nablus: "Don't worry about the demographic density of the Arabs. I was born in Petach Tikva, we were entirely surrounded by Arab villages. They have all since disappeared."[129]

Morris put the emphasis where it belongs. The important thing is not the moral character of the settlers or of the Israeli population, nor to what extent the extremist statements cited above are representative of either. What matters is that settler ideology, as described, is well known, widespread, and rightly perceived to have real influence on Israeli politics. It would be irrational for any Palestinian not to perceive this as a menace and to react accordingly.

The effects of the settlements

To the menace of settler ideology and Israeli government policy must be added the menace of the settlements themselves. A full description of their effects, and those of the occupation in general, lies well outside the scope of this essay. For an extended account of daily life in one area, Gaza, the reader is referred to the work of Israeli journalist Amira Hass, *Drinking the Sea at Gaza: Days and Nights in a Land under Siege.*[130] Here is a brief description of their impact from Amos Elon:

> In the Gaza Strip some of the well-established, prospering set-tlements are only a few hundred meters away from the vast refugee camps, populated by third- and fourth-generation Palestinian refugees. In five minutes a visitor might feel as if he were passing from Southern California to Bangladesh—through barbed-wire entanglements, past watchtowers, searchlights, machine-gun positions, and fortified roadblocks: a bizarre and chilling sight.
>
> The Palestinians are infuriated as well by seeing their olive groves uprooted or burned down by settlers while their water faucets go dry and their ancestral land reserves and scarce water resources are taken over for the use of settlers who luxuriate nearby in their swimming pools and consume five times as much water as the average Palestinian. The settlements them-selves occupy less than 20 percent of the West Bank, but through a network of so-called regional councils they control planning and environmental policy for approximately 40 percent of the West Bank, according to figures recently pub-lished by B'tzelem, the Israeli human rights organization.[131]

Elon's description is not of a static situation; it marks a stage in a continuing and slowly intensifying pattern of encroachment. The inexorable degradation of Palestinian living conditions and opportunities is the result not only of actions by the settlers themselves, but also of the Israeli authorities. Their support for the settlers is sometimes enthusiastic, sometimes begrudging, but in the end ruinous to the population of the Occupied Territories. Against this background the sporadic and feeble attempts to restrain settler excesses are laughable.

For one thing, settlements, with a few exceptions considered "illegal" by the Israeli government, are built on previously confiscated land. Gabriel Ash, a journalist who grew up in Israel, describes the whole process, and his account is worth citing at length.

> Since 1948, the first battalion, thrown into action once a settlement has been decided, is composed of bureaucrats—mapmakers, hydrologists, civil engineers, lawyers, judges, and apparatchiks. Their job is to figure out which land can be confiscated from Palestinians...
>
> Land can be expropriated for "public" use, namely Jewish use; or it can be declared as "abandoned" if it belonged to a refugee. Often, however, the settlement begins as a military camp because "security" is the best legal justification for confiscating private Palestinian property—a house, an orchard, a field. The NAKHAL brigade is a special paratroop unit whose job includes providing personnel for new settlements disguised as military camps.
>
> Often the land is designated "state land" in order to ward off legal challenge in the specially designed military "appeal committee," which rubber-stamps the armed robbery. "State land" is land Israel reserves for the exclusive benefit of Jews...
>
> Sometimes the appearance of fairness requires that land taken from Palestinians spends a few years in decontamination, for example, as parkland, environmental reserve, etc., before it is "thawed" for its final destination as a new Jewish settlement. This is particularly the case in East Jerusalem.
>
> In the end, it doesn't matter how the land is procured. The Settlement of Shilo, established in 1985, is 45 percent land declared "public," 52 percent land expropriated for "security" reasons, and 3 percent land expropriated for "public" use....
>
> After the bureaucrats come the bulldozers, followed by the mobile homes, the construction workers, and finally the settlers...

When families finally move into a new settlement, the war just begins. A settlement (unlike a Palestinian village) needs room to grow, land reserves, an abundance of cheap water, etc., which the state of Israel will provide, often by using resources denied to the target village or town. For example, each settler in Hebron consumes over nine times more water daily than his water-starved Palestinian neighbor.

In addition, a settlement needs access—a road to connect it with other settlements. Roads are a key mechanism for confiscating Palestinian property. Between August 1994 and September 1996, 4,386 dunam of private land (there are about 4.5 dunams per acre) were confiscated for the purpose of constructing seventeen "bypass" roads. Roads are long and wide and their trajectory can be shifted here and there to achieve maximum impact in terms of houses that must be demolished, orchards that need to be uprooted, and growth that can be stifled... For example, road 447, which shortens the trip to the Settlement of Ariel by a full five minutes, "necessitated" uprooting one thousand olive trees and confiscating 75 dunams from residents of the two Palestinian villages which Ariel targets. In addition, every road that connects two Jewish settlements doubles as a road that separates two Palestinian towns. Palestinians cannot use "Jewish" roads.[132]

Despite the overwhelming government presence in the semi-official settlement process, settlers are sometimes dissatisfied with its workings, and, having little fear of government intervention, take matters into their own hands. Usually this involves ongoing harassment at a fairly low level.[133] On occasion it is more than that. Here is a 2002 AP press description of one incident:

Sobbing as they filled a truck with furniture and piled themselves into dusty cars, six Palestinian families set out from this tiny village of old stone houses, leaving it completely abandoned.

Once home to 25 families, members of the Sobih clan said they were fleeing after four years of worsening attacks by Jewish settlers, who have set up illegal outposts on nearby hilltops. The attacks have become increasingly frequent in recent months, they said.

"Our life here is more bitter than hell," Kamal Sobih, a thin, bearded man of 40, said Friday.

Groups of masked Jewish settlers have charged into the village, coming at night with dogs and horses, stealing sheep, hurling stones through windows and beating the men with fists and rifle butts, Palestinian residents said.

An electricity generator has been scorched by fire, knocking out power to the village. Three large water tanks were tipped over and emptied.[134]

Though this was the first recent recorded incident of a whole village being emptied, such attacks are not uncommon, and no one can say how large a role they play in the process of dispossession. And the authorities? The report continues:

An Israeli army spokesman, who insisted his name not be used, said soldiers try to prevent conflict between settlers and Palestinians, but that forces are primarily in the area to protect Israelis from attacks by Palestinian militants.

Not that the settlers are helpless:

...every settlement now has its own native militia, which has mortars, light and heavy-caliber machine guns and sniper rifles. According to current estimates by Israeli military intelligence officials, about 20,000 of these heavily armed settlers would use their weapons against the government if they were told to abandon their homes as a condition of a peace accord.[135]

These weapons are not merely defensive but allow the settlers to act with virtual impunity. In 2003, Chris McGreal reported in *The Guardian*[136] that:

> Armed Israelis are systematically wrecking trees that have stood for hundreds of years and frequently provide the only livelihood for Palestinian families.
>
> Rights groups estimate that more than 1,000 trees have been damaged or destroyed in recent weeks, some planted in the Roman era.

It was not only that trees were destroyed. A Palestinian farmer, head of the village council, stated that:

> I myself had picked five sacks when the settlers came down the hill with knives and guns. They slashed open our sacks and emptied the olives on to the ground. They put guns against our heads and made us stand there while they did it.
>
> The settlers have built a road near the bottom of the hill. They told us that we are not allowed to cross the road any more and that all the land the other side, all our olive trees up the hill, are now theirs.

"In one incident," McGreal reports, "the settlers beat a 70-year-old man, stripped him, and forced him to walk back to his village naked."

As with settler ideology, so it is with the settlements. The point is not to retail a collection of horror stories: indeed, the worst horrors, stemming from Israeli military incursions, have not been mentioned. Nor have the consequences of industrial pollution and settler sewage in the Occupied Territories been discussed.[137] What matters is how the occupation and the settlements belong to a complex of circumstances that constitute a mortal threat to the Palestinians. It is time to complete the picture with a preliminary look at violence in the Occupied

Territories, and with an equally preliminary assessment of Palestinian options.

Immediate consequences of the occupation

That the occupation should meet with violent resistance was inevitable and hardly unexpected. Whether the forms this violence took were justified is not at issue here; it will be discussed later. There were at least two reasons for Palestinian attacks. The first was old: some Palestinians still had hope of regaining their land. This was a miscalculation but not an inexcusable one; the hope of effective support from "the Arab world" was not yet entirely forlorn. The second reason was old too, but in a new incarnation. The inhabitants of the Occupied Territories had now come under the sovereignty of a "Jewish state"—as feared before 1948, Jews would now hold the power of life and death over non-Jews. The inhabitants of the Occupied Territories would not have even the civil rights that the "Jewish state" had granted, on sufferance, to the Arab inhabitants of Israel. So again, it was entirely reasonable for the Palestinians to resist, if not with every form of violence, at least with *some* form of violence. Again, this would be a right any group would claim in similar circumstances.

To this violence the Israelis responded with considerable savagery and questionable methods including what was quite explicitly termed collective punishment. Dayan, for instance,

> ...made no bones about it: it was collective, or,—as he put it, "neighbourhood" punishment... That is how he described the destruction of some seventy houses in the wake of a guerilla attack on Israeli soldiers. He told the villagers: "today we demolished twenty homes [sic]. If this is not enough we will demolish the whole town, and if you don't like this policy, the bridges are open before you for departure."[138]

Israeli practices were brutal but again, to the extent that they were an attempt to consolidate the occupation, no special crime:

to the occupation there was at least some military rationale, and Israel had the same limited rights of self-defense as all other illegitimate states. But we have seen that this was no mere occupation. The settlements were not, and as we have seen were not perceived to be, a security requirement. They and the ideologues behind them testified, in the clearest possible fashion, to an intention to displace the occupied population. This both caused and justified an increasingly bitter resistance. There were increasingly vicious attempts to repress it, resulting in more and more damage to Palestinian lands, cities, and livelihoods. Border closures stifled employment opportunities in Israel; tanks ripped up roads and broke sewer lines beneath them; curfews and, above all, checkpoints made anything remotely resembling normal economic life impossible. So, to the direct harm of the settlements must be added the indirect harm resulting from the violence they spawned.

Let us ignore all but one starkly quantifiable human cost and look at the findings of the Nutritional Assessment Survey carried out by CARE International, Johns Hopkins University School of Public Health and Al-Quds University School of Public Health, and the Global Management Consulting Group. It reported

> …an increase in the number of malnourished children with 22.5 percent of children under 5 suffering from acute (9.3 percent) or chronic (13.2 percent) malnutrition. The preliminary rates are particularly high in Gaza with the survey showing 13.2 percent of children suffering from acute malnutrition, putting them on par with children in countries such as Nigeria and Chad.
>
> Other early findings show that the rate of anemia in Palestinian children under 5 has reached 19.7 percent (20.9 percent in the West Bank and 18.9 percent in Gaza), while anemia rates of non-pregnant Palestinian women of childbearing age are 10.8 percent (9.5 percent in the West Bank and 12 percent in Gaza).[139]

These figures and the general conditions that may be inferred from them indicate that the Palestinians in the Occupied Territories had more to fear than mere dispossession, humiliation, and lack of opportunity. Their lives, or the lives of their families, are constantly in very real danger. But to complete an assessment of their situation, it is necessary to explore their alternatives.

Nowhere to go

Dayan invited the Palestinians to leave if they didn't like their treatment. That the "Arabs" of Palestine—once their existence had been discovered—could go elsewhere had been an article of faith since the earliest days of Zionism. To drive them from their homes, it was supposed, would be unfortunate, but no catastrophe: unlike the homeless Jews, the Palestinians had all the vast regions of Arabia to make a new beginning. Today it is regularly suggested that the Arab world could and should easily accommodate the Palestinians, most likely in Jordan. Can these helpful hints for unhappy Palestinians be taken seriously?

Behind the suggestions lie an even more basic assumption, voiced as far back as 1918 by Vladimir Jabotinsky, the prototypical Zionist hardliner:

> The matter is not... an issue between the Jewish people and the Arab inhabitants of Palestine, but between the Jewish people and the Arab people. The latter, numbering 35 million, has [territory] equal to half of Europe, while the Jewish people, numbering ten million and wandering the earth, hasn't got a stone...[140]

We have already questioned Zionism's right to represent the Jewish people and the whole notion that "peoples" have rights to "homelands." We have also questioned both the attack on the notion of the Palestinian people and the importance of that notion to the Israel/Palestine conflict. But to say the Palestinians—like the Jews—needn't be considered a people is not to portray them as having the whole Arab world to play in: Benny Morris, like Jabotinsky, implicitly suggests this by subtitling his *Righteous Victims* "A History of the Zionist-*Arab* Conflict." Similar assumptions abound in the discourse of Ben-Gurion and Weizmann. This sort of wishful thinking stems from a broader and deeper assumption—that in some politically important sense the Palestinians are "Arabs," and part of the "Arab people." This is a highly misleading notion, ultimately harmful to the Palestinians, and for once the blame cannot be laid at the feet of the Zionists.

In the West, the notion of an Arab people, comprising all those who speak Arabic, goes well back into the nineteenth century. This idea, at the time, was a relatively innocuous "they're-all-the-same" sort of racism, somewhat like the sort that sees only "blacks" and or "orientals" and not quite distinct African and Asian ethnic groups. Ironically, Arab nationalism got its start largely from Westernized Lebanese and Syrians (often Christian) who adopted this colonial concept, partly out of admiration for Western ways, partly as an attempt to form politically cohesive opposition to Ottoman and European domination. The British in particular were sympathetic to the idea as a counterweight to Ottoman, later Turkish and French, ambitions.

British sponsorship of the "Arab revolt" against the Ottomans gave Arab nationalism substantially more credibility than it deserved. From its beginnings before the First World War until sometime well after 1948, Arab nationalism was a top-down ideology with little relation either to political reality or to the self-perception of Arabic-speaking Middle Easterners. Opposition to Zionism, followed by Nasser's sponsorship of Arab nationalism, and more recently by the relentless pressure of Western stereotyping, have all contributed to the acceptance by Arabic-speaking Middle Easterners that they are some sort of "people" with some sort of common interests. Academics have contributed to this perception almost out of politeness, out of deference to aspirations now popular throughout the Arabic-speaking Middle East.

But aspirations are not reality. Israel's most powerful pre-Camp David enemy, Egypt, is, oddly enough, inhabited by people who perceive themselves as Egyptians. Many older Egyptians have stories about the first time, in the 1940s or early 1950s, that they heard themselves referred to as Arabs, and about their bafflement or dismay on hearing this. Nasser's repeated attempts to form unions with other Middle Eastern countries foundered at least partly because their inhabitants or leaders considered his protestations of Arab nationalism a disguise for Egyptian or "Nasserist" expansionism. And today in Cairo it is commonplace to hear complaints about "the Arabs" from the Gulf States who come as playboys or sex tourists. Lebanese, Syrians, and urbanized Jordanians, whatever they call themselves, share with Egyptians a certain stereotype of what might be called Arabians, whom they perceive much as ignorant Westerners perceive all Arabic-speaking Middle Easterners: as half-civilized nouveaux riches, hardly a step up from a camel-riding nomadic existence or—worse—as "peasants." Conversely, the original Hashemite ally of the British, Prince Feisal, surprised none other than the ur-Zionist Chaim Weizmann by being "contemptuous of the Palestinian Arabs whom he doesn't even regard as Arabs!"[141] In parts of North Africa, the antagonism is even more acute: many Berbers in Algeria, for instance, despise their Arabic-speaking fellow-citizens. And this is more than mere bickering: the urbanized Levant, Egypt, and North Africa are very different culturally, politically, and anthropologically, not only from one another, but also from the inhabitants of the Arabian peninsula. Not even language and religion, which also vary, serve as unifying forces. It makes as much sense to tut-tut about the frequent conflicts between "Arab" nations as it would to express surprise that Christian or white Europe should have seen so many wars in the first half of the twentieth century.

Though Arab nationalism may in the final analysis prove to have been a positive force in the Middle East, it certainly has carried with it political liabilities whose dimensions become increasingly clear. On the broadest level it makes the disunity in the Middle East, seen as the "Arab world," into a sign of pathetic fractiousness and political incompetence. The notion of Arabic-speaking Middle Easterners as one "people" obscures the simple fact that there are many distinct nations in the Middle East whose identities are increasingly robust and whose interests are often sharply conflicting. There is no more shame in this than there is in the general inability of the human race to "just get along." On a more specific level, Arab nationalism and the notion of an "Arab people" have both helped and hurt the Palestinian cause. It has helped the Palestinians by garnering them support from the "Arab world," but it has hurt them by allowing the Zionists to believe and to convince others that the Palestinians do not really have their backs to the wall: why, they can just go live with their Arab brethren!

This suggestion is ludicrous on several levels

In the first place, even if the Palestinians were in some politically significant sense "Arabs" and even if they were regarded by their neighbors as fellow-Arabs, that would hardly trivialize their dispossession. If you lose your home to a flood or fire, should we shrug and say: as an American or Canadian or European, you can "just go live" elsewhere, because there is "plenty of room" in those places? Ethnic or national similarity does not magically conjure up food, clothing and shelter, or the willingness of others to help you. The Christian Protestants of Ulster are not welcome to live among their English-speaking, Christian neighbors to the south, nor the Christian Serbs to live among their Christian neighbors, the Croatians. As the similarities are attenuated, the comfort that can be expected from them diminishes: if Norwegians were to lose their homes, we would not marvel at

Third, and most important, even if the Jordanians were ever so willing to help the Palestinians, the notion that they could take them in is fatuous. It completely ignores the scale of what is proposed. According to the *CIA World Factbook*, the population of Jordan is approximately 5,611,202 (July 2004 estimate). The estimated population of the U.S. is 293,027,571. According to Amnesty International, some 3.5 million Palestinians inhabit the Occupied Territories.[142] So, if the population of the Occupied Territories were transferred to Jordan, that would amount to a refugee influx equal some 62.5% of its population. This would be equivalent to the U.S.—of course a far richer country per capita— admitting about 183,125,000 people! In 2001, the U.S. admitted 1,064,318 *immigrants* from all countries. The U.S. ceiling on *refugees* from all countries—a far less desirable category—was a mere 80,000 in 2001; it declined to 70,000 since then. This is substantially less that three *one-thousandth* of one per cent of the population; the equivalent Jordanian quota would be about 1,600 people. The "Jordanian option" simply does not exist.

The Palestinians are not some advance guard of the "Arab world." Whether or not they form an ethnic group—a "people"— they resisted Zionism for over sixty years before some Arab states went to war on their behalf. Since then, most of Israel's wars have been over territory, not Arab attempts to help the Palestinians. Egypt in 1956, 1967, and 1973 fought over the Sinai Peninsula, the Suez Canal, and Israeli access to the Red Sea, not to bring the Palestinians back to their homes. Syria's main concern is regaining the Golan Heights. Jordan and Egypt have made a separate peace with Israel, and Lebanon is deadly to the Palestinians. The "Arab world" truly sympathizes with the Palestinian cause, but certainly not to the extent of risking substantial forces or resources. Nor should this be surprising, because Palestinians and other "Arabs" have far less in common than they themselves might like to think. The Palestinians for all practical purposes stand alone, and they have nowhere to go.

the reluctance of Bulgarians or Portuguese to take in thei "fellow-Europeans." And even if there were some special obliga- tion on the part of "Arabs" to accommodate the Palestinians, any failure to do so might reflect badly on these "Arabs," but it would have no tendency whatsoever to make the situation of the Palestinians any less desperate. Nor does any of this have any- thing to do with whether the Palestinians are in some cultural or anthropological sense a "people." What we called "the Yugoslavs" forty years ago may not count as a people; this does not make Yugoslavs any more or less welcome to "their fellow Slavs" or "their fellow Europeans."

Secondly, facts, not obligations or affinities, define the situa- tion of the Palestinians. No neighboring "Arab" country has in fact been willing to take the Palestinians in. Egypt and Syria have been so plain about this that they are never even suggested. Lebanon is the site of the greatest ethnic massacre of Palestinians ever, at the hands of Israel's Christian clients in the Shatila and Sabra refugee camps. Is this a reasonable destination for dispos- sessed Palestinians? The prime candidate, in Zionist ideology, is Jordan. Jordan also killed many Palestinians during "Black September," 1970, and the Jordanian U.S. Embassy's website carries newspaper articles that state in the plainest language that Jordan has no intention of taking in any more refugees. It is true that urban Jordanians and Palestinians have much in common; indeed that many Jordanians, perhaps even a majority, are them- selves considered Palestinian. But just for that reason, the admis- sion of more Palestinians is unthinkable: the rulers of Jordan and their supporters are *not* in any sense Palestinian and have no desire to destroy the existing political arrangements. Moreover, Jordan's economy is in no position to carry a large influx of dis possessed people, nor are the Jordanians so stupid as to tak promises of copious financial assistance seriously. The intern tional community has repeatedly shown itself, wherever refuge congregate, unwilling to live up to its promises of support.

An overview

The current situation can be assessed by returning to the Zionist claim that the settlements are not the problem, because Palestinians simply don't want peace. This claim has two parts. The first is that the settlements can't be the problem because the Palestinians rejected peace *before* the settlements became an issue. The second is that the settlements can't be the problem because the Palestinians rejected a peace offer that *included* dismantling most settlements. The second assertion will come up for scrutiny when negotiations are discussed. For now, it will be enough to look at the first assertion.

For the Palestinians to have refused peace, they must have been offered it, and the offer must have been reasonable. This must at least mean "not on condition that you pretty much give up everything you want." Omit this condition, and the result is foolishness: of course each side wanted peace provided the other was consigned to the permanent status of a politically impotent minority. One could add: and of course, each side preferred peace to violence given sufficiently large concessions from their opponents. Did the Palestinians—at least up to the negotiations of the late 1990s—"refuse peace" in a reasonable sense of that expression?

The Palestinians could not have done so before the occupation. Until 1967, Israel had nothing to offer the Palestinians unless it was willing to cease being a Jewish state and permit unlimited right of return. Only this would have ended the ethnic sovereignty of Jews over Palestinians which was the heart of the dispute. Israel never dreamed of making such an offer, so the Palestinians never dreamed of a peaceful settlement with Israel.

After the occupation, the situation changed dramatically. There was indeed a chance at peace, because the Israelis did have something to offer the Palestinians: the West Bank and the Gaza strip in which to create a sovereign state of their own. Such a proposal seems to have been contemplated but never seriously considered. It was the settlements—not exactly the occupation, but the settlements—that closed this window of opportunity. Given not only the settlements, but also the intentions of the settlers and the government's settlement policy, it became crystal clear that Israel would not give the Palestinians room for a sovereign state. It *could* not do so, given its agenda. If this ever changed, it was only *after* ferocious Palestinian resistance made the Israelis reconsider their commitments. Since it was Israel that instituted the settlements, it was Israel that closed the window.

Those sympathetic to Zionism might reply: even if the settlements meant that Israel no longer had anything to offer, that really made no difference. The Palestinians, as their record of terrorism reveals, would not have accepted any offer. The Palestinians are committed to the destruction of Israel, and that means peace is unattainable. If that is in some measure the fault of Zionism, it is also the fault of the Palestinians. To see whether this reply works, it is necessary to look at more than the situation as described above. One must also look at the alternatives available to both Israelis and Palestinians, which are crucial to determining the rights and wrongs of the current situation.

Palestinian and Israeli Alternatives

NEITHER ISRAEL NOR THE PALESTINIANS CAN BE JUDGED WITHOUT understanding the courses of action open to them: what, after 1948, could they do? In the case of the Palestinians, as we will see, this is comparatively simple. In the case of the Israelis, there is a complication: to some extent it is at least supposed that Israel's alternatives depend on Palestinian attitudes. This claim of dependence is dubious, but it will be addressed by a brief look at the Palestinians' attitudes after Israeli alternatives are explored.

Palestinian alternatives

This subject is in a sense quickly exhausted. After 1948, the Palestinians didn't have any alternatives, because they had nothing to offer the Israelis. They could not offer their remaining land, because they needed it to survive, and because Israel didn't see any need for Palestinian assent to the ever-intensifying process of dispossession. The Palestinians also could not offer passivity. Not to resist the settlements would have been virtually suicidal, but Israel was deeply committed to the settlements. So the Palestinians had no choice but to resist, as effectively as possible. This was their only reasonable strategy; their "alternatives" were reduced to choosing what form of resistance to adopt.

It is sometimes supposed that the Palestinians should have adopted nonviolent resistance as their strategy; even that their "failure" to do so is some dark indication of their character. Such opinions are voiced in apparent ignorance of the fact that the

Palestinians have always used a mixture of violent and nonviolent responses—petitions, strikes, marches. This means in part that many Palestinians have never resisted by any but nonviolent means. The results have been less than impressive. In addition, the entire first intifada, brutally repressed, used forms of "violence"—so juvenile and tentative—kids throwing rocks—that they hardly deserve, in the face of the massive professional army thrown against them, that description. But this is not enough for the critics; they envisage huge crowds throwing themselves before (more likely under) the tanks of the IDF.

No one can say with certainty that such a strategy would not work, especially if the Palestinians were prepared to die in large numbers to effect it. But do the Palestinians, or anyone else, have rational grounds for supposing that it *would* work? Such expectations would have to be based on past experience, and the past is not accommodating. Non-violence has never "worked" in any politically relevant sense of the word, and there is no reason to suppose it ever will. It has never, largely *on its own strength*, achieved the political objectives of those who employed it.

There are supposedly three major examples of successful nonviolence: Gandhi's independence movement, the U.S. civil rights movement, and the South African campaign against apartheid. None of them performed as advertised.

Gandhi's nonviolence can't have been successful, because there was nothing he would have called a success. Gandhi's priorities may have shifted over time: he said that, if he changed his mind from one week to the next, it was because he had learned something in between. But it seems fair to say that he wanted independence from British rule, a united India, and nonviolence itself, an end to civil or ethnic strife on the Indian subcontinent. What he got was India 1947: partition, and one of the most horrifying outbursts of bloodshed and cruelty in the whole bloody, cruel history of the postwar world. These consequences alone would be sufficient to count his project as a tragic failure.

What of independence itself? Historians might argue about its causes, but I doubt any of them would attribute it primarily to Gandhi's campaign. The British began contemplating—admittedly with varying degrees of sincerity—some measure of autonomy for India before Gandhi did anything, as early as 1917. A.J.P. Taylor says that after World War I, the British were beginning to find India a liability, because India was once again producing its own cotton and buying cheap textiles from Japan.[143] Later, India's strategic importance, while valued by many, became questioned by some who saw the oil of the Middle East and the Suez Canal as far more important. By the end of the Second World War, Britain's will to hold onto its empire had pretty well crumbled, for reasons having little or nothing to do with nonviolence.

But this is the least important of the reasons why Gandhi cannot be said to have won independence for India. It was not his saintliness or the disruption he caused that impressed the British. What impressed them was that the country seemed (and was) about to erupt. The colonial authorities could see no way to stop it. A big factor was the terrorism—and this need not be a term of condemnation—quite regularly employed against the British. It was not enough to do much harm, but more than enough to warn them that India was becoming more trouble than it was worth. All things considered, the well-founded fear of violence had far more effect on British resolve than Gandhi ever did. He may have been a brilliant and creative political thinker, but he was not a victor.

How about the U.S. civil rights movement? It would be difficult and ungenerous to argue that it was unsuccessful, outrageous to claim that it was anything but a long and dangerous struggle. But when that is conceded, the fact remains that Martin Luther King's civil rights movement was practically a federal government project. Its roots may have run deep, but its impetus came from the Supreme Court decision of 1954 and from the subsequent attempts to integrate Central High School in Little Rock, Arkansas. The students who braved a hell to accomplish this goal are well remembered. Sometimes forgotten is U.S. government's almost spectacular determination to see that federal law was respected. Eisenhower sent, not the FBI, not a bunch of lawyers, but one of the best and proudest units of the United States Army, the 101st Airborne, to keep order in Little Rock and to see that the "federalized" Arkansas national guard stayed on the right side of the dispute. Though there was never any hint of an impending battle between federal and state military forces, the message couldn't have been clearer: we, the federal government, are prepared to do whatever it takes to enforce our will.

This message is an undercurrent throughout the civil rights struggles of the 1950s and 1960s. Though Martin Luther King still had to overcome vicious, sometimes deadly resistance, he himself remarked that surprisingly few people were killed or seriously injured in the struggle.[144] The surprise diminishes with the recollection that there was real federal muscle behind the nonviolent campaign. For a variety of motives, both virtuous and cynical, the U.S. government wanted the South to be integrated and to recognize black civil rights. Nonviolence achieved its ends largely because the violence of its opponents was severely constrained. In 1962, Kennedy federalized the National Guard and sent in combat troops to quell segregationist rioting in Oxford, Mississippi. Johnson did the same thing in 1965, after anti-civil rights violence in Alabama. While any political movement has allies and benefits from favorable circumstances, having the might of the U.S. government behind you goes far beyond the ordinary advantages accompanying political activity. The nonviolence of the U.S. civil rights movement sets an example only for those who have the overwhelming armed force of a government on their side.

As for South Africa, it is a minor miracle of wishful thinking that anyone could suppose nonviolence played a major role in the collapse of apartheid.

In the first place, the African National Congress was never a nonviolent movement but a movement that decided, on occasion and for practical reasons, to use nonviolent tactics. (The same can be said of the other anti-apartheid organizations.) Much like Sinn Fein and the IRA, it maintained from the 1960s an arms-length relationship with MK (Umkhonto we Sizwe), a military/guerrilla organization. So there was never even a commitment to Gandhian nonviolence within the South African movements.

Secondly, violence was used extensively throughout the course of the anti-apartheid struggle. It can be argued that the violence was essentially defensive, but that's not the point: nonviolence as a doctrine rejects the use of violence in self-defense. To say that blacks used violence in self-defense or as resistance to oppression is to say, I think, that they were justified. It is certainly not to say that they were nonviolent.

Third, violence played a major role in causing both the boycott of South Africa and the demise of apartheid. Albert Luthuli, then president of the ANC, called for an economic boycott in 1959; the ANC's nonviolent resistance began in 1952.[145] But the boycott only acquired some teeth starting in 1977, after the Soweto riots in 1976, and again in 1985–1986, after the township riots of 1984–1985. Though the emphasis in accounts of these riots is understandably on police repression, no one contests that black protestors committed many violent acts, including attacks on police stations.

Violence was telling in other ways. The armed forces associated with the ANC, though never very effective, worried the South African government after Angola and Mozambique ceased to function as buffer states: sooner or later, it was supposed, the black armies would become a serious problem. (This worry intensified with the strategic defeat of South African forces by Cuban units at Cuito Cuanavale, Angola, in 1988.) In addition, violence was widespread and crucial in eliminating police informers and political enemies, as well as in coercing cooperation with collective actions. It included the practice of necklacing, with a tire set around the neck of the target and set on fire.

Though much of the violence was conducted by gangs and mobs, it was not for that fact any less important politically: on the contrary, it was precisely the disorganized character of the violence that made it so hard to contain. And history of the period indicates that the South African government fell not under the moral weight of dignified, passive suffering, but because the white rulers (and their friends in the West) felt that the situation was spiraling out of control. Economic problems caused by the boycotts and the administration of apartheid were also a factor, but the boycott and the administrative costs were themselves, in large measure, a response to violent rather than nonviolent resistance.

In short, it is a myth that nonviolence brought all the victories it is supposed to have in its ledger. In fact it brought none of them.

How does this bear on the Israel-Palestine conflict? In that situation, success is far less likely than in the cases we have examined. Unlike Martin Luther King, the Palestinians are working against a state, not with one. Their opponents are far more ruthless than the British were in the twilight of empire. Unlike the Indians and South Africans, they do not vastly outnumber their oppressors. And neither the Boers nor the English ever had anything like the moral authority Israel enjoys in the hearts and minds of Americans, much less its enormous support network. Nonviolent protest might overcome Israel's prestige in ten or twenty years, but the Palestinians might well suppose they do not have that long.

The Palestinians will continue to choose, sometimes violence, sometimes nonviolence, most often a mixture of the two. They will presumably base their choices, as they have always done, on their assessment of the political realities. It is a sort of insolent naïveté to suppose that, in their weakness, they should defy the lessons of history and cut off half their options. The notion that a people (in any sense of the word) can free itself literally by allowing their captors to walk all over them is in historical terms a fantasy.

In short, the Palestinians had to use violence of some sort: it might not work, but there was at least some historical precedent for it working. This, of course, does not license all types of violent resistance. The issue of terrorism will be discussed later.

Israeli alternatives

If the Palestinians have no alternative but violent resistance, what about the Israelis? It might be said, and has been said, that Israel also has no alternative other than a military response to such resistance; that Israelis and the Palestinians are locked together in some fatal struggle. Matters of right in this area have been supposed to parallel matters of fact: if the Palestinians have a right to defend themselves, even violently, doesn't Israel? But the parallels are inaccurate. Because Israel does, in fact, have an alternative to military responses, its right of self-defense does not apply.

Israel's alternative is unilateral withdrawal from the Occupied Territories. This course of action has been recommended since 1998 by The Council for Peace and Security, an organization originally headed by Aharon Yariv, who joined the Haganah (the main Zionist armed force) in 1939 and was at various times a general, the first commander of the IDF staff college, head of military intelligence, and cabinet minister in the Meir and Rabin governments.[146] The group comprises some 1,000 "security experts," including ex-army and intelligence officers with impressive credentials. Some of its members want Israel to hang on to some of its settlements, but on the whole something very close to complete withdrawal is contemplated.

In the opinion of this group, withdrawal will improve, not harm Israel's security. The main reasons are obvious. First, Israel expends vast resources to defend the settlements, and it cannot be easier to protect civilians scattered all over the landscape than to protect a single border. Second, because of the settlements, the existing border cannot be properly sealed; this constraint would vanish with withdrawal. It is eloquent testimony to the desirability of this option that almost invariably, when Israel is really concerned about its internal security, it does in fact temporarily close the border, roughly along the pre-1967 "Green Line." Within its borders, Israel could erect whatever barriers and fortifications it liked to tighten its frontiers. Third, Palestinians in the Occupied Territories will be able to establish a state of their own—the group recommends that Israel assists them. They will no longer have the motive of self-defense for engaging in violence. The extent to which these changes will reduce attacks is the subject of much speculation, but it would be unreasonable to suppose that withdrawal offered no grounds for expecting such a reduction.

The chief disadvantage alleged is that Israel will now lose its "buffer" of the Occupied Territories, so that in consequence the Palestinians or conceivably neighboring states would be in a better position to mount attacks. This problem is vastly overblown. In the first place, it has already been noted that buffer zones need not be within one's own borders. States do on occasion announce that military operations close to certain vulnerable borders would not be tolerated. Israel is more than powerful enough to do the same, whether or not such announcements were judged consonant with international law. Second, and for similar reasons, nothing would prevent Israel from making retaliatory or even pre-emptive strikes across its borders if genuinely necessary. This is in fact the strategy Israel has employed against neighboring states, with considerable success. In 1981, it even got away with bombing the Oisraq nuclear reactor in Iraq, a country that does not even border on Israel. There is little doubt that after withdrawing from the Occupied Territories and thereby placating at least Europe, it could get away with such strikes again.

Third, only on the most pessimistic analysis can it be supposed that the government of a Palestinian state would not want to restrict terrorism against Israel: with a state, the Palestinians would have much to lose from such attacks and, given military realities, virtually nothing to gain. Fourth, there is a good chance that international forces could be enlisted to monitor the border: withdrawal would put Israel in compliance with both U.S. recommendations and with various UN resolutions, thereby greatly enhancing its standing in at least the Western world. Finally, in the worst case, the decision would not be irrevocable. If Israel really did find itself in an intolerable security situation as a result of its withdrawal, there is little doubt it would have the power to reoccupy the territories, particularly if it did so before allowing a buildup of forces on the other side.

No strategy is without risks, but the risks of the alternatives must also be considered. Two of these have already been stated—porous borders, and a large Palestinian population that really must resort to violence for its own defense. Two other factors are relevant. First, the increasing anger of not only Arab and Islamic states and populations, matched by Israel's increasing diplomatic isolation, cannot be anything but a security liability. Second, Israel's security position vis-à-vis its neighbors is constantly improving. Its nuclear lead is compounded by an even greater lead in delivery systems such as ballistic missiles, cruise missiles, and satellite technology. The same can be said for its lead in conventional weapons. Equally important, Israel has signed peace treaties with two of its neighbors. Lebanon, with the very minor exception of Hizbollah attacks, poses no threat. Syria is certainly no match for Israel, and in any case it is hard to see how a Palestinian state could worsen Israel's position in relation to its one more or less active enemy. The worry of smaller borders related primarily to Egypt and Jordan, the countries least likely, given the treaties, to pose any threat. Even if Israel has worries beyond its borders about states such as Iran, or perhaps some future Pakistani régime, these cannot be increased by withdrawal from the Occupied Territories. There is, then, every reason to suppose that unilateral withdrawal is a viable alternative.

What makes this option so significant is that it is instantly available to Israel and has been, at any time, for years. *It requires no negotiations, no change in Palestinian attitudes, no trust, and no improvement in the effectiveness of the Palestinian authority.* An Israeli major in the Israeli armored corps showed an appreciation of the situation when he said that:

> Make no mistake, Israel has no other reason for remaining in the Occupied Territories than to preserve the existing settlements, even when they are deep within Palestinian centers of population. Maybe the Palestinians are not interested in peace— one of the most commonly heard justifications for our recent invasions—and truly want to push us into the sea. Even then, we would be much better off defending ourselves from the 1967 borders rather than from inside the narrow alleys of Jenin, Ramallah, and Bethlehem. This is why I think that the occupation runs against the most basic interests of the state of Israel, even to the extent of threatening its very existence.[147]

The political difficulties involved in getting Israelis to accept the proposal are irrelevant to its viability: they simply mean that Israel might not choose it, and that decision would remain Israel's responsibility. As for the settlers, they pose no problem at all: they can either leave or fend for themselves. Colonial history suggests, moreover, that settlers are not nearly so fierce in their resistance to displacement as they would like themselves and others to believe. This has proven to be the case throughout sub-Saharan Africa and in Algeria. There, despite a large, heavily armed and well-organized underground movement, settler opposition collapsed when, in 1962, the French government opened fire on a settler demonstration, killing 80 and wounding 200. Presumably, overcoming settler opposition would not require such drastic measures in Israel.

It is sometimes alleged that complete withdrawal from the Occupied Territories is "impracticable" because the facts on the ground are too deeply entrenched: Israeli settlements are just too extensive and important to uproot. One can hardly take this seriously. If it was "practicable" for hundreds of thousands of stateless Palestinians to leave their homes, why is this impracticable for half as many Israeli citizens in far more comfortable and peaceful circumstances? Throughout modern history, from the waves of U.S. immigration to the peaceful post-World War II population transfers, there have been far greater shifts than this movement of a few miles. In many cases, if the settlers prefer, they can simply return to their homes in the United States. "It's impracticable" seems here a stand-in for "Aw, gee, these towns are too nice to let the Arabs have them."

The significance of the withdrawal alternative is not that it represents a just solution. Arguably, justice would require much more than that—not only the abolition of Jewish sovereignty in Israel but a full right of return, with compensation, for the Palestinians, and the eviction of Jewish inhabitants occupying Palestinian property. But the existence of the withdrawal alternative effectively completes the case against Israel. Its willful and pointless rejection of that alternative places Israel decisively in the wrong.

In the first place, Israel has a right of self-defense, but it does not apply in the Occupied Territories. If the U.S. invaded Jamaica and dotted it with settlements, neither the settlers nor the armed forces could invoke any right to defend themselves against the Jamaicans, any more than a robber who invaded your house.[148] So it is with Israelis in the Occupied Territories. Their right of self-defense is their right to the least violent defensive alternative. Since withdrawal (perhaps followed by fortifying their own 1948 border) is by far their best and least violent defense, that is all they have a right to do.

In the second place, since Israel can withdraw at will and close its border, Israel can put an end to virtually all the violence. That violence is occasioned by the settlement policy, which is Israel's sole reason for the occupation. Since that occupation has no defensive or strategic rationale, Israel has no good reason to prolong it. Since Israel is willfully pursuing an unjustifiable strategy that it can end at no cost, it is responsible for all the consequences of that strategy. It follows that all the violence, and all horrors of the occupation, are to be laid at Israel's doorstep.

Much is often made of Israel's "humane" occupation strategies. By this is apparently meant that, although Israel commits human rights violations and war crimes,[149] it could do worse. Indeed it could: it could, as some Israelis like to fantasize, level Palestinian cities with nuclear weapons or conventional explosives. But what makes the occupation so reprehensible is even more its gratuitousness than its severity. Israel does not need to pose a mortal threat to the Palestinians. It does so for no good reason, so it is responsible for the Palestinian response to that threat and for its own counter-moves. (The Palestinians are also, of course, responsible; whether they are culpable will be explored in the next chapter.) After the Nazi era, it is small comfort indeed to know that Israel could have done even worse.

Third, the idea that Palestinian hostility antedates the settlement policy and will persist if the settlements are dismantled now becomes of relatively minor importance. Whether or not the settlements are the cause of Palestinian hostility, they are the chief obstacles to peace. This is because unilateral withdrawal and the peace it would bring are entirely independent of Palestinian hostility. Should that hostility persist after withdrawal, violence would still go down, and Israel would still be in a better position to deflect it. In any case, at least one version of the "implacable hostility" argument is unsound: the claim that the occupation and the settlements could not be the cause of the violence because the violence preceded them. Alan Dershowitz, for instance, says that a resolution of the Presbyterian Church

> ...effectively blames the Israelis for Palestinian slaughter of civilians by asserting that the occupation is the "root" of terrorism. This canard ignores the reality that the Palestinian leadership opted for murder and violence as the tactic of choice well before there was any occupation.[150]

I take "the occupation" to involve a reference to the settlements that go with it. The argument depends on a false presupposition, namely that there is one set of activities properly called "the violence." But there were two sets of activities. The first was the Palestinian response to a mortal threat, the prospect of Jewish sovereignty within what became pre-1967 Israel. (The attacks on Israel between 1948 and 1967 can be seen as an extension of this response, a reaction to dispossession and the imposition of Jewish sovereignty on those Palestinians remaining in Jewish-controlled territory.) The second was a response to a second mortal threat, the settlements. That pre-1948 Zionism provoked the first response obviously doesn't mean the settlements didn't provoke the second.

An example supports this claim. If, say, white nationalists come into your neighborhood to set up a white state, and you fight them, that is one response. Suppose you are driven out and go elsewhere. Then, white nationalists conquer your new neighborhood and settle there with a view to extending their racial hegemony. You fight back. That is a second response. The first white nationalist campaign caused the first response, and the second one, the second response. That both responses were violent doesn't mean that the second response wasn't caused by the second campaign. The Palestinians fought twice, against two distinct threats. When they fought a second time, it was because of the second threat. That they fought earlier against an earlier threat doesn't change this.

Nevertheless, the matter of Palestinian attitudes and willingness to make peace does still loom over the discussion. Morris, Horovitz, and others have a point whose weight is hard to determine, but whose relevance is clear. If the Palestinians in particular and the "Arabs" in general are eternally bent on Israel's destruction, if they are consumed with inextinguishable hatred, then there is a futility to the situation that pat solutions like immediate withdrawal cannot dissipate. Sooner or later, one might think, the terrorism or some other form of violence will start up all over again, so why even bother dreaming of peace?

Part of the answer is already available. The peace treaties with Jordan and Egypt show absolutely no sign of breaking; this makes it hard to believe that "the Arab world" insists on Israel's destruction. Unilateral withdrawal, moreover, because it improves Israel's security situation, is even more justified if Arab intentions are solidly hostile. Israel would certainly benefit, not only from its more defensible position, but also from an improved reputation on the international stage.

However, no final verdict on Israel or on Palestine can be reached until the question of Palestinian attitudes and strategies has been addressed.

Palestinian Attitudes and Strategies

THREE TOPICS LOOM LARGE IN THE DISCUSSION OF PALESTINIAN hostility and "intransigence": negotiations, Palestinian or Arab hatred, and terrorism. None of these items are of decisive importance to the case against Israel, because none prevents Israel from leaving the Occupied Territories to end the conflict. However, these topics are very important in the minds of Israel's defenders. They will be discussed in the order listed.

Negotiations

The course of Israeli-Palestinian negotiations has been studied in minute detail. Rivers of ink still flow concerning whether or not Ehud Barak made a "generous offer" in 2001 at Camp David, whether Arafat rejected that offer, whether an agreement was more or less reached at Taba in the same year, to what extent the parties were prepared to compromise, to what extent they wanted the process to fail, and so on. Seldom if ever in the whole course of the Israel-Palestine debate has so much energy (more heat than light) been expended on matters of so little consequence.

There are three reasons why negotiations don't matter much.

The first is that, as argued previously, the option of unilateral withdrawal makes them unnecessary. Negotiations make much more sense after withdrawal, when there is a sovereign state to negotiate with: experience as well as logic confirms that agreements made with the PLO have limited value precisely because the PLO does not have the authority of a full-fledged government. Israel would certainly not lack for bargaining chips, such as the ability to provide a land corridor between the West Bank and Gaza, after withdrawal.

If negotiations are not needed to bring peace, they might at least be useful as an indicator of *willingness* to make peace. But why would you want to know *that* when willingness to make peace isn't necessary either, when unilateral withdrawal brings peace even if the Palestinians are *un*willing? Negotiations seem to be useful only as a general indication of Palestinian attitudes. The problem is, they're a very weak indicator. Suppose it could be established—though we will see it cannot—that in a particular course of negotiations, "the Palestinians" could have had peace but rejected it. For one thing, that would show only something about the negotiators, not about "the Palestinians." More important, it would show very little. Perhaps, in such a hypothetical case, the Palestinians rejected a real peace offer because they didn't want peace. But there would be other very simple explanations. Maybe, for instance, there was some misunderstanding of the offer, or some misreading of the sincerity behind it, or some miscalculation about the viability of the government making it, or the ability of that government to enforce its provisions. Maybe there was overconfidence, an unfounded belief that more could be obtained. Maybe the negotiators were in a bad mood and would come to regret their decision. The interminable debates about past negotiations themselves testify to how difficult it is to prove any of these explanations, so the failure of negotiations pretty clearly doesn't tell us much.

Third, it is just silly to proclaim, as Zionists often do, that the failure of negotiations has some sort of permanent and fateful implication for the prospects of peace. If negotiations failed last month, if it seems that the Palestinians didn't want peace last month, why does that mark some point of no return? How about making an offer next month? Maybe attitudes have changed. The issues involved in the Israel/Palestine dispute don't *have* points of no return: it's not as if they're arguing about who's going to save a sinking ship. Are the negotiators exhausted; are their hearts broken? Take a rest, or get some new negotiators. Do particular negotiations such as Camp David and the Taba reveal some unbridgeable gap between the parties? We are about to see reasons for doubting such claims, but there are endless disputes about everything connected with these meetings. If bickering about the past has yet to resolve the controversy, it probably never will. What better way, then, to settle these disputes than for one side or the other to make a crystal clear offer, one which is easily seen to produce peace if accepted and which has solid support behind it? If such an offer cannot be made, then the negotiation process can't be very important. If it can be made, then why is the murky course of prior negotiations of any great significance?

Suppose, however, that we accept the presupposition of the negotiations debates: that it would be highly significant if the Palestinians had rejected some real peace offer from Israel. Did this happen? A full-scale discussion of this question is beyond the scope of this essay, the competence of its author, and probably of the materials available to sustain it. There are, however, shortcuts to at least a tentative verdict.

For a start, many of the issues negotiated and much of the discussion about negotiations concern matters that are peripheral to a settlement. Just as Jewish sovereignty was the make-or-break issue of the pre-1948 conflict, so Palestinian sovereignty is the make-or-break issue of the post-occupation conflict. Before 1948, Zionist commitment to Jewish sovereignty left no room for compromise. After the occupation and especially after the settlement movement, there could be no peace without a sovereign Palestinian state that could plausibly provide protection from settler ambitions. Whether or not the Palestinians did or didn't obsess over other issues such as the holy places in Jerusalem, or a full right of return,[151] or even the legitimacy of the Israeli state, doesn't change this. The settler movement was and is a mortal threat. Without that threat, peace is possible. With it, no.

By that yardstick it is futile, for instance, to argue about how much land the Palestinians were offered, or what proportion of the settlements were to be removed. Not that these issues are unimportant: having renounced all of pre-1967 Israel, the Palestinians have already compromised enormously when they demand total withdrawal from the Occupied Territories. Given that the settlements are utterly unnecessary to Israel, there is no reason a single one should remain. But the discussion of territorial claims cannot even get started unless the Palestinians are offered real sovereignty, because without it they are offered nothing. To be "given" a billion dollars is to be given nothing unless it is really yours. No matter how much land is "given up" by Israel in a proposal, unless the Palestinians get genuine sovereignty they have not been offered one square inch.

With this in mind, the complex course of negotiations reduces to something much simpler. Israel's offers supposedly reached some climax of generosity in 1999-2001; so we can concentrate on that period. To simplify further, we need not look at the territorial offers at all—the main focus of the debates—but can simply ask: were the Palestinians offered a sovereign state? Is any feature of the Israeli proposals incompatible with Palestinian sovereignty? The answer is not far to seek. Our authority is Professor Menachem Klein, Senior Scholar at the Jerusalem Institute for Israeli Studies, Professor at Bar Ilan University, who served as advisor to the Israeli delegation to the Camp David Summit in July 2000.

Professor Klein is not much given to jargon or circumlocution: he dismisses the pro-Israel claims of generous offers and Palestinian intransigence as "nonsense." On one crucial point he is very clear:

> Israel presented a map to Yasir Abd Rabbo and then presented
> this orally in Stockholm and at Camp David. It was leaked to
> [the Israeli newspaper] *Yediot Aharanot*. It shows Israel control-
> ling a Greater Jerusalem that goes to the Dead Sea and connects
> with the Jordan Valley where Israel would have sovereignty over
> a strip of land west of the River, and thereby keep control over
> the external borders of the Palestinian state.[152]

What happened at the borders of the Palestinian "state," in other words, would be entirely at the discretion of the Israeli state. The Israeli proposal had other serious defects. It left the Palestinians with a territory riddled with settlements and Israeli-controlled access roads, with supervised ports, immigration, and airspace, with something that could not effectively function as a state. But the border restrictions represent the starkest, clearest denial of Palestinian sovereignty. They are all by themselves, without regard for the other state-destroying features of the offer, enough to support the conclusion that the Palestinians, far from being offered 80 or 90 or 95 or 98 percent of the Occupied Territories, were offered nothing at all. A territory is not yours unless you control it, and you do not control it unless you have sovereignty over it. You do not have sovereignty over it if you do not have a state, and you do not have a state if you do not control its external borders. To be offered territory you do not control is to be offered nothing.

After Camp David, in December 2000, Barak resigned, leading to an election campaign that went against him. Sharon, clearly ahead, was elected in February 2001. Just before he took office, in January 21-27, 2001, there were more negotiations at Taba. The Israeli side made much improved, though somewhat vague, proposals. The only authoritative record of those talks is a document drawn up by EU Special Representative Ambassador Moratinos. His account of the negotiations was, in the words of the document itself, "acknowledged by the parties as being a relatively fair description of the outcome of the negotiations."[153] The Israelis seemed prepared to make important concessions relevant to Palestinian sovereignty over airspace, borders, demilitarization, and the contiguity of Palestinian territory, though in all cases Moratinos reports something short of agreement. Taba is generally conceded to represent the furthest negotiations have advanced towards peace. It suggests the contours of a settlement to which the Israeli and Palestinian delegations might eventually have assented: a demilitarized but sovereign Palestinian state with full control over its borders—perhaps with Israeli observers involved—and a contiguous territory produced in part by land swaps.

Whether the outcome of negotiations would have produced a genuinely sovereign state, no one can say. But the progress from Camp David to Taba was the progress from a clearly unacceptable offer to a possibly not unacceptable non-offer. The Israeli negotiators did not make any definitive proposal, let alone a proposal representing the position of the state of Israel. They could not do so, because the government of Israel was in a state of transition and in no position to make official commitments on such matters. When the Sharon government took power, for good reason or bad, the Taba proposals never gained official status.

In other words, Israeli-Palestinian negotiations give no indication whatever that "the Palestinians" or Arafat or the PLO rejected peace, or indeed that they refused to compromise. Arafat was right to reject Barak's offer. Even if this torpedoed the peace process—and Taba suggests otherwise—acceptance would have done the same, because without genuine sovereignty the Palestinians would have had no security from Israeli expansionism and, therefore, would have had to continue their resistance. In particular, they could not accept living within Israeli-controlled borders, a situation that would permit Israel to do what it liked in the Occupied Territories. What it liked, as experience had shown, often constituted a mortal threat.

Perhaps, though, the negotiations are besides the point because the Palestinian negotiators did not represent Palestinian sentiment. Perhaps that sentiment makes peace impossible, just as so many Zionist polemics claim. On this account, the Palestinians are consumed with unquenchable hate, so that nothing will stop their attacks on Israel. (One wonders where this leads: to a case for extermination?) It is time to examine this claim.

Hate

The condition of the Palestinians in the Occupied Territories is often compared to that of black South Africans under apartheid. The comparison is sometimes made by those in a position to know. In 2001, Archbishop Desmond Tutu gave a compelling address entitled "Apartheid in the Holy Land."[154] South African Defense Minister Joe Modise made the same comparison in 1994.[155] Nelson Mandela, on a visit to Gaza in 1999, said that "It is a realization of a dream for me to be here to come and pledge my solidarity with my friend Yasser Arafat." Addressing a special session of the Palestinian assembly, he remarked that "the histories of our two peoples correspond in such painful and poignant ways that I intensely feel myself at home amongst my compatriots."[156] The Israeli academic Uri Davis has argued for the comparison at length in *Israel: An Apartheid State*.[157]

Whatever the details of the occupation, it does seem safe to say that the condition of the Palestinians is no better than that of those who endured Apartheid. One could be far more cautious and say that, if the Palestinians are not under an apartheid régime, at least they are no better off than blacks were in the 1960s in the U.S. (In fact, it would be too cautious: apart from the effect of the settlements and of Israeli armed strikes in civilian areas, the scenes of humiliation and worse at the checkpoints are clearly the work of sadists. Israeli doctors have protested 600 cases in which ambulances were delayed and 39 in which women were forced to give birth at checkpoints.[158] On one occasion, twin newborn girls died there.[159]) How are these comparisons relevant to the hypothesis that Palestinians are consumed by hate?

Well, here is a passage by James Baldwin, published in 1962:

> And there is, I should think, no Negro living in America who has not felt, briefly or for long periods, with anguish sharp or dull, in varying degrees and to varying effect, simple, naked and unanswerable hatred; who has not wanted to smash any white face he may encounter in a day, to violate, out of motives of the cruelest vengeance, their women, to break the bodies of all white people and bring them low, as low as that dust into which he himself has been and is being trampled; no Negro, finally, who has not had to make his own precarious adjustment to the "nigger" who surrounds him and to the "nigger" in himself.[160]

Journalists do not produce this passage as evidence of some pathology in Baldwin; they speak instead of its "stony beauty" and of his "raw anger."[161]

This is of course hatred and, like anti-Semitism, it is racial hatred. No one seems to find it in the least bit surprising, and no one clucks sympathetically to express their sad dismay at the twisted minds of those Negroes. *Of course* many blacks hated whites, indiscriminately, at least into the late 1950s and early 1960s. *Of course* many Palestinians hate Israelis, and this hatred sometimes takes on a racial character: is this somehow surprising, given that the government of Israel and the Zionists never cease to portray themselves as the truest representatives of the entire Jewish people? This is not pathology but normalcy and no evidence for some collective, unquenchable Palestinian madness.

But, one might say, however justified or excusable or understandable Palestinian hatred, it is there, and it makes peace impossible. Is there some relevant truth in this?

In the first place, unquenchable hatred would change nothing. Since it is widely and authoritatively held that the occupation is a security liability for Israel, the "hatred" thesis would lead to a further, very strong argument for unilateral withdrawal. This makes one wonder what relevance to the conflict the hatred thesis is supposed to have.

Even if the hatred thesis were relevant, why should it be accepted? That Palestinian hatred is unquenchable is a large claim about a particularly murky subject, the prevalence of a certain psychology in a sizeable population. Yet the basis of this claim is mysterious: how on earth do you establish unquenchability? There is plenty of historical evidence that suggests otherwise.

The Palestinians have not hated Israelis or Jews from all eternity. In the late 19th century, Palestinian notables, if less than delighted at the idea of massive Jewish immigration to Palestine, were quite sympathetic to the idea of a Jewish homeland.[162] Ordinary Palestinians had little to do with Jews, and there was no record of conflict between the two ethnic groups. This is why Palestine seemed to the more informed Zionists a better bet than Western Europe.

What bred Palestinian hatred of Jews and Israelis was just like what bred Israeli and Jewish hatred of Palestinians.[163] The hatreds were the product of war, not the cause of it. Jewish leaders quite regularly and very early on attributed the war not to any deep-seated racial antagonism, but to conflicting desires for territorial sovereignty. Thus Jabotinsky:

> Has ever been known that a people would willingly give up its soil? No more would the Palestinian Arabs yield their sovereignty without force.[164]

And later, Ben-Gurion agreed:

> If I were an Arab leader, I would never make terms with Israel. That is natural: we have taken their country. Sure, God promised it to us, but what does that matter to them? Our God is not theirs... There has been anti-Semitism, the Nazis, Hitler, Auschwitz, but was that their fault? They only know but one thing: we have come here and stolen their country. Why would they accept that?[165]

So it is unreasonable to suppose that the war was born of hatred rather than the hatred of war.

Though philosophers of history debate the existence of historical laws, there are least historical generalizations which are overlooked simply because they are so banal. One is that wars, even "good wars," breed hatred. We might not be surprised that Nazi Germany hated its (real or imagined) enemies. But we should also not be surprised that the Allies had similar feelings. Here is one account of American portrayals of Japanese:

> A common technique used by propagandists was to liken the Japanese to animals like snakes and rats. But the most common animal used to portray the Japanese was the monkey. In several posters and editorial cartoons, the Japanese were drawn up as monkeys hanging from trees or lumbering around like big gorillas. The image of a subhuman primate was key to undercutting the humanity of the enemy...

A description of one image conjures up striking parallels to the talk of some of the less respectable Middle Eastern "experts"today:

> Figure 2 shows scientists and scholars baffled by their monkey-like Japanese specimen. One of the scholars holds a document reading "International problem: What goes on in the Japanese mind," as if the Japanese were a specimen whose behavior was tested and observed like a lab rat. Despite Japan's military prowess and technological skills proven in the Pacific,

the notion that the Japanese were intellectually inferior was still a stubbornly held popular view.[166]

These attitudes reached the highest levels, including the presidency. Here is an account of Roosevelt's efforts to understand his foes:

> He had set one Professor Krdlicka, of the Smithsonian Institute, to work on a private study of the effect of racial crossing... The President has asked the Professor why the Japanese were as bad as they were. The Professor had said the skulls of these people were some 2,000 years less developed than ours (this sounds very little, doesn't it?). The President asked whether this might account for the nefariousness of the Japanese and had been told it might, as they might well be the basic stock of the Japanese.[167]

Another writer refers to how First World War "stirred up hatred of Germans and German culture in the United States."[168] In Europe, books of atrocity stories depicted Germans "as apes and pigs, creatures with oversized feet and hands."[169] Hatred arises in wartime both as a natural and as a consciously engineered reaction.

Since there seems to be nothing atypical of Palestinian wartime hatreds, there is no reason to suppose they will not dissipate as such hatreds usually do. Turks and Greeks, the most bitter enemies, were brought together by Greek assistance to Turkish earthquake victims. The French and Germans killed one another literally in the millions in 1871, 1914-1918, and 1939-1954. In the fifties there was still much bitterness; in the sixties it was the exception rather than the rule; in the seventies and eighties there was residual mistrust. Now the French and Germans get along very well. And in Spain, with a million dead in the civil war in the 1930s, you do not hear of feuding republicans and fascists.

Perhaps even more important, often where there is continued animosity there is virtually no violence. That is the situation between Native Americans and the descendants of white settlers who almost wiped them out. Japan perpetrated horrible atrocities in China: the Japanese are not loved, but do they, or should they, fear a Chinese attack? Is it likely that the Vietnamese or Cambodians or Laotians will wreak vengeance on the Americans for the millions who died in Indochina? The Chaco Wars of 1932–1935 between Bolivia and Paraguay killed some 100,000 people, but one does not hear of clashes between Bolivians and Paraguayans. These wars were of course far bloodier than the Israel/Palestine conflict. It is not just that hatred dissipates; it is also that it often ceases to be a danger. There is simply no evidence to support the view that Palestinian (or Israeli) hatred will be any different.

There is one outstanding issue that bears heavily on the question of Palestinian attitudes but whose importance goes much further. What about Palestinian terrorism? On the one hand, this is taken as an expression of absolutely extraordinary hatred: what sort of beings could perpetrate such atrocities? The idea here is that terrorism is the work of crazed beasts. A quite different lesson is sometimes drawn: that the Palestinians are coldly calculating, fiendishly ingenious murderers with whom peace is utterly impossible. On this account, to put it bluntly, they deserve everything they get or, if some innocents are harmed, their blood is entirely on the hands of the terrorists.

Neither reaction to Palestinian terrorism is as important as may appear. If the Palestinians are beasts or calculating murderers, then—as in the case of the unquenchable hatred theory—all the more reason to disengage from them and move to fully closed, defensible borders. But the issue of terrorism is so sensitive and looms so large in thinking about the Israel/Palestine conflict that it needs the full-dress discussion found in the next chapter.

Terror

NOT SO LONG AGO IT WAS COMMON KNOWLEDGE THAT RADICAL Zionists brought terrorism to Palestine. No one thought this an enormity. As recently as 1977, J. Bowyer Bell took time off from a distinguished academic career at Harvard, MIT, and Columbia to write a remarkably cheerful book called *Terror out of Zion: Irgun Zvai Leumi, LEHI, and the Palestine Underground, 1929-1949*. Its ending is quite moving:

> Those of the underground believed their state could only be won by resort to force, and most assume it can only be so maintained. This they see as their legacy. For this small state, this remnant of their dream, for this they called for terror out of Zion and not in vain.[170]

That these attitudes were acceptable in the recent past has no tendency to justify Palestinian terrorism: maybe past attitudes were wrong, or maybe the Zionists were justified and the Palestinians are not. Maybe the type of terrorism employed makes a difference. Because the "war on terror" has made terrorism such a hot button issue, it is worth stepping back and discussing it in more general terms. For a start, what does the word mean?

Many apparently respectable definitions of "terrorism" are not just wrong, but outlandishly, foolishly wrong. This has not prevented them from commanding wide acceptance, even from almost opposite ends of the political spectrum. Chomsky and

Donald Rumsfeld, for instance, will live in lexicographic harmony. The former says:

> I understand the term "terrorism" exactly in the sense defined in official US documents: "the calculated use of violence or threat of violence to attain goals that are political, religious, or ideological in nature. This is done through intimidation, coercion, or instilling fear."[171]

The definition borrowed by Chomsky—as he undoubtedly knows—is nonsense. It implies that uncalculated use of violence against civilians—the spur-of-the-moment, unorganized torching of randomly selected immigrant houses, for instance—is not terrorism. It implies that threatening intervention in East Timor or Rwanda would have been terrorist. It implies that those who flagellate themselves in a religious procession are terrorists, as are those who threaten sinners with hellfire. It implies that the Warsaw Ghetto uprising and invasion of Normandy were terrorist campaigns. It implies that virtually any attack against terrorists is also terrorism. (The same can be said of threatening any such attacks.) And it also implies that the Buddhist monks who set themselves ablaze to protest the Vietnam war were terrorists.

Terrorism is not any old violence or threat of violence, for any old political purpose. This is clear if we go back to a time before the word had become quite such a battleground. When, in 1957, the Algerian rebels set off bombs at bus stops, in cafés, in a casino, and in a stadium, hardly anyone denied that this was terrorism. Nor did anyone, except perhaps some extreme right-wingers, deny it when the colonists' *Organisation de l'Armée secrète* set off bombs in Algerian shops, or rolled a gasoline truck down on an Arab quarter. Airline hijackings were considered terrorism by virtually everyone except some of their perpetrators.

"Terrorism," when polemics are set aside, normally involves attacks against civilians. The attacks are, if not utterly random, in some sense arbitrary. The particular victims may be carefully selected; years may go into the planning. But the victims were selected because they were representative members of some large group, not because of their individual traits or positions in society. Anyone in the café or stadium, and in many other cafés or stadiums, would have made just as suitable a target. In fact, the point of the exercise was to transmit just this message: it doesn't matter who you are or where you are, as long as you belong to the relevant population. In some cases, that population may include everyone in a country, because the idea is not so much to attack a particular group as to show that one is incapable of protecting its citizens. (Even several populations of several countries may be the target.) But some element of randomness used to be thought central to the tactic. If a particular individual was targeted, a police informer or government minister, that was assassination, not terrorism. And you could not commit terrorism against soldiers, unless perhaps their army was entirely uninvolved in operations against you.

Some attacks on civilians strain against this definition, because they don't seem random enough. What if there is an attack on dormitories for defense industry workers or housing on an army base? How about the attack on the USS Cole, where it is a stretch to suppose that the victims were in some way fighting a war against their attackers? But a definition is not to be discarded simply because there are problem cases: we wouldn't discard a definition of "car" because it didn't tell us enough about Ford Rancheros or three-wheel vehicles like the old Isetta or Messerschmitt. Terrorism, at its core, seems to involve "random" attacks against civilians, for any purpose, even apolitical. If the aim is to take the heat off the coke business, or scare people away from competitors' products, does that mean we're not dealing with terrorism?

One of the few mistakes Chomsky's definition doesn't make is insisting that the goal of terrorism is to instill terror. What the word tempts us to think would be obvious is instead false.

Suppose you plan a random attack on civilians who don't scare easily who will respond instead with righteous indignation. You might not intend to terrorize the population; maybe you simply want them to make rational calculations about the success of their government's policies. You would still be a terrorist. Terrorism does not presuppose any political or psychological objectives, much less particular ones.

"Terrorism," on this account, can be defined as random violence against non-combatants. "Non-combatants" need not be civilians, but must designate those not involved in hostilities against the attackers: workers in defense industries are one of many borderline cases. "Random" means only that the victims are selected not because of their importance as individuals, but because they are representative of some larger population.

When terrorism is discussed, two quite distinct questions are almost invariably conflated. The first is whether terrorism is better or worse than some other practices (e.g., "state terrorism"), or, on the other hand, "morally equivalent" to those practices. It is rare that a defender or critic of terrorism answers this question without triumphantly proclaiming that his work is done: if terrorism is equivalent to something like state terrorism, then somehow its moral status has become clear. If it is equivalent to something like murder, then clearly, the author supposes, it must be wrong. This is a blunder: equivalence or the lack thereof settles nothing. There is a second question to be asked: whether, in fact, state terrorism, or for that matter murder, is sometimes justified. Only then does it make sense to proceed to a verdict on the particular instances of terrorism being examined.

Why this error? It probably belongs to a phenomenon frequently encountered in ethics courses. I have frequently noticed, with some irritation, a suspicious transformation. As soon as people discuss morality and especially particular moral issues, they become suddenly and inexplicably far more noble and sensitive than they are in daily life. The very same individuals who will without qualms vote for increased defense spending or support a hawkish leader proclaim in anguished tones how terrible it is to take another human life. The same people who rage about an uncaring world accept, without second thought, highway speed limits, knowing full well that if they were, say, halved, many innocent children would be spared death, mutilation, or a lifetime of paralysis. We all accept, in fact, that the added convenience of the higher speeds is well worth a few horribly maimed lives. So, when we accept that terrorism is or isn't morally equivalent to some other brutal practice, our work is far from done. We must then, as I intend to show, ask when—not if—such brutal practices are justified. We must, that is, judge terrorism according to the standards we actually have, not those we pretend to have. This is not much to ask. It is only human not to live up to one's principles, but at least we can be clear about what principles we actually espouse.

Is there some moral equivalence between terrorism and other acts of war?

We can now ask: are terrorist attacks significantly different, from a moral standpoint, from the normal practices of modern warfare? In particular, are they significantly different from tactics employed by the U.S. and Israel, whose governments claim to abhor terror?

One popular answer—and Chomsky's—is that America and Israel are on the same low moral plane as the Palestinians, because these countries practice "state terrorism." States certainly can commit terrorist acts. They can do so not only by police and paramilitary repression, but also in wartime. If air strikes are called down on randomly selected schools, housing projects, or hospitals, that's terrorism. It is indeed equivalent, from a moral standpoint, to the terrorism practiced by Palestinians, because it is the deliberate killing of innocent civilians.

On the other hand, leftist accusations of "state terrorism" often stretch the expression far too much. If, as I suspect, Israeli raids on Palestinian cities and camps disguise deliberate but arbitrary killing of civilians as "collateral damage," that too is terrorism. But no amount of genuinely collateral damage indicates terrorism, nor does destroying civilian infrastructure in order to cripple an enemy's military capacity, nor is it terrorist simply to wage unjustified war. Though the U.S. may have engaged in terrorism during the Vietnam conflict, it is not clear that it has done so since then. It is not clear that it ever actually wants to cause civilian casualties, that it intentionally targets civilians at random. Why should it? The U.S. sticks to easy military objectives. It hasn't fought without crushing air superiority since at least the Second World War, in other words, ever since air power mattered. It has no military reason to kill civilians, and it probably doesn't want to. It leaves that sport to the individual initiative of its lower ranks. So state terrorism is not, in my opinion, a standard contemporary tactic employed by the U.S. It may be employed by the Israelis, but if so, Israeli practices deviate from contemporary standards of what is acceptable in warfare.

There is, however, another element of contemporary warfare that might be morally equivalent to terrorism, and that is "collateral damage." What then about "collateral damage?" The phrase is associated with American military briefings and has migrated to Israel. The critics, therefore, spare no effort to show that the U.S. and Israel do, in fact, willfully kill innocent civilians. But it is not easy to show this, because you can't get inside people's heads: how do you prove their claimed intentions are not their real ones? In Israel's case, there is no doubt that individual Palestinian civilians have been deliberately shot, but not on any great scale: were Israel really to go after Palestinian civilians, none would be left. On the other hand, it is quite clear that Palestinian and Iraqi terrorists do deliberately seek to take civilian lives. The U.S. and Israel are quite right to say that they do not plan in the same way. A lot of their victims really are "collateral damage."

However, the issue is not whether a distinction can be made between collateral damage and terrorism; it is rather whether this distinction has moral importance. The answer depends on a further distinction: there is more than one kind of "collateral damage." One kind of collateral damage is, in important ways, morally distinct from terrorism. The other is not.

Suppose, for instance, some naval battle in which a destroyer is sunk in shallow water. After the fighting is over, divers inspect the vessel and are horrified to discover it carried several dozen civilians—children, perhaps—who were being transported to safe exile in a nonbelligerent country. This is unexpected collateral damage: no one imagined, and no one should have imagined, this terrible but also terribly unusual circumstance.

But when the Americans—or for that matter the Israelis—speak of collateral damage, they are not speaking of the unexpected kind. On the contrary, they know with certainty—the commanders, the soldiers, the decision-makers—that civilians are in the firing line and that they will be killed. To suppose, for example, that the attack on Iraq would not produce the death of innocent civilians would have been frivolous. This is expected collateral damage, innocent deaths that no reasonable person could fail to expect.

Expected collateral damage involves knowingly killing innocent civilians. Terrorism involves intentionally killing innocent civilians. The conceptual difference is discernable, but the moral difference is too academic even for an academic. (If there is a morally relevant difference, how important is it?) An example will make this plain. Suppose Joanne decides she wants to kill Jack by running him over in her SUV. She knows he goes to a movie at the Paramount every Friday night. She plans to drive into that movie line at high speed. She will hit him and, as she knows full well, some of the people standing behind and in front of him. She also knows full well that, when she hits them, they will be killed. She executes her plan. According to most legal codes, she is guilty of homicide; not only of Jack, but of anyone else she kills. It's literally collateral damage, but it's not accidental. Certainly to the dead it doesn't matter that she did not intend to kill them, but only decided to perform an action that she knew would kill them. If this difference doesn't matter, neither does the difference between terrorism and expected collateral damage.

Before finishing with moral equivalence, it is worth considering whether any of the acts described so far are really that much worse than practices that are certainly considered an acceptable part of modern warfare. Since terrorism is usually considered the worst of these acts, it's a good basis for comparison. Ordinary, legal warfare produces horrors with which terrorism can rarely if ever compete. The most respectable actions of the most respectable nation may be utterly free of any terrorist taint. They may conform to the laws of war, international law, and the Geneva Convention. They may show impeccable respect for the strictures of human rights organizations, the resolutions of United Nations, and the wishes of Lady Di. But conventional, squeaky-clean, NGO-approved, UN-sanctioned, Geneva-Convention-friendly high explosive frequently turns human beings into a bloody mist, or blows off half a face, or empties its eye-sockets. And it is not just that this can happen to innocents, including children. It is also that we know this will happen to them. All of us know it when we support or participate in a war.

Justifications

The normal assumption in debates about the Israel/Palestine conflict is that, if actions can be classified as terrorism, or murder, or their equivalents, they must be wrong. That's false: by commonly accepted standards, some of these acts can be right. To argue this, I will work backwards from the previous section, starting with conventional warfare and ending with terrorism.

What, then, of the ordinary brutalities of war? We may believe that there aren't many worse things than inflicting the horrors of war on other human beings, but certainly there are a few: letting Hitler win would have been one of them. You can say that, in such situations, "there are no right actions," or "this is a lesser evil, but still an evil," or "killing is never justifiable." But the last one just doesn't seem to be true. As for the first two, if we ought to have fought Hitler, how is that—lesser evil and all—not right? Common sense suggests that our morality, at least, approves of such warfare.

So our conventional morality, even restricted by the concerns expressed in international conventions, does sanction horrible violence. Does it sanction violence against civilians? Before answering this question, it might be worth considering whether it should really loom as large as it does today. Of course it suits those who possess powerful conventional armed forces to suppose that killing other soldiers somehow can't count. But this is a bit odd: if it is bad to kill a civilian, can it be so much better to kill that same person once he is conscripted to fight, perhaps in a hopeless cause against an enemy he has virtually no chance of threatening, much less harming? It's all very well to say that the guy's rulers are to blame for his broken limbs and torn flesh, but blame is generous. The people who actually inflicted the injuries could also be to blame. Certainly, it's hard to see much difference between an impotent conscript soldier forced to fight a hopeless battle and a civilian human shield. We can say, with a shrug, that these people shouldn't have been put in harm's way. Yet we knew they were, we knew they had no choice, and we decided to inflict the harm. You would think this would at least give us pause, even when the civilian becomes a soldier.

Next there is the question of whether these standards ever sanction state terrorism.

State terrorism was once a standard element in warfare. Gradually, and for a while, it became a bit less acceptable. From roughly the end of the 17th century, when it became bad form to take cities and slaughter the civilian population, on through the end of the First World War, it was by no means inevitable that war involved the indiscriminate murder of civilians. As H.G. Wells predicted in *The War in the Air* (1908), this would change, and really it was the Nazis who changed it. The world was shocked when, in 1937, Nazi aircraft dropped 100,000 pounds of bombs on the Spanish town of Guernica, killing 1,500 people—about a third of the population. This is sometimes considered the defining moment of modern state terrorism. But in the course of the Second World War, allied governments and their populations alike decided that these tactics were really quite a good idea: hence the saturation bombings of Germany and, of course, their incendiary and nuclear equivalents in Japan. And so it came to pass that the burning children alive was once again reinstated into warfare.

Do we still consider state terrorism acceptable? It's not clear. Many people disapprove of the saturation bombings of Dresden, Hamburg, and Tokyo, and of the use of atomic weapons against Hiroshima and Nagasaki. But, in the first place, much of this disapproval depends on the belief—as far as I know, correct—that the bombing campaigns were based on mistaken assumptions about the effectiveness of such actions or their alternatives. What then if the assumptions had been correct? What if the bombings were essential to ending the war without even greater loss of life? In the second place, if virtually no one has advocated state terrorism regarding any post-World War II situation, it may be because never, since then, have Western powers been seriously threatened. (The Chinese may have been a formidable opponent in the Korean War, but no one saw them as a threat to the American mainland.) So it is not at all clear that we do reject, in principle, state terrorism, and with it the deliberate targeting of civilians for political ends.

What then of expected collateral damage?

When we put our stamp of approval on the mutilation of children, we place a great deal of weight on good intentions. What matters isn't that children were mutilated; what matters is that our hearts are in the right place. We aren't bloodthirsty like the other guys. But you would think that good intentions get us only so far. Past a certain point, as the law itself affirms, you are responsible for being a dumbass, for believing your own lies, for ignorance and negligence. This is a responsibility that American neo-cons, for all their chirping about "moral compass," take pains to evade. And leftists are eager to help them, to look for evil motives with a desperation that suggests, should such motives be lacking, everything is ok.

To put it in official language, American officials tirelessly explain collateral damage with statements like this:

> It was inevitable there would be regrettable civilian losses. Our
> forces made every effort to minimize innocent casualties, often
> to the point of putting their own lives at risk.[172]

Doesn't a good effort, after all, make all the difference? Americans and Israelis alike are baffled: why can't the rest of the world understand this?

Collateral damage fans will repeat that their forces make all efforts to avoid civilian casualties. But this claim distorts the real situation. Joanne may make all efforts to avoid killing the other people in line, too, but she knows damn well that she will kill them all the same. And this isn't like a car manufacturer who knows that, despite his best efforts, he will produce defective cars in which people will die. The car manufacturer doesn't kill anyone. He doesn't even impose a risk on anyone; he sells risky cars. The government and the public, individually and collectively, decide how to manage this risk. The victims of collateral damage have no such choice. A much greater risk is forced on them. And someone is killing them, knowingly killing them, because it would be a bit inconvenient to do otherwise.

Reasons

You would think that, if we accept this sort of brutality against civilians, it is only when we think there is excellent reason to do so. Not at all. We're pretty relaxed about standards for killing and mutilating civilians. For one thing, we don't seem to require great certainty that the acts in question really are necessary. Take for example the great American meditation on the Vietnam War. It is conceded—not universally, but widely—that the war was some sort of mistake, involving too much fear of communist expansion, or too much faith in various South Vietnamese saviors, or too much confidence in air power, or misguided schemes to win hearts and minds. Few people claim that these mistakes were unavoidable, that America had no inkling its policy was headed for trouble. Yet most American critics of the Vietnam War see it only as a "tragic mistake." And for most of these critics, the tragedy was primarily the loss of 50,000 American lives, not the loss of one to four million Southeast Asian lives. There is no hue and cry to punish those who made what—were we speaking of a plane crash or a tainted food scandal —we would think of as criminal errors. Instead, we hear that it's not easy to be a president, or a general, or a state department analyst, or a commanding officer, or a marine. Give the guys a break.

This attitude is not peculiar to the Vietnam War. If you look at analyses of World War I, there is almost a general consensus that it was the work of idiots. But they're just idiots, and the whole era is often seen through a pleasantly misty veil of indulgence for bygone naïveté. (The returning soldiers were not so forgiving, but their indignation doesn't come down through history.) In short, we don't really feel that you simply must not make mistakes when it comes to reasons for war. On the contrary, we are very charitable about such mistakes. A few million innocent deaths? Life is full of uncertainties...

It's not just that we countenance the death and mutilation of innocent people on the basis of foolishly mistaken factual beliefs. It's also that we don't require a very serious reason for such actions. Opinions about the Korean War illustrate this. We scarcely know the circumstances that led up to it. We do know that it concerned, well, Korea, not an invasion of California. Why did the U.S. have to fight there? We're not sure; according to *MASH*, there didn't seem to be much of a reason. But that's good enough. The war may have been "senseless" in some vague way, and it's important that our troops had to endure the mud and cold and "Chinese human wave attacks." But war is war. A terrible thing, to be sure, but no crime, even when the objective is nebulous. There may be strategic reasons not to have nebulous objectives—this is an important post-Vietnam strategic doctrine— but not moral reasons. When it comes to justifying the mutilation of innocents, nebulous reasons will do.

Lest this account seem too cynical, compare our wooly moralizing about war to the crystal clarity of our moralizing about, say, raping an eight year-old girl. Now that provokes real anger, an outrage that brooks no blather about mistakes or intentions, no shrugs about the vicissitudes of life. It's something we take very seriously. Why the difference?

It's not that a sex crime is somehow a matter of "private morality;" a government that (instead of which) inflicted child-rape would be hated beyond imagining. But we do lower our standards when it comes to politics: because we expect countries to act like vicious beasts, the mutilation of children in war does matter less to us than a single mutilated child found in an empty lot. And it's not simply that the brutalities of war affect us less. It's also that we cannot help thinking they are sometimes, under not very stringent restrictions, justified. The other guy's atrocities horrify us, not our own.

The Case Against Israel

Terrorism

In short, here's where we stand on mutilating children:

> 1) If it's deliberate, part of a bombing campaign to demoralize a civilian population, its morality is perhaps somewhat questionable. We shouldn't do such things when we're not fighting a really big war against an enemy who seems to threaten our survival. But if we are, it might be ok.

> 2) If it's not deliberate, it's fine. It's ok in any war that we have any fairly good reason to fight given possibly false, but not too ill-founded beliefs about the world. In such circumstances it's quite acceptable to take actions that we know with moral certainty—certainty for all practical purposes—will mutilate children.

In other words, the crucial point about collateral damage is not that it mutilates children and is therefore wrong; it's that it mutilates children and may at times be right. There really isn't any question about this. Even if every war the U.S. has fought since 1945 was wrong, we can easily conceive of wars that are right, or at least in which we were right to participate. Most of us think that such wars have actually occurred. And such wars involve just the sort of collateral damage we're talking about.

This is why there can't be any serious issue about justifying terrorism. Yes, it sometimes mutilates children for political purposes. This is clearly wrong if done in an obviously bad cause, or for very stupid reasons. But—I am not in a position to change or judge almost universally accepted moral principles—otherwise it can certainly be ok. That's why we so often cause it to happen.

Why then, would any of us feel entitled to find terrorism morally repugnant? Imagine trying to make such a claim. You say: "To achieve my objectives, I would certainly drop bombs with the knowledge that they would blow the arms off some children. But to achieve those same objectives, I would not plant or set off a bomb on the ground with the knowledge that it would have that same effect. After all, I have planes to do that, I don't need to plant bombs." As a claim of moral superiority, this needs a little work.

Like war, and killing, and playing soccer, terrorism is sometimes justified, sometimes not. One would hope that it would be justified only on the strongest of reasons, but, if our attitudes to war are any guide, this isn't the case. Pretty good reasons will do fine. Perhaps, Bin Laden's reasons for 9/11 were so very stupid that he committed a great crime. Perhaps, the terrorists who ravage Algeria today are so insanely, profusely brutal that their evil is patent. But there are very few other cases as clear-cut. What is absolutely clear, clear beyond any shadow of a doubt, is that we all accept the mutilation of children as a suitable means to certain political ends. No self-induced, self-serving revulsion against terror will change this.

Whether to engage in terrorism—like whether to start a war— is a very serious strategic issue, fraught with uncertainty. But it is no more than that. I would not pronounce judgment on Palestinian terrorism because I do not, God-like, have all the facts on the ground at my disposal. I do not know if some other tactic would work as well, with less cost. I do know, and have argued here, that the Palestinians don't have any obviously viable nonviolent alternatives. It is also apparent that Palestinian terrorism has done great damage to the Israeli economy and that, for all the brutal retaliation it understandably provokes, from the Palestinian standpoint these very high costs may still be worth bearing, because the alternative seems to be total dispossession and very likely death in the thousands. I also know that the Palestinians have very substantial rights of self-defense that do apply to their present circumstances. Anyone who believes the Palestinians should renounce terror ought at least to provide a plausible argument that some other strategy will be more effective—and I do not see such an argument on the horizon.

The Palestinians have often said that, given an army like Israel's, they would never engage in terror. Perhaps they would be as scrupulous as we are, or ten times more so. One thing is certain: could the Palestinians trade terrorism for conventional, legal, approved warfare, thousands more innocent human beings would be reduced to bloody lumps of flesh. Why this would be morally preferable is not entirely clear to me.

Other Reasons for Supporting Israel?

THE PREVIOUS CHAPTERS HAVE ESTABLISHED—AS MUCH AS THINGS of this sort can be established—that Israel, and the Zionist movement that created it, has consistently been in the wrong in its conflict with the Palestinians. The Zionist movement took their land, that is, it deprived them of sovereignty over that land. The Palestinians had done nothing to provoke this usurpation. Sovereignty was the right of the Palestinians, of the inhabitants of Palestine, not of the settlers who came with the express purpose of establishing an ethnic state that could reasonably be seen as a mortal threat to the Palestinians and as a grievous assault on their rights. Given this threat, the Palestinians were right to make no concessions of sovereignty to the Zionists and, given that the Zionists would not abandon their project, there was no room for compromise. However, a real opportunity for peace arose with the Israeli conquest of the Occupied Territories in 1967, when the Palestinians made concessions they did not, as a matter of right, have to make. This opportunity was decisively abandoned by the Israelis, not so much by the occupation itself as by an extremist settler movement and the policies that supported, nurtured, and sustained it.

The settler movement constituted a new mortal threat to the Palestinians, worse than the previous one. The Palestinians were entitled—indeed rationally compelled—to resist this threat, and they were justified in supposing that violent resistance was required. Moreover, nothing in the character of that resistance supports the claims that the Palestinians are consumed by anything more than the entirely normal hatred that is born of warfare and that generally dissipates with peace. The claim that Palestinians are permanently bent on destroying Israel and consumed by inextinguishable hatred now shows itself to be baseless. The Palestinians' desperate attempts to defend themselves against catastrophic dispossession are no evidence whatever for that claim. What you say and feel when someone has trapped you and is progressively making your life intolerable is no evidence for how you will act when that person relents and departs.

What makes the Israeli position particularly indefensible is its utter gratuitousness. There is no conceivable reason for Israel to promote the settlements that have been the cause of so much misery. The settler movement is built on pseudo-Biblical foolishness, bad history, greed, and—worse—a sort of racist messianism that deserves no tolerance, consideration, or respect. Israel could have not only peace but vastly increased security tomorrow if it chooses: (it has all the options, and the Palestinians none). The fussing about negotiations, trust, and hatred are nothing but self-deceiving excuses for more bloodshed. Given these circumstances it would seem that no one, Jewish or non-Jewish, should support Israel.

Yet there are sometimes motives for supporting even the most immoral states. Other countries may want to do so for reasons of expediency, even a higher sort of expediency: maybe a bad state nevertheless helps advance good values. Are there such reasons? Because the only country seriously interested in supporting Israel is the United States, we can narrow the question to: does the U.S. have reasons to support Israel? Having addressed this question, it will be time for a final verdict, which must include consideration of a common complaint that Israel is judged by some double-standard.

In a recent UN vote demanding that Israel "desist from any act of deportation and cease any threat to the safety of the elected president of the Palestinian Authority," 133 nations supported the resolution. The U.S. and Israel could count only on their faithful allies, Micronesia and the Marshall Islands. In other words, not one NATO or EU country was on their side. The same can be said of every Latin American country, every East Asian country, and every African country. The U.S. stance is not one of principle; the U.S. disapproves of Israel's threats. It can hardly be one of expediency. How does a nation get itself into this position? More to the point, what keeps it there? The reasons for the alliance are historical, not practical, and its survival causes nothing but trouble.

How Israel became an ally

Jewish organizations (representing only part of the Jewish spectrum of opinion) and prominent Zionists have always exerted an important pro-Israel influence in Washington: there is nothing surprising, unusual or even particularly improper about this sort of lobbying. But the U.S. would never have allied itself with Israel merely to serve Zionist interests. The alliance with Israel was above all a child of the Cold War.

From before 1948 until the mid-1950s, both the U.S. and the Soviet Union attempted to extend their influence in the Middle East by helping both Zionists and Arabs. Both sides hastened to recognize Israel. But the U.S. imposed an arms embargo on Israel in 1948 and maintained it with minor exceptions until the Hawk missile sale of 1962. (Even then, according to some authorities, the sale was to be linked to the repatriation by Israel of some 100,000 to 150,000 Palestinian refugees!) The U.S. also signed a mutual defense pact with Saudi Arabia in 1951 and initially endorsed the 1952 coup that brought a nationalist government to Egypt. As for the Soviets, as late as 1956 the Soviet Union was supplying Israel with cheap oil to circumvent the Arab boycott, and Israel refused to supply NATO with military bases to counter a Soviet threat. But starting in the early 1950s, Israeli-Soviet relations soured and Arab-Soviet relations prospered. What changed the face of Middle East politics was not Zionist lobbying, but Egypt's Gamel Abdel Nasser.

Nasser, as much an Egyptian as an Arab nationalist, quite naturally sought to improve his position by exploiting great power rivalries. This alienated him from a United States increasingly concerned about Soviet influence in the Middle East. In March 1955, Nasser refused to join the anti-communist Baghdad Pact. A month later, at the Bandung Conference, he moved to form a neutral bloc of exactly those nations the West was trying to recruit against the Soviet Union. Next, he announced a sale of cotton to Communist China, a country then embroiled in a frightening confrontation with the U.S. over Quemoy and Matsu. The West's alarm compounded when he built on barter agreements with the Soviet bloc to conclude, in September 1955, a major arms deal with Czechoslovakia. Its impact was felt throughout the Arab world and beyond.

In May 1956, while the Quemoy-Matsu crisis was still smoldering, Nasser recognized China. With his modern weaponry and vigorous diplomacy, he was widely seen as the leader of the entire Arab world. The West became dismayed enough to withdraw financing for his most important development project, the Aswan Dam. In response, Nasser nationalized the Suez Canal. In the ensuing 1956 Suez invasion, America sided with Egypt against Israel, Britain, and France, but only to co-opt the Soviet Union, which had stated that any further Franco-British advances into Egyptian territory would be met by force. For the superpowers, that marked the end of serious efforts to play both sides of the street.

The 1956 war for the first time showed Israel as a militarily capable power that could, on its own, defeat Arab forces armed with Soviet weaponry. And to the U.S., communist-backed Arab forces began to seem worth defeating. Nasser maintained increasingly close relations with the Soviet Union, and the launch of Sputnik in October 1957 aggravated American anxieties about a worldwide Soviet threat. Egypt's union with Syria in February 1958 made its ties with the USSR all the more disturbing.

By October 1958, when the Soviet Union announced it would provide financing for the Aswan Dam, the lines were clearly drawn. The Arabs, led by Egypt, were on the Soviet side, and the Israelis became the very useful proxies of the West. One of the first services Israel rendered to the West was when, in July 1958, it allowed "a British and American airlift of strategic materials through Israeli airspace to prop up the embattled Jordanian monarchy that was being challenged by a radical nationalist uprising fomented by Egypt's Nasser."[173] This is the origin of the United States' deep commitment to Israel. Zionist influences certainly helped form this commitment, but they were never decisive. In the end, it was American security concerns that cemented the U.S.-Israel alliance.

With the fall of the Soviet Union, the rationale for the alliance ceased, but the alliance itself rolls on, its inertia abetted by the disinclination of Americans to put any obstacle in its course. Stale ideology has enshrined a counter-productive alliance at the heart of American foreign policy.

The alliance today

Nowadays, the alliance with Israel is typically defended on nebulous grounds: Israel is "our friend," it "shares our values," it is "a staunch ally in the war on terror." These phrases disguise the fact that, in contrast to most alliances, there is virtually no confluence of Israeli and American interests.

That Israel is "our friend" implies an affection for which there is little evidence: even discounting spy scandals and the USS Liberty incident, the relationship is certainly prickly enough. So, the only sense in which Israel is truly "our friend" is that Israel is our ally. This of course begs the question at hand. No one would dispute that Israel is our ally in the sense that we have allied ourselves with her; at issue is whether this alliance is to America's advantage.

As for "sharing values," this is too nebulous to take seriously. Alliances involve common interests, not common mentalities. Iran and the United States, at least in its post-Reagan incarnation, share deeply felt family values. In the Second World War, Italy and France probably shared more values than Italy and Germany, or France and Russia; the alliances did not reflect these facts. And it must be said that, though Israel does indeed believe in democracy, the American conception of democracy would not permit territorial control of three million Palestinians for thirty-five years without any role in the election of their ultimate rulers, the Israeli government. Nor does it seem democratic to grant more or less automatic citizenship, with voting rights, to all members of one ethnic group—even an atheist Jew has the privilege—and to no others.

Presumably democracy is in any case not the only value that concerns Americans. What about non-discrimination? Israel's land policies, whose implementation is entrusted almost at arms length to semi-official bodies such as the Jewish National Fund, are greatly preoccupied with the task of obtaining and preserving land for the exclusive use of Jews. Even the most impeccably democratic voting system cannot reconcile such institutional and social realities with American values. If the U.S. has good reason to ally itself with Israel, that alliance must have shared objectives rather than a mere appearance of shared values.

With communism no more a common enemy, the Israelis had to worry about the appearance of a common cause. In this respect, 9/11 was a godsend because it enabled Israel to present itself as a comrade in the war on terror. But to say the U.S. and Israel both want to fight terror is a bit like saying that the U.S.

and Iran both want to defend themselves against external attacks. In this blatantly insufficient sense, the U.S. and Iran do indeed have some basis for an alliance, namely a common interest in weapons development. Even enemies can share an interest in certain military technologies. An alliance requires a deeper sort of common interest, objectives that involve more than the technical means to further possibly opposing ends.

This is not the case when it comes to American and Israeli efforts against terror. Terrorism experts tell us that Al Qaeda is a semi-organization whose roots lie in Sunni Wahabist fundamentalism. It has made sympathetic noises but done nothing useful for the Palestinians, who are so little inclined to fundamentalism that, in the 1970s, the Israelis thought it wise to encourage the Moslem Brotherhood as an alternative to Arafat.[174] The defeat of Al Qaeda would help Israel as little as the defeat of Hamas will help the U.S. "The war on terror" does not name a common cause but an abstraction, so vague as to give the false impression that such a cause exists. Even supposing that both American and Israeli struggles against terror are entirely legitimate and productive, there is simply no significant linkage between them.

On the other hand, the claim and pretense of linkage is itself strategically damaging to the U.S. Hizbollah and Hamas want to attack Israel, not America. But, of course, the more Israel induces the Americans to strike directly at these terrorist organizations, the more they will turn their attention to the United States. The false claim that America and Israel have these common enemies itself does much to make Israel's enemies our own. This hardly speaks for the alliance.

Even if America's and Israel's wars on terror are quite different struggles, Israel might still, through its expertise and technology, be a valuable ally. But for this to be true, the U.S.-Israel alliance would have to have technical advantages outweighing any political or strategic disadvantages. This is not the case.

For one thing, the technical advantages of doing business with Israeli firms should not be confused with the technical advantages of the U.S.-Israel alliance. Israel, of course, benefits at least as much as the U.S. from technological cooperation. So, if only for defense and commercial reasons, it would want such cooperation to continue whether or not the political alliance with the U.S. continued. Countries need not be allies to do business with one another, which is why the U.S., even as it was planning its attack on Saddam Hussein, continued to buy his oil. Moreover, Israel's technical excellence is impressive but hardly indispensable. Other advanced Western countries, not to mention American firms, could do the same work, and the latter alternative would naturally have security advantages. Israel's technological contributions to America's arsenal may benefit the United States, but not more so than readily available alternatives.

On the other hand, Israel does nothing but harm the strategic and political position of the United States. This is apparent whether you look at the purported advantages of the alliance, or at its known disadvantages.

The purported advantages

It is often claimed that the U.S. alliance with Israel is motivated by oil politics. This is implausible. Why would American concerns about its oil supply prompt it to ally itself with the one power in the world that drives its suppliers to distraction? Were it not for that alliance, the U.S. would be able to apply much more direct and finely tuned pressure on oil-rich governments. Israel is (a) best positioned to pressure states which are not significant oil producers—Lebanon, Syria, Jordan, Egypt; (b) utterly superfluous for pressuring the very feeble Gulf states; and (c) politically unsuitable, as the Gulf Wars showed, for pressuring militarily strong producers like Iraq under Saddam Hussein and Iran. And what is true of oil is true, *mutatis mutandis*, of other U.S.

economic interests: Israel is more a hindrance than a help in furthering them.

The portrayal of Israel as America's stationary aircraft carrier is equally unconvincing in this context. Again, this made a certain paranoid sense when the enemy was communism, because the states bordering on Israel were considered the most likely to go communist. But the U.S. does not need or want Israel to strike through Jordan and Syria to Gulf oil fields. This "solution" would be much more of a problem than simply occupying the oil fields with American troops. The U.S. today would have no more difficulty securing or controlling Middle East oil supplies than the Allies did during World War I, long before Israel existed. The one thing that might conceivably come in handy—lots of expendable ground troops—only friendly Arab governments, not Israel, could provide.

As for more immediate objectives, there is no common interest at all. America has absolutely no desire for Israeli settlers to dispossess the Palestinians of the little that remains to them, no desire whatever to persecute the Palestinians in any way. Israel benefits from these activities; America merely pays the price, in dollars and lives. This is an offense not only to morality but to common sense.

Why the alliance should end

Despite the air of unshakeable piety that surrounds the U.S.-Israel alliance, it has never been, even at its height, the sacred bond that we habitually suppose it to be. Even after the Yom Kippur war, when the U.S. replenished Israel's arsenal, U.S. aid to Egypt was very substantial and preceded the Camp David agreements of 1977. In 1974, for instance, Nixon signed a treaty providing Egypt with nuclear technology "for peaceful purposes." Saudi Arabia, still at war with Israel, is armed by the United States. And how soon we forget the amazing fact that, in 1990, the U.S. and Syria were military allies.

In fact, America would be far better off on the other side of the Israel/Palestine conflict. It would instantly gain the warm friendship of Arab oil producers and obtain far more valuable allies in the war on terror: not only the governments of the entire Muslim world, but a good portion of the Muslim fundamentalist movement! The war on terror, which seems so unwinnable, might well be won at nominal cost, and quickly. Perhaps, the mostly likely scenario would simply involve an embargo on Israel sponsored by the U.S. in cooperation with the United Nations. There is a chance that Israel would prove intransigent; it has great military resources and could probably buy the materials it needs through sales of military technology. If this happens, Israel might have to be made the object of the kind of coalition forged against Iraq in the first Gulf War. Of course, against Israel the coalition would be far broader and stronger, including all the countries of the former Soviet Union, Iran, Libya, Pakistan, and many others. And though Israel is quite strong enough to persist in its policies without U.S. support, it could not stand up to such a coalition.[175] Israel would be forced to follow its own best interests and make peace.

Perhaps most important, switching sides would revitalize America's foundering efforts at non-proliferation. There are two main reasons why other countries resist these efforts: fear of American attack, and the outrageous exemption of Israel from non-proliferation initiatives. It is simply absurd to suppose that any serious effort to stem the development of nuclear weapons can proceed in the absence of any attempt to disarm Israel, which is estimated to possess between 200 and 500 nuclear warheads. Having launched its own satellites, it clearly has the capacity to hit targets anywhere in the world, and it possesses cruise missiles that have hit targets 950 miles away. Until it is forced either to disarm or to establish good relations with its neighbors, the pace of proliferation will simply increase. On the other hand, U.S. efforts to neutralize the Israeli nuclear threat would win support for non-proliferation efforts from Pakistan and Iran. In these circumstances, in a radically different political environment, the problem of North Korea would no longer seem intractable. Meanwhile, the U.S. contents itself with hollow victories such as Libya's recent gesture, the nuclear disarmament of a country that never had nuclear weapons in the first place.

In short, one has only to conceive the end of the U.S.-Israel alliance to be overwhelmed with the benefits of such a move—very likely, even to Israel itself. That once-beneficial alliance, a legacy of the Cold War, has turned poisonous to America's security and its future.

Is Israel judged by a double standard?

One often hears this. Here is a moderate version of the "double standards" claim, voiced by Ian Buruma in his review of a work by Bernard Lewis:

> Lewis is at his best when he identifies Western double standards in dealing with the non-Western world. The *bien-pensants*, he says, are obsessed with Israeli violence against Arabs, while ignoring far worse brutality among the Arabs.[176]

Much is unclear here; even whether double standards are really at issue. To ignore one side's misdeeds may simply mean that one is focused on the other side, and there can be good reason for this. I suspect that Lewis has in mind such *bien-pensants* as Noam Chomsky and Norman Finkelstein in the U.S., or Uri Avnery and Uri Davis in Israel, perhaps also Kenneth Roth of Human Rights Watch. These vigorous critics of Israeli excesses are all Jewish. Their focus on Israel is no evidence of double standards, but of where they feel their responsibilities lie. This is not bias but admirable rectitude: we would not have condemned but praised a Northerner who fought Union cruelties and ignored Confederate ones, or an Englishman who fought English excesses in colonial India but ignored Indian ones.

Other Western authors may simply feel that they can better contribute to a solution by criticizing Israel than by criticizing brutalities "among the Arabs," which presumably means throughout the Arab world. It is not clear how excoriating torture in Morocco, for instance, will bring peace to Palestine. One need not pay attention to all brutalities on all sides all the time: the 18th century English abolitionists were not remiss when they were "obsessed" about white slavers and ignored the African slave traders who provided the merchandise. But English defenders of slavery used the "double standards" defense, as did their American counterparts who reproached abolitionists for obsessing about the South and "ignoring" labor conditions in the North.

Suppose, though, that Lewis has found some less dubious examples of bias against Israel. Are there really all sorts of dastardly *bien-pensants* who, in some unspecified yet reprehensible way, obsess about Israeli violence and ignore far worse Arab brutalities? Such claims are false, though the complexities of the situation make their falsity less than obvious. There are two sorts of cases to consider on the Arab side, reports of human rights violations in Arab countries, and reports of Palestinian terrorism. These are to be compared with reports of human rights violations and atrocities committed by Israel.

Consider first the treatment of Israeli and Arab brutalities. Sometimes Israeli brutalities do command more attention in the press. This is not because there is a double standard, but because they are more public. The atrocious incursions into the Occupied Territories have aroused great outrage because they were undertaken in full view of thousands of people and, partly in consequence, of the press. There are multiple confirmed eyewitness reports, often with footage. Israel's more private atrocities, committed behind prison walls or in interrogation rooms, attract very little attention outside partisan circles. Conversely, if Arab brutalities have received less attention in recent years, it is because, like Israel's more private atrocities, they occurred in prisons or in remote areas. However, the disparity of press coverage does not seem to result in the application of double standards. In the press, Arab countries have quite as bad a reputation for brutality and human rights violations as Israel. Among human rights organizations, the same is true. The most causal look at the pages of Amnesty International or Human Rights Watch reports confirms this.

Consider, then, the comparison of Israeli brutalities with Palestinian terrorism. Where the news media are concerned, we get unending and very graphic reports on both sides; there is no question of a double standard. (Again, this suggests that coverage is determined by the public nature of the events.) In recent years, Palestinian terrorism is excoriated, not only on the right, but on the left as well. To find *western* radicals cheering Palestinian terrorist exploits, you have to go back to the 1970s.

But, perhaps, we have the wrong *bien-pensants* and are ignoring the ones Lewis chides. It is true that some Western writers "are obsessed with Israeli violence against Arabs, while ignoring far worse brutality among the Arabs"? Certainly, there are some political writers biased in favor of the Palestinians; that there are double standards in this sense is beyond trivial. There are also, as one would expect, some political writers biased in favor of Israel. Unless Lewis conducts an exhaustive survey indicating that one type of bias is far more prevalent than the other, he is arm waving. What's more, Buruma and Lewis are guilty of the very one-sidedness they denounce: they obsess about the bias of pro-Palestinian intellectuals while ignoring the bias of pro-Israeli intellectuals.

One complication in assessing bias on these issues is the danger of confusing bias against Israel with unbiased judgments against Israel and for the Palestinians. To decide that one side is almost entirely wrong and the other almost entirely right, does not necessarily involve a double standard. We don't think that a judge is biased simply because he assigns full blame to one side or another. One wonders, then, where the bias really is: some of us can recall similar claims of bias coming from Southern segregationists or defenders of apartheid. There is a further difficulty, which is that a *single* standard can rightly assess one act worse than another even though they appear, on the surface, exactly similar.

This is quite common; in fact, it is enshrined in law. A husband shoots his wife; a wife shoots her husband; the wife gets a lighter sentence. Is that indicative of a double standard? Perhaps, but not necessarily: maybe the husband shot his wife in a drunken rage, while the wife shot her husband in self-defense. Even if the wife is found guilty of a lesser charge, that may not involve a double standard but simply the recognition of mitigating circumstances. This has relevance both for Palestinian and for "Arab" brutalities.

Palestinians claim self-defense. Even if this does not justify their actions, it may well be a mitigating circumstance. Arab régimes, for the most part, brutalize those who seek to overthrow them. This is distasteful but hardly a wild deviation from the practices current today: witness how America has treated violent anti-American revolutionaries at home and abroad. Israel, on the other hand, is seen by many as lacking any good reason for its occupation. Its crimes in the Occupied Territories appear to sustain nothing more than a land grab and are committed not to satisfy any real need, but to feed the fantasies of Biblical fanatics. For Lewis or Buruma to cry "double standard" is not to refute these claims; it is simply to dismiss them out of hand. Perhaps, by one set of standards, that is, according to ordinary Western moral criteria, Israel is far more at fault than the Palestinians or the Arab régimes. To establish bias, sneers are not enough: it will be necessary to show why, exactly, so many of us, and so many Israelis, are misguided in thinking Israel has no good reason to be in the Occupied Territories. This the accusers have not done.

There is another problem with the "double standards" complaint. If Israel's admirers don't want that country held to a higher standard, why do they unceasingly declare that Israel is, in fact, a paragon of moral or political excellence? The rhapsodists don't have a wide expressive range: invariably we hear that Israel is a beacon of some sort.

This litany comes from small-time libertarians like the Prodos Institute—"Israel is a beacon of Western values, Capitalism, and success—smack in the middle of the Middle East."[177] It surfaces in local papers like Gannett's Florida publication, *The News-Press*: "this small struggling state, fallible, run by human beings and therefore liable to the failings and vices that afflict human nature, is nonetheless a beacon of light in history born of humanity's darkest age."[178] It comes from focused pro-Israel sources like LionPAC, which describes itself as "Columbia University's pro-Israel political action group," and whose political coordinator tells us, "you need to understand why Israel is vitally important to the world as a beacon of democracy and self-determination."[179] Rabbi Benzion Klatzko, Los Angeles-based leader of the Jewish Awareness Movement, says that "Israel has nothing to be ashamed about in defending itself and that it is a beacon of light for all nations to follow."[180] The indefatigable pro-Israel journalist Gary Fitleberg writes that "Israel is a beacon of democracy and freedom, and the only such nation in the bad neighborhood known as the Middle East."[181] One major Jewish organization, Aish, publishes an elaboration on this theme: "The TRUTH is, Israel stands as a BEACON of DEMOCRACY and FREEDOM, in a predominately TYRANICAL [sic] region where terrorism is promoted as the most effective means to a desired end, where women are exploited and treated little better than animals, where children are used to draw fire, for the purposes of propaganda, and where any views held contrary to the extremists' views are often illegal, and in most cases may result in the death penalty."[182] On Benjamin Netanyahu's site, Israel is called "A Great Beacon of Light on the Darkness of Terror."[183] Last, but not least, John Kerry states that "The State of Israel continues to be a 'light unto nations,' a beacon of freedom and democracy in the Middle East."[184] Double standards for Israel are as much a cause of celebration as protest.

The breathless exaltation of Israel's moral standards has a sort of feedback effect: to the direct consequences of Israel's crimes it adds the important indirect consequence of setting a bad example. In this sense, Israel's self-proclaimed and American-confirmed high moral status actually makes its crimes worse. The very same actions, committed by another country, would not be as alarming because they would not have the same, very real, consequences for world moral standards. Israel is touted as the Middle East's only democracy, with the implication that this must mean it is more humane and shows greater respect for human rights. Israel, unlike the Arab countries, is a destination for thousands of worshipful tourists, not only Jews but also evangelical Christians,[185] who sing the praises of Israeli society and Israeli values. The overall message is that Israel is a "respectable" country with "respectable" and legitimate concerns, with appropriate policy objectives; a country you can trust. This means that Israeli crimes, unlike otherwise equivalent Arab crimes, have a much greater corrupting effect on world moral standards. It is the difference between, say, the Nobel Committee and Augusto Pinochet coming out in favor of torture.

Consider, for example, the pronouncements of Amnesty International, surely a guardian of these standards. Its military adviser, David Holley, with a sort of honest martial bonhomie, tells the world that the Israelis have "a very valid point" when they refuse to allow a UN investigative team into Jenin: "You do need a soldier's perspective to say, 'Well, this was a close quarter battle in an urban environment, unfortunately soldiers will make mistakes and will throw a hand grenade through the wrong window, will shoot at a twitching curtain, because that is the way war is.'"[186] The idea that Israel was somehow justified in inserting itself, with crushing violence, *into* the "urban environment" is simply taken for granted: hardly a case of Israel being held to some higher moral standard. One does not hear Western journalists, much less Amnesty International, making excuses for Egyptian or Syrian or Algerian brutalities on the grounds that they are defending their country from, say, a takeover by repressive and fanatical Islamic fundamentalists.

So, if there is a double standard, it in fact favors Israel. This has the effect of eroding Western moral standards. It is precisely Israel's treatment of the Palestinians—its indisputable willingness to fight militants with strategies that are known from repeated experience to kill and cripple young children—that has legitimized America employing the same tactics: gone are the days when killing children represents any deterrent to a proposed strategy. This is a perfectly good reason for considering the Israeli brutalities worse. They are worse because, coming from a country that manages to portray itself as the very incarnation of Western values, they corrupt those values.

A verdict

Israel is the illegitimate child of ethnic nationalism. The inhabitants of Palestine had every reason to oppose its establishment by any means necessary. No one is required to submit to a sovereignty from which they are excluded, much less a sovereignty arrogated to one ethnic group and excluding all others. Given the life-and-death powers of the proposed state and the intention of its proponents to maintain ethnic supremacy within its borders, the Palestinians were justified in taking the project as a mortal threat, and, therefore, to resist it by any means necessary. The inhabitants of early 20th century Palestine were, for the most part, poor and unsophisticated people, unwelcome elsewhere. They could not accept the Zionists' scornful invitation to leave. And had they been able to accept it, they had no reason to do so. It is admirable to fight those who come to dispossess or dominate you rather than flee.

It is over fifty years since Israel's foundation, and that is time enough to forget and forgive. Had Zionism been content with what it had acquired in 1948, the Palestinians' fight to regain what had been taken from them might by now be running out of moral steam. One might say: to make unending war on Israel will cost many innocent lives on both sides. Would it not be better to let an old injustice go unrighted, or at least to attempt to right it by peaceful means? At some point, if property alone is involved, peace trumps justice.

But Zionism was not content with what it had acquired in 1948. With the acquisition of the Occupied Territories in 1967, Israel had a chance to make handsome amends for the crimes on which it was built. Saintliness or selfless optimism were not required. Israel could have sponsored and supported, with true generosity, the establishment of a sovereign Palestinian state by backing those amenable to reconciliation and attacking those who were not. This might not have been a just settlement, but it would have worked. It was something that might have been expected of flawed human beings, even those with blood on their hands.

Instead, as so often happens, an ethnic nationalism born of persecution became a vehicle for bigotry, insolent self-righteousness, sadism, fanatical nonsense, and naked greed. This was largely the work of those who had no part in fighting for the Jewish state and who had never sought refuge in Palestine. The Zionist author Jon Kimche writes in 1973:

> After the war, Diaspora Jewry had become a potent factor that could not be ignored as it has been before 1967. World Jewish financial support became a more significant factor in Israeli

policy-making than did the new immigrants or members of
Israel's parliament. World Jewry—especially the money-provid-
ing sector—became an essential element of new Israeli society
and politics, a constant, mounting challenge to the more egali-
tarian and socialist Israel of the pre-war days.[187]

"World" Jewish support meant primarily American Jewish
support: the support of a community that, by and large, had *not*
suffered extensive persecution despite its pretensions to the contrary. The "new immigrants" to whom Kimche refers were mainly
poor and poorly received North African Jews, not the pampered
middle class American Jews who later came to provide the vanguard of the settler movement. American and, indeed, many
Israeli Jews are increasingly disenchanted with this vanguard
and its work. Rightly so. The settlers reopened and deepened
Palestinian wounds just when they might have healed. The
settler movement substituted for peace a new mortal threat,
worse than the first one. The ever-greater pattern of encroachment brought endless bloodshed and suffering. It did indeed
bring hatred, on both sides. The difference was that Israeli
hatred had all the power of the modern state behind it, with the
will and means to visit daily agony on millions. No doubt, hatred
contributes to Palestinian resistance as well, but that resistance
would be justified whatever emotions accompanied it.

Worse happens in the world, and happens every day. But
rarely does evil have such trifling motivation. The most brutal
African conflicts are at least struggles over scarce resources exacerbated by the fateful incompetence of colonial "nation-building." The brutalities of the settler movement and its sponsors are
the work of "haves" who have got it in their head that God wants
them to have more, and to crush, slowly and painfully, all those
who stand in the way of their fifth-rate vision. These spoilt brats
who, in the memorable words of Amos Elon, "believe they know
exactly what God and Abraham said to each other in the Bronze

Age,"[188] not only make life unlivable for millions, but spare no effort to implicate the entire Jewish people in their crimes. In this they are fabulously successful, though at last a significant number of Jews are attempting to reverse this "achievement."

What is to be done? This is not the place to formulate specific strategies. Suffice it to say that no nation and no person of any ethnicity should support Israel. Nor is that nearly enough. They should work to isolate that nation and, by marshaling the most extensive international sanctions possible, to force Israel out of the Occupied Territories. That is not an extreme proposal but the bare minimum that the current situation demands.

Finally, no one should be deterred from vigorous anti-Israeli action by the horrors of the Jewish past. On the contrary: Israel's current policies are themselves an insult and a threat to Jews and to Israelis everywhere. Concern for the past requires a quite different attitude. When it comes to the lessons of history, we can do no better than to heed the words of Irena Klepfisz, who was born in Warsaw in 1941 and whose father died a hero in the Warsaw Uprising:

> Am I to feel better that the Palestinians ... were not shot by the Israelis but merely beaten? As long as hundreds of Palestinians are not being lined up and shot, but are killed by Israelis only one a day, are we Jews free from worrying about morality, justice? Has Nazism become the sole norm by which to judge evil, so that anything that is not its exact duplicate is considered by us morally acceptable? Is that what the Holocaust has done to Jewish moral sensibility?[189]

Let no one throw up the Nazi era as some excuse for Israel, or wax sentimental about the Zionist dream. This has not been some exercise in moral reasoning whose object is simply to find fault. The situation is urgent, and dangerous to all involved. The lies, obfuscations, and self-deceiving nonsense that sustain

Israel's occupation—something it could end tomorrow—cost Jewish as well as Palestinian blood.

Afterword

AS THIS ESSAY WENT TO PRESS, ISRAEL COMPLETED ITS WITH-
drawal from the Gaza strip. It is far too early to assess the
full meaning of this move, but perhaps something can
be said about some of its implications.

First, the withdrawal does bring some relief to the
Palestinians in Gaza. The Jewish settlements and the measures
taken to preserve them were a cruel burden, now lifted. To that
extent the withdrawal is a welcome concession, but it gives the
Palestinians nothing whatever on a permanent basis.

Israel still controls the borders, the airspace, the coastline
and indeed everything that happens in the Gaza strip. Israel
therefore has not ceded any sovereignty over that area. The
Palestinians have neither the power nor the recognized legal
status to challenge any Israeli decision concerning their fate.
New and terrible constraints might be imposed on them without
warning, negotiation, or even prior notice. At most, the Israeli
withdrawal holds some promise of future progress towards a
resolution of the conflict. It does not in itself represent a substantial step forward.

Second, right-wing Israeli demagogues insist that the withdrawal from Gaza is a "reward for violence." When there is armed
conflict, any concession of any sort, on either side, can always be
seen this way. The whole of Israel and the Occupied Territories
can be seen as such a reward, for the Israelis. If no so-called
rewards of this sort were ever allocated, there would almost
never be any peace. And rewards are neither necessary nor sufficient for the continuation of violence. The Palestinians, like

many people resisting a stronger power, pursued violent strategies for decades, even when the strategies brought no such rewards. Moreover, every successful peace settlement rewards violence without a continuation of violence.

Third, the relief brought by Israeli withdrawal is not nearly sufficient to remove a mortal threat to the Palestinians. Israel continues to build settlements in the West Bank and has done nothing whatever to confer sovereignty on the Palestinians in any part of the still-Occupied Territories, including Gaza. This means that the Palestinians are still at the mercy of Israel, that Palestinians continue to live and die at Israel's good pleasure. It means that the encroachment on their vital living space and resources continues.

There may indeed be self-interested reasons for the Palestinians to change their tactics; this is well beyond my capacity to judge. But there is no fundamental and obvious moral reason for them to do so. They are still subjugated, still endangered, and still have a right to defend themselves. For a large number of them, in Gaza, the threat has become less immediate, but only in a trivial sense: Israel can send troops back into the strip, which it still controls, at any moment, and indeed has reserved the right to do just that. For this reason, at this point, the Palestinians have no reason to feel any less vulnerable, less threatened, than before.

Let us hope, for both Palestinians and Israelis, that this will soon change.

Sources

This is not a bibliography but a mere list of some important works. Full references can be found in the endnotes.

BEN-GURION, DAVID, *Letters to Paula*. Translated from the Hebrew by Aubrey Hodes. Pittsburgh (University of Pittsburgh Press) 1971 [1968].

BRENNER, LENNI. ED., *51 Documents: Zionist Collaboration with the Nazis*. New Jersey (Barricade Books) 2001.

CHOMSKY, NOAM, *The Fateful Triangle: The United States, Israel and The Palestinians*. Updated Edition. Cambridge, Massachusetts (South End Press) 1989, 1999.

CHRISTISON, KATHLEEN, *Perceptions of Palestine: Their Influence on U.S. Middle East Policy*. Updated Edition with a New Afterward. Berkeley (University of California Press) 2001.

COHEN, AHARON, *Israel and the Arab World*. Abridged Edition With a New Introduction & Concluding Chapter by the Author. Boston (Beacon Press) 1970, 1976.

FINKELSTEIN, ISRAEL, and SILBERMAN, NEIL ASHER. *The Bible Unearthed: Archaeology's New Vision of Ancient Israel and the Origin of Its Sacred Texts*. New York (Simon and Schuster) 2003.

FINKELSTEIN, NORMAN, *Image and Reality of the Israel-Palestine Conflict*. London (Verso) 1995.

FISHER, STANLEY NETTLETON, *The Middle East: A History*. Third Edition. New York (Knopf) 1979.

FROMKIN, DAVID, *A Peace to End all Peace: The Fall of the Ottoman Empire and the Creation of the Modern Middle East*. New York (Avon Books, by arrangement with Henry Holt and Company), 1990 (1st ed. 1989).

HARKABI, YEHOSHAFAT, *Israel's Fateful Hour*. New York (Harper and Row) 1988.

HASS, AMIRA, *Drinking the Sea at Gaza: Days and Nights in a Land under Siege*. Translated by Elana Wesley and Maxine Kaufman-Lacusta. New York (Henry Holt and Company)1999 (original edition 1996).

HIRST, DAVID, *The Gun and the Olive Branch: The Roots of Violence in the Middle East*. New York (Thunder's Mouth Press/Nation Books) 1977–2003.

HOLDEN, DAVID and JOHNS, RICHARD, *The House of Saud*. London (Pan Books) 1982 [Sidgwick and Jackson 1981].

KEINON, HERB, "A Yom Kippur War—25 Years Later: A victory remembered as a defeat," *Jerusalem Post*, Friday, October 9, 1998.
http://www-origin.jpost.com/com/Archive/09.Oct.1998/Features/Article-12.html

KIMCHE, JON, *Palestine or Israel: The untold story of why we failed*. 1917–1923–1967–1973, London (Secker and Warburg) 1973.

KIMMERLING, BARUCH and MIGDAL, JOEL S., *The Palestinian People: A History*. Cambridge, Massachusetts (Harvard University Press) 2003.

MORRIS, BENNY. *Righteous Victims: A History of the Zionist-Arab Conflict, 1881–2001*. New York (Random House, Vintage Books) 2001.

Palestine Royal Commission, Report. London 1937. [Peel Commission]

RABKIN, YAKOV M., *Au nom de la Torah: Une histoire de l'opposition juive au sionisme*. Saint-Nicholas, Québèc (Presses de l'Université Laval) 2004.

RABKIN, YAKOV M., "A Glimmer of Hope: A State of All Its Citizens," *Tikkun*. July/August 2002.
http://www.tikkun.org/magazine/index.cfm/action/tikkun/issue/tik0207/article/020711f.html

ROUSSILLON, ALAIN, "Republican Egypt: revolution and beyond", in M.W. Daly, ed., *The Cambridge History of Egypt, Volume Two: Modern Egypt from 1517 to the End of the Twentieth Century*. Cambridge (Cambridge University Press) 1998.

SHAHAK, ISRAEL, and MEZVINSKY, NORTON, *Jewish Fundamentalism in Israel*. London (Pluto Press) 1999.

SEGEV, TOM, *The Seventh Million*. New York (Hill and Wang) 1993.

SEGEV, TOM, *One Palestine Complete: Jews and Arabs under the British Mandate*. New York (Henry Holt) 2000.

SMITH, GARY, ed., *Zionism: The Dream and the Reality*. London (David & Charles Newton Abbot) 1974.

THOMPSON, JUDITH JARVIS, "In Defense of Abortion," *The Rights and Wrongs of Abortion, A Philosophy and Public Affairs Reader*. Princeton (Princeton University Press) 1974.

WEBER, MAX. "Politics as a Vocation" ["Politik als Beruf," 1918], in H.H. Gerth and C. Wright Mills, eds., *From Max Weber: Essays in Sociology*, New York (Oxford University Press) 1958 [1st ed. 1946].

WEIZMANN, CHAIM, *Trial and Error: The Autobiography of Chaim Weizmann*. New York (Harper and Brothers) 1949.

Endnotes

1. "Among the civilian deaths [in Jenin] were those of Kamal Zgheir, a fifty-seven-year-old wheelchair-bound man who was shot and run over by a tank on a major road outside the camp on April 10, even though he had a white flag attached to his wheelchair; fifty-eight-year-old Mariam Wishahi, killed by a missile in her home on April 6 just hours after her unarmed son was shot in the street; Jamal Fayid, a thirty-seven-year-old paralyzed man who was crushed in the rubble of his home on April 7 despite his family's pleas to be allowed to remove him; and fourteen-year-old Faris Zaiban, who was killed by fire from an IDF armored car as he went to buy groceries when the IDF-imposed curfew was temporarily lifted on April 11." Human Rights Watch, "Israel, the Occupied West Bank and Gaza Strip, and the Palestinian Authority Territories." Jenin: IDF Military Operations. (May 2002) Vol. 14, No. 3 (E), p. 4, available at
http://www.hrw.org/reports/2002/israel3/israel0502.pdf

2. "One of President Woodrow Wilson's Final Addresses in Support of the League of Nations, 25 September 1919, Pueblo, CO," cited at
http://www.firstworldwar.com/source/wilsonspeech_league.htm

3. WOODROW WILSON, "Fourteen Points" Speech, January 8, 1918,
http://www.firstworldwar.com/source/fourteenpoints.htm

4. This is the view of Michael Hirst, as expressed in "At War With Ourselves—America's push for other people's national self-determination can backfire." *Harpers Magazine*, July 1999. His view is typical of current interpreters.

5. *UN Charter*, Chapter I, Article 1. See http://www.un.org/aboutun/charter/

6. For example, Hitler said: "For us there are only two possibilities: either we remain German or we come under the thumb of the Jews. This latter must not occur; even if we are small, we are a force. A well-organized group can conquer a strong enemy. If you stick close together and keep bringing in new people, we will be victorious over

the Jews." Adolf Hitler, November 9, 1921. Munich, quoted at
http://www.schoolshistory.org.uk/ASLevel_History/sourcematerial_earlynaziideology.htm

7. See ESTHER KAPLAN, "The Jewish Divide on Israel," *The Nation*, June 24, 2004.

8. David Hirst, *The Gun and the Olive Branch: The Roots of Violence in the Middle East* (New York: Thunders Mouth Press/Nations Books, 2003), p. 392.

9. AHARON COHEN, *Israel and the Arab World*. Abridged Edition With a New Introduction & Concluding Chapter by the Author. (Boston: Beacon Press, 1976), p. 52.

10. See FROMKIN, p. 294: "As of 1913, the last date for which there were figures, only about one percent of the world's Jews had signified their adherence to Zionism."

11. Available online at:
http://www.m-w.com/cgi-bin/dictionary?book=Dictionary&va=zionism&x=18&y=16

12. Available online at http://www.bartleby.com/61/86/Z0018600.html

13. The most compact account is in DAVID HIRST, *The Gun and the Olive Branch: The Roots of Violence in the Middle East,* (New York: Thunder's Mouth Press/Nation Books, 1977–2003), pp. 135–141.

14. See FROMKIN, pp. 276–301.

15. The Declaration stated that, "His Majesty's Government views with favour the establishment in Palestine of a national home for the Jewish people, and will use their best endeavours to facilitate the achievement of this object, it being clearly understood that nothing shall be done which may prejudice the civil and religious rights of existing non-Jewish communities in Palestine, or the rights and political status enjoyed by Jews in any other country."

16. HIRST, p. 160. The intimate, extensive and decisive participation of Weizmann and other Zionists in the framing of the Balfour Declaration is clearly and fully described in Weizmann's memoirs. See CHAIM WEIZMANN, *Trial and Error*, pp. 187–207.

17. WALTER LAQUEUR, *The Israel Arab Reader* (New York: Bantam Books, 1976), pp. 6–11. See also the judgment of David Fromkin, who says that "the crux of the Zionist idea [was] that the renaissance of the Jewish nation should occur within the context of a political entity of its own." FROMKIN, p. 293.

18. SEGEV, p. 49.

19. CHRISTOPHER SYKES, *Two Studies in Virtue* (London: Collins 1953), p. 160, n1, quoted in MICHAEL PRIOR, *Zionism and the State of Israel: A Moral Inquiry.* (London: Routledge, 1999), p. 18, and HIRST, p. 140.

20. Cited in WALTER LEHN, *The Jewish National Fund.* (London: Kegan Paul, 1988), p. 326f, n. 101.

21. Chaim Weizmann: *Excerpts from his Historic Statements, Writings and Addresses.* (New York: The Jewish Agency, 1952), p. 48. Cited in HIRST, pp. 161, 165.

22. CHAIM WEIZMANN, *Trial and Error: The Autobiography of Chaim Weizmann* (New York Harper and Brothers 1949), p. 68. A fragment of this comment is cited in MICHAEL PRIOR, *Zionism and the State of Israel: A Moral Inquiry* (London Routledge 1999), p. 18.

23. Notoriously, Herzl wrote in his diaries: "We must expropriate gently... We shall try to spirit the penniless population across the border by procuring employment for it in the transit countries, while denying it any employment in our country... Both the process of expropriation and the removal of the poor must be carried out discreetly and circumspectly." RAPHAEL PATAI, ed., *The Complete Diaries of Theodor Herzl*, vol. 1 Harry Zohn, trans. (New York: Herzl Press and T. Yoseloff, 1960), pp.88–89. According to Benny Morris, "The transfer idea... goes back to the founders of modern Zionism and, while rarely given public airing before 1937, was one of the main currents in Zionist ideology from the movement's inception." Morris goes on to elaborate on and document this claim. See BENNY MORRIS, *Righteous Victims: A History of the Zionist-Arab Conflict, 1881–2001* (New York: Random House, Vintage Books, 2001), p. 139.

24. See NORMAN FINKELSTEIN, *Image and Reality of the Israel-Palestine Conflict.* (London: Verso, 1995), pp. 64–87. I am not qualified to say who is right in this dispute.

25. BENNY MORRIS, *Righteous Victims: A History of the Zionist-Arab Conflict, 1881–2001* (New York: Vintage Books, 1999), 2001, p. 75.

26. MOSHE PEARLMAN and DAVID BEN-GURION, *Ben-Gurion Looks Back in Talks with Moshe Pearlman* (London: Weidenfeld and Nicholson, 1965), p. 62.

27. STANLEY NETTLETON FISHER, *The Middle East: A History*, 3rd ed. (New York: Knopf, 1979), p. 458.

28. MORRIS R. COHEN, "Zionism: Tribalism or Liberalism?," in *Zionism: The Dream and the Reality: A Jewish Critique* (New York: Barnes & Noble, 1983), p. 51.

29. Ibid., 49.

30. JON KIMCHE, *Palestine or Israel: The untold story of why we failed. 1917–1923, 1967–1973* (London: Secker and Warburg, 1973), p. 86.

31. Cited in HIRST, p. 171. When Weizmann spoke of trusting that a Jewish state would come about by the sweat and blood of the Jewish people, he followed up with very similar verbiage: see HIRST, p. 161.

32. WALTER LAQUER, *A History of Zionism* (New York: Schocken, 1976), p. 452.

33. HIRST, p. 220f. Some of the outrage was no doubt directed at the White Paper's restrictions on Jewish immigration rather than specifically at its rejection of the Jewish state. But the emphasis of the protests was on immigration to Palestine, not on immigration to anywhere that might be a refuge from persecution. This conformed to the Zionist agenda, not to the dictates of compassion. Segev reports that "The Jewish Agency's business, David Ben-Gurion said at the height of the Holocaust, was to build the Land of Israel. He did not want to judge which was more important, building the country or saving a single Jewish child from, say, Zagreb. Sometimes, he added generously, it may well be more important to save a child from Zagreb. But the Jewish Agency's job was to save Jews by bringing them to Palestine; saving them where they were or sending them to other countries was the business of bodies like the World Jewish Congress, the American Jewish Congress, and the Joint Distribution Committee..." If it came to saving Jewish children at Zionism's expense, Ben-Gurion wasn't interested. The Jewish Agency, at the time Ben-Gurion spoke, had become an international body which he chaired, and which represented the World Zionist Organization. See SEGEV, *The Seventh Million*, p. 83.

34. http://www.jewishvirtuallibrary.org/jsource/Zionism/zionism.html

35. http://www.mfa.gov.il/mfa/history/modern%20history/centenary%20of%20zionism/

36. Provisional Government of Israel, Official Gazette: Number 1. Tel Aviv, 5 Iyar 5708, 14.5.1948, Page 1, "The Declaration of the Establishment of the State of Israel."
http://www.knesset.gov.il/docs/eng/megilat_eng.htm, accessed July 17, 2004.

37. LAWRENCE KRADER, *The Formation of the State* (Englewood Cliffs, New Jersey: Prentice-Hall, 1968), p. 22, quoted in ROBERT NOZICK, *Anarchy, State, and Utopia* (New York: Basic Books, 1974), p. 116.

38. MAX WEBER, "Politics as a Vocation" ["Politik als Beruf," 1918], in H.H. GERTH and C. WRIGHT MILLS, eds., *From Max Weber: Essays in Sociology* (New York: Oxford University Press, 1958), p. 78.

39. It is worth noting, though, the view of I.F. Stone: "... Israel is creating a kind of moral schizophrenia in world Jewry. In the outside world the welfare of Jewry depends on the maintenance of secular, non-racial, pluralistic societies. In Israel, Jewry finds itself defending a society in which mixed marriages cannot be legalized, in which the ideal is racial and exclusionist. Jews might fight elsewhere for their very security and existence—against principles and practices they find themselves defending in Israel." I.F. STONE, "For a New Approach to the Israeli-Arab Conflict" *The New York Review of Books*, August 3, 1967.

40. Quotas that affected Jewish immigration to the U.S. were not imposed until 1921 and did not apply until 1922, well after the Zionist program of constructing a Jewish state had already precipitated violence in Palestine. After that, Zionists were, of course, concerned with getting Jews to Palestine, not with fighting or circumventing quotas elsewhere.

41. The prestige of the bi-nationalists far outstripped their strength. The very neutral *Encyclopedia Britannica* speaks of Martin Buber advocating "the unpopular cause of Jewish-Arab cooperation in the formation of a bi-national state in Palestine.
http://www.search.eb.com/eb/article?query=martin+buber&ct=eb&eu=18101&tocid=8 89

42. AHAD JA'AM [ASHER GINZBERG], "After the Balfour Declaration," in *Zionism: The Dream and the Reality* ed. Gary Smith (London: David & Charles Newton Abbot, 1974), p. 88f.

43. See SEGEV, p. 408: "... These proposals reflected more of a mood than a feasible plan."

44. See FINKELSTEIN, Ibid, p. 11.

45. See FINKELSTEIN, Ibid, p. 11.

46. HIRST, p. 135.

47. SEGEV, p. 105.

48. Quoted in HIRST, p. 155.

49. Baruch Kimmerling and Joel S. Migdal, *The Palestinian People: A History* (Cambridge, Massachusetts: Harvard University Press, 2003), p. 79.

50. Ibid., p. 11.

51. Herzl already envisaged, in private, the need for force. See Hirst, p. 138f.

52. See, for example, "Facing Reality," *The Jewish Times*, Volume II, no. 35. June 2003. Available at http://www.mesora.org

53. Segev, p. 338f.

54. Ibid., p. 340.

55. Kimmerling and Migdal, p. 100.

56. Noam Chomsky, *Middle East Illusions: Including Peace in the Middle East, Reflections on Justice and Nationhood* (London: Rowman & Littlefield, 2003), p. 33.

57. Cohen, p. 97.

58. Noam Chomsky, discussion at http://www.znet.org, Monday, October 06, 2003, posted at http://vancouver.indymedia.org/news/2003/10/71313_comment.php

59. Hirst, p. 140.

60. Cited in Hirst, p. 171.

61. See Finkelstein, pp. 21–50

62. Segev, p. 273

63. From the Jewish National Fund web site: http://www.jnf.org/site/PageServer?pagename=history

64. See Kimmerling and Migdal, p. 100.

65. See Finkelstein, pp. 15, 103.

66. See Michael B. Oren, "Wingate: Friend Under Fire," *Azure*, Winter 2001. http://c4israel.org/articles/english/e-u-01-2-oren-ordewingate.html

67. Aharon Cohen says that even those Zionists who favored the Peel Commission proposal of partition (1937) did so on "the hope that even a puny Jewish state would immediately make possible unhampered immigration and settlement." "Coming generations will take care of the future," argued its proponents. Cohen continues: "Arab leaders, who

had followed the internal Jewish struggle on partition, could read into that enthusiasm an intention to use the proposed Jewish state as a point of departure from which to transform the whole country into a Jewish state in the future." COHEN, P 113.

68. Israeli Ministry of Foreign Affairs, *From Mandate to Independence*. 5 July 1998,
http://www.mfa.gov.il/MFA/Foreign%20Relations/Israels%20Foreign%20Relations%20si nce%201947/1947-1974/FROM%20MANDATE%20TO%20INDEPENDENCE

69. MORRIS, p. 168. Palestinian anxieties were exacerbated by the pronouncements of Zionists outside the mainstream, such as the LEHI and other "revisionist" organizations. Paul Johnson, in *A History of the Jews* (New York: Harpers, 1988), p.588, says that "neo Zionists," when advocating a Greater Israel, "could quote ... from Herzl and Ben-Gurion as well as Jabotinsky." The Jewish Virtual Library states that "Lehi's goals were maximalist: conquest and liberation of Eretz Israel; war against the British Empire; complete withdrawal of Britain from Palestine; and establishment of a "Hebrew kingdom from the Euphrates to the Nile." http://www.jewishvirtuallibrary.org/jsource/History/lehi.html

70. Martin Buber, in PAUL MENDES-FLOHR, ed., *A Land of Two Peoples: Martin Buber on Jews and Arabs* (Gloucester: Peter Smith, 1994), p. 237. Buber also speaks of "the Biltmore Program" (which envisioned Jewish rule over all of Palestine), p. 219. See also Hirst, p. 234ff. He describes how the World Zionist Congress of 1942 pushed Zionism towards explicitly demanding a Jewish state with unrestricted immigration. Immediately after the war, the Zionists specified that their state should be "undiminished and undivided," a formula that ruled out territorial compromise.

71. FISHER, p. 671.

72. DAVID BEN-GURION, *Letters to Paula*, trans. Aubrey Hodes (Pittsburgh: University of Pittsburgh Press, 1971), p. 154f. SEGEV, in *One Palestine Complete* (p. 403), cites two not entirely revealing snippets of this important text.

73. FINKELSTEIN, p. 103. Finkelstein gives helpful references in his own note.

74. See FROMKIN, 263–275.

75. Benny Morris, correspondence with Kathleen Christison, *CounterPunch*. October 2/3, 2004, http://www.counterpunch.org/christi-son10022004.html

76. Even activist Assyrians today demand at most a very limited and subordinate form of "autonomy," and their stated goals contrast vividly with those of Zionism. One Assyrian activist expressed his views as follows: "I assure you that most of the Assyrian people will return to their country if they feel that they are secure in their homeland. We are not demanding to have power, only that we feel secure in our homeland." In such a context, the issue of territorial compromise can't even arise. Note that this Assyrian spokesman, at least, does not appear to believe that distant memories of a cloudy past constitute a contemporary entitlement to political supremacy. See EMMA MARSHALL, "Iraq's Forgotten People."
http://www.zyworld.com/Assyrian/Iraq%E2%80%99s_forgotten_people.htm

77. Similar sentiments were voiced by Chris Patten, former governor of Hong Kong and European commissioner for relations. He wrote: "Europe's recent history of gas chambers and gulags, our 'Christian' heritage of flagrant or more discreet anti-Semitism, do not entitle us to address the Islamic world as though we dwell on a higher plane, custodians of a superior set of moral values." His views are expressed in "Huntington's Logic Isn't Europe's," *The Daily Star*, Lebanon, Friday, July 02, 2004,
http://dailystar.com.lb/article.asp?edition_id=10&categ_id=5&article_id=5814

78. JUDITH JARVIS THOMPSON, "In Defense of Abortion," in *The Rights and Wrongs of Abortion: A Philosophy and Public Affairs Reader* (Princeton: Princeton University Press, 1974), p. 8.

79. See, for instance, FINKELSTEIN, p. 17.

80. In this connection, one must be suspicious of appeals to, for example, the Balfour Declaration, Wilson's 14 principles, and the decisions of the United Nations. In the first two cases, it is patent that Palestinians had not the slightest input into the formulation or application of the principles. In the third, we have an organization over whose actions colonial nations—Britain, France, and the U.S.—all with ambitions in the Middle East, have always held veto power. Their will can be effectively opposed only by Russia and China, who have similar ambitions and certainly cannot claim in any sense to represent anyone in the area. This is quite unlike what is required in private land claims, when the adjudicator is meant to represent a government neutral between, and in some sense representative of, the parties involved. In these circumstances, it is hardly plausible to appeal to "international" principles whose claim to represent world opinion is highly dubious, and whose application is inevitably tainted by unacceptable bias.

81. ISRAEL FINKELSTEIN, and Neil Asher SILBERMAN *The Bible Unearthed: Archaeolog's New Vision of Ancient Israel and the Origin of Its Sacred Texts* (New York: Simon and Schuster, 2003), p. 1.

82. Ibid., p. 202.

83. Ibid., p. 191.

84. See HIRST, p. 135.

85. An exhaustive discussion of this phenomenon may be found in YAKOV M. RABKIN, *Au nom de la Torah: Une histoire de l'opposition juive au sionisme* (Saint-Nicholas, Québèc: Presses de l'Université Laval, 2004).

86. Yakov M. Rabkin, "A Glimmer of Hope: A State of All Its Citizens," *Tikkun.* July/August 2002, http://www.tikkun.org/magazine/index.cfm/action/tikkun/issue/tik0207/article/020711 f.html.

87. Cited in SEGEV, *The Seventh Million* p. 28. Segev, in turn, cites a Hebrew work by Natan Michael Gelber.

88. Ibid., p. 19f. The text of the agreement, with commentary from a contemporary Zionist publication, can be found in LENNI BRENNER, ed., *51 Documents: Zionist Collaboration with the Nazis* (New Jersey: Barricade Books, 2001), pp. 47-49.

89. TOM SEGEV, *The Seventh Million*, p. 29.

90. See HARKABI, p. 218.

91. HERB KEINON, "Yom Kippur War—25 Years Later: A victory remembered as a defeat," *Jerusalem Post*, Friday, October 9, 1998, http://www-origin.jpost.com/com/Archive/09.Oct.1998/Features/Article-12.html

92. MATTHEW DORF, Jewish Telegraphic Agency, "Yom Kippur War changed U.S.-Israel ties." http://www.jewishaz.com/jewishnews/980925/yomkip-pr.shtml, accessed July 13, 2004.

93. ALAIN ROUSSILLON, "Republican Egypt: Revolution and Beyond," in *The Cambridge History of Egypt, Volume Two: Modern Egypt from 1517 to the End of the Twentieth Century* (Cambridge: Cambridge University Press 1998), p. 360f.

94. Ibid., p. 363f.

95. KIMCHE, p. 237.

96. DAVID HOLDEN and RICHARD JOHNS, *The House of Saud* (London: Pan Books, 1982), p. 248.

97. Ibid., p. 253.

98. Ibid., p. 232.

99. Ibid., p. 264.

100. See HIRST, p. 338.

101. WALTER REICH, "The Enemy at the Gates," *New York Times Book Review*, May 23, 1004, p. 14. ALAN DERSHOWITZ takes a somewhat similar line in *A Case for Israel*. (Hoboken: John Wiley, 2003), p. 159.

102. BENNY MORRIS, letter to the *New York Review of Books*, 51:6, April 8, 2004, p. 77.

103. See FINKELSTEIN, pp. 123–149.

104. THOMAS HOBBES, *Leviathan*, II p. 21.

105. Ibid.,

106. It's not clear whether what follows is really less extreme than Hobbes would allow. Hobbes says that resistance is permitted "if it be only to defend their persons," and that the right to resist state authorities ceases if a pardon is offered. This suggests that violent self-defense is a right only if there is no other alternative. Invading aggressors do have another alternative, namely, to withdraw.

107. KIMCHE, p. 260f.

108. Ibid., p. 260.

109. Ibid., p. 264.

110. CHOMSKY, NOAM, *The Fateful Triangle: The United States, Israel and The Palestinians* (Cambridge, Massachusetts: South End Press, 1999), pp. 104.

111. Cited in HIRST, p. 348.

112. HIRST, p. 358, and CHOMSKY, *The Fateful Triangle*, p. 103.

113. Quoted in CHOMSKY, *The Fateful Triangle*, p. 105.

114. Quoted in HIRST, p. 368.

115. CHOMSKY, *The Fateful Triangle*, p. 104.

116. Ibid., p. 481.

117. See, e.g., Kimmerling and Migdal, p. 275f.

118. Harkabi is cited below. Another extensive study is Israel Shahak and Norton Mezvinsky, *Jewish Fundamentalism in Israel* (London: Pluto Press, 1999). The reliability of this work has been contested, but it contains ample citations whose accuracy and significance are easily verifiable. See also Hirst, p. 500 et. seq.

119. Yehoshafat Harkabi, *Israel's Fateful Hour* (New York: Harper and Row, 1988), p. 140.

120. Harkabi, p. 145.

121. Ibid., p. 145f.

122. Ibid., p. 146.

123. Ibid., p. 147f.

124. Ibid., p. 149f.

125. Ibid., p. 153.

126. Cited in Shahak and Mezvinksy, p. 62.

127. Harkabi, p. 144.

128. Amos Elon, "Israelis & Palestinians: What Went Wrong?," *New York Review of Books*, December 19, 2002.

129. Morris, p. 567.

130. Full reference: Amira Hass, *Drinking the Sea at Gaza: Days and Nights in a Land Under Siege*. Translated by Elana Wesley and Maxine Kaufman-Lacusta (New York: Henry Holt and Company, 1999)

131. Ibid.,

132. Gabriel Ash, "Settlements: A User Guide." Printed on Thursday, May 15, 2003 at 12:40:02 CDT. http://www.yellowtimes.org/article.php?sid=1354

133. The patterns are well described in Jeffrey Goldberg, "Among the Settlers: Will They Destroy Israel?" *The New Yorker*, June 17, 2004, Issue of 2004-05-31, Posted 2004-05-24,
http://www.newyorker.com/printables/fact/040531fa_fact2_a

134. "Palestinians Abandon West Bank Village, Citing Attacks, Harassment by Jewish Settlers."
http://abcnews.go.com/wire/World/ap20021019_191.html

135. ROBERT I. FRIEDMAN, "And Darkness Covered the Land." *The Nation*, Sunday, 16 December 2001 (December 24, 2001 Issue),
http://www.bintjbeil.com/articles/en/011216_friedman.html

136. CHRIS McGREAL, "Bitter harvest in West Bank's Olive Groves: Jewish settlers wreck fruit of centuries of toil to force out Palestinian villagers." *The Guardian*, Friday, November 14, 2003,
http://www.guardian.co.uk/israel/Story/0,2763,1084731,00.html

137. On these topics, see "The Socio-economic Impact of Settlements on Land, Water, and the Palestinian Economy," Foundation for Middle East Peace, Washington, DC 1998, http://www.fmep.org/reports/v8n4.html#9

138. HIRST, p. 377.

139. Care International (news release, "Survey Finds High Rates of Malnutrition and Anemia in the West Bank and Gaza Strip," August 05, 2002, the complete survey is available at
http://www.usaid.gov/wbg/reports/Nutritional_Assessment.pdf

140. Cited in MORRIS, p.79. The explanatory insertions in square brackets are his. We have seen Ben-Gurion make the same assumption at 35.

141. FROMKIN, p. 324.

142. Amnesty International, *Israel and the Occupied Territories: Surviving Under Siege: The impact of movement restrictions on the right to work.* September 2003, http://www.amjerusalem.org/pdf/surv-under-sige2.pdf

143. A.J.P. Taylot, English History 1914–1945 (Oxford: Oxford University Press, 1965), p. 152

144. MARTIN LUTHER KING JR., *Why We Can't Wait* (New York: Signet Books, 1964), p. 39f.

145. Even then, nonviolence was taken with a grain of salt. Oliver Tambo, writing as Deputy President of the ANC in 1966, said that "Mahatma [Gandhi] believed in the effectiveness of what he called the 'soul force' in passive resistance. According to him, the suffering experienced in passive resistance inspired a change of heart in the rulers. The African National Congress (ANC), on the other hand, expressly rejected any concepts and methods of struggle that took the form of a self-pitying, arms-folding, and passive reaction to oppressive

policies. It felt that nothing short of aggressive pressure from the masses of the people would bring about any change in the political situation in South Africa."

146. See http://www.peace-security.org.il/engfound.html. This page belongs to the site of the organization and contains ample documentation of its position.

147. RAMI KAPLAN, interview with *The International Herald Tribune*, Tuesday, April 30, 2002.

148. Unlike Hobbes' rebels, the robber has an alternative to defending himself, namely, to withdraw. His violence would not be a legitimate defense of his person, but an illegitimate defense of his invasion. This would violate what Hobbes' "fundamental law of nature," *"That every man, ought to endeavour Peace, as farre as he has hope of obtaining it..."* (Leviathan I.14) In law, too, the right of self-defense applies only when you cannot simply put yourself out of danger.

149. These are amply documented by Human Rights Watch and Amnesty International.

150. ALAN DERSHOWITZ, "Presbyterians' Shameful Boycott," *Los Angeles Times*, August 4, 2004.

151. "Right of return" refers here to the right of Palestinian refugees, and/or their descendants, to return to the homes they lost before 1948. Comically, the phrase is also used to designate the proclaimed right of Jews—even Jews whose great-great-great-great-great grandparents never set foot in Palestine—to become citizens and inhabitants of Israel.

152. Menachem Kleinm, "The Origins of Intifada II and Rescuing Peace for Israelis and Palestinians," a lecture delivered in Washington on October 2, 2002, at the invitation of the Foundation for Middle East Peace and the Middle East Institute.
http://www.pepeace.org/current_reprints/10/Rescuing%20Peace.htm, accessed July 23, 2004.

153. http://www.haaretzdaily.com/hasen/pages/ShArt.jhtml?itemNo=130196&contrassID=2&subContrassID=5&sbSubContrassID=0&listSrc=Y.

154. The address was published in *The Guardian*. Monday, April 29, 2002. It is available at
http://www.guardian.co.uk/israel/comment/0,10551,706911,00.html, accessed July 25, 2004.

155. http://www.anc.org.za/anc/newsbrief/1994/news0715

156. "Nelson Mandela gets warm welcome in Gaza: Former South African leader calls on Israel to pull out of occupied lands," CNN, October 20, 1999, http://www.cnn.com/WORLD/meast/9910/20/mandela.arafat/

157. (London and New Jersey: Zed Books, 1987).

158. *Associated Press*, "Israeli Doctors Criticize Army Roadblocks That Keep Ailing Palestinians From Medical Help," October 29, 2002, http://abcnews.go.com/wire/World/ap20021029_1287.html

159. GIDEON LEVY, "And the Twins Died," *Haaretz*, 8/01/2004 http://www.haaretz.com/hasen/objects/pages/PrintArticleEn.jhtml?itemNo=380975

160. From "Notes of a Native Son" in *Collected Essays*, (New York: Library of America, 1998), p. 29.

161. Colm Tóibín, "The Henry James of Harlem: James Baldwin's struggles," The Guardian, September 14, 2001, http://books.guardian.co.uk/lrb/articles/0,6109,551979,00.html

162. See HIRST, p. 135.

163. An example of the latter: Herut MK Michael Kleiner outraged MKs when he proposed to Sharon that the IDF carpet bomb Palestinian cities. He was responding to Sharon's request that the MKs in the committee propose ways to deal with the terror problem. When Sharon said Israel has no intention of harming the civilian population that is not involved in terror, Kleiner interrupted. "Are the 100,000 people who attended Salah Shehadeh's funeral innocent?" GIDEON ALON, "Sharon to panel: Iraq is our biggest danger," *Haaretz*, August 13, 2002 http://www.haaretzdaily.com/hasen/pages/ShArt.jhtml?itemNo=196942&contrassID=2&subContrassID=1&sbSubContrassID=0&listSrc=Y, that most members of the Knesset were outraged is compatible with the existence of such sentiments in a significant minority of the population.

164. Quoted by Juda L. Magnes, "A Solution through Force?" in ed. Gary V Smith *Zionism: The Dream and the Reality:A Jewish Critique*, (New York: Barnes and Noble, 1973), p. 112.

165. Quoted by Nahum Goldmann, *The Jewish Paradox: A personal memoir of historic encounters that shaped the drama of modern Jewry,* Translated by STEVE COX (New York: Fred Gordon Books/Grosset & Dunlap, 1978), p. 99.

166. ANTHONY V. NAVARRO, "A Critical Comparison Between Japanese and American Propaganda during World War II," http://www.msu.edu/~navarro6/srop.html#U.S.

167. Cited inaccurately in Navarro's paper. The reference is to JOHN SBREGA, *Anglo-American Relations and Colonialism in East Asia, 1941–1945*, (New York: Garland, 1983), p. 285. The original source is Sir Ronald I. Campbell (British Embassy in Washington, D.C.) to Sir Alexander Cadogan (Foreign Office), 6 Aug 1942, PREM 4-42/9, Public Record Office, London. I am indebted to Dr. Sbrega for this information.

168. ALLAN M. WINKLER, "Selling Our Message," *History News Network*, November 24, 2001, http://hnn.us/articles/408.html

169. RUTH HARRIS, "The Child of the Barbarian" *Rape, Race and Nationalism in France during the First World War: Past and Present*, Vol 141, (1993), 188.

170. J.BOWYER BELL, *Terror out of Zion: Irgun Zvai Leumi, LEHI, and the Palestine Underground, 1929–1949*, (New York: St.Martin's Press, 1977), p. 353.

171. From an interview with Chomsky on zmag.org, http://www.zmag.org/chomsky_interview_5.htm, accessed July 25, 2004.

172. From a news story in *The Herald*. The story is no longer available but was last found at
http://www.theherald.co.uk/news/archive/23-5-19103-23-48-54.html

173. MICHAEL RUBNER, review of *Decade of Transition: Eisenhower, Kennedy, and the Origins of the American-Israeli Alliance*, by ABRAHAM BEN-ZVI, *Middle East Policy*, Volume VI, Number 3, February 1999,
http://www.mepc.org/public_asp/journal_vol6/9902_rubner.asp

174. This policy prepared the ground for the emergence of Hamas in the 1980s. See
http://www.pbs.org/newshour/booboo/middle_east/July-dec01/hamas_12-4.html

175. According to Andrew Cordesman, a senior analyst at the Center for Strategic and International Studies in Washington, that Israel could fight for two years before needing U.S. help.
http://www.nj.com/news/ledger/index.ssf?/base/news-1/101834340582787.xml

175. "Lost in Translation: The two minds of Bernard Lewis," *The New Yorker*, Issue of 2004-06-14 and 21, Posted 2004-06-07,
htttp://www.newyorker.com/critics/books/?040614crbo_books.

177. See "Israel Campaign," http://israel.prodos.org/, viewed January 17, 2005.

178. ROBERT ROSENBAUM, "Israel remains vital ally for U.S.," *The News-Press*, December 21, 2004,
http://www.news-press.com/apps/pbcs.dll/article?AID=/20041221/OPINION/412210394/1001/ARCHIVES

179. JULIE CARSON, "All Agree on Israel At Candidate Forum," *Columbia Daily Spectator*, February 16, 2004
http://www.columbiaspectator.com/vnews/display.v/ART/2004/02/16/403083406f800?in_archive=1, and http://sky.prohosting.com/lionpac/aboutus.shtml

180. Paraphrase from "Jewish professor condemns actions of Israel," *Daily Bruin Online*, Wednesday, April 24, 2002,
http://www.dailybruin.ucla.edu/db/articles.asp?ID=19398

181. GARY FITLEBERG, "Only in Israel," *Chronwatch*, Saturday, June 19, 2004, http://www.chronwatch.com/content/contentDisplay.asp?aid=7993

182. Comment at
http://www.aish.com/jewishissues/mediaobjectivity/Standing_Up_for_Israel.asp

183. See http://www.netanyahu.org/greatbeacofl.html

184. "JohnKerry.com—Kerry Statement on the 56th Anniversary of Israel's Independence," http://www.johnkerry.com/communities/jewish_americans/independence.html

185. For example: "1,200 evangelical Christians, coming from Europe and Far East, arrived in Israel these past two days. Tomorrow morning, they will take part at a gathering near the Temple Mount to "support tourism in Israel." This is the largest event of this type since the Intifada started in 2000." (Guysen.Israël.News 6.9.4).

186. BBC, "Expert weighs up Jenin 'massacre'," Monday, April 29, 2002, 14:31 GMT 15:31 UK,
http://news.bbc.co.uk/hi/english/world/middle_east/newsid_1957000/1957862.stm.

187. KIMCHE, p. 270.

188. AMOS ELON, "Israelis and Palestinians: What Went Wrong?" *The New York Review of Books*, December 19, 2002.

189. From *Dreams of an Insomniac: Jewish Feminist Essays, Speeches, and Diatribes*, (Portland: Eighth Mountain Press, 1990), p. 130f.

Index

101st Airborne Division, U.S. Army 132
Abolitionists 182
Abortion 64–65
Abraham 74, 112, 190
Affirmative action 34
African National Congress (ANC) 133–135
African nationalism 19
Aid to Israel, by France 95
Aid to Israel, by U.S. 94, 172–180
Aish 185
Al Qaeda 177
Algeria 17, 19, 123, 138, 156, 169, 187
Ali, Mohammed 42
Al-Khalidi, Yusuf Zia 41
Amalekites, ancient 44, 110–111
American Heritage Dictionary 24
American Revolution 21
American West, settlement of 45–46
Amnesty International 1, 6, 126, 183, 186
Anemia, in Palestinians 120–121
Angola 134
Anti-Semitism 5–6, 150, 152
Apartheid, South Africa 130, 133–135, 149–150, 184
Arab nationalism 122–123
Arab Revolt (1916) 122

Arab-Israeli War (1948) 93
Arabs, stereotypes of 121–123
Arafat, Yasser 48, 50, 99–100, 143, 148–149, 177
Archaeology magazine 73
Ariel, Israeli settlement 116
Ariel, Yisrael 110
Armenians 35, 70
Army, U.S. 132
Ash, Gabriel 115–116
Ashanti 70
Assassination 157
Assimilation, of Jews 82–85
Assyrians 62, 74, 110
Aswan Dam 174–175
Auschwitz death camp 152
Austria 16, 71
Aviner, Rabbi Shlomo 108–109
Avnery, Uri 181
B'tzelem 114
Baghdad Pact (1955) 174
Baldwin, James 150
Balfour Declaration 6–7, 25–27, 38, 45, 46–47, 89
Balfour, David 60
Bandung Conference (1955)
Bangladesh 114
Barak, Ehud 61, 143, 147–148
Bar-Ilan University 110, 146
Belgium 51, 61
Bell, J. Bower 155
Ben-Gurion, Amos 59
Ben-Gurion, David 27–28, 40, 47–48, 50, 52, 55–56, 59, 81, 151
Berbers 17, 123
Bible 67, 73–76, 109
Bible Unearthed, The (Finkelstein) 73–74
Biblical claims to

Palestine 67–76
Bill of Rights, U.S. Constitution 33
Biltmore Program for Palestine (1942) 58
Bin Laden, Osama 169
Bi-nationalism 38–39, 47–48, 50–55, 89
Black September Conflict (1970) 95, 96, 125
Blood and Soil ideology 105–106
Boers 134
Bohemians 70
Bolivia 154
Book of Deuteronomy 110
Book of Joshua 74
Border closures, by Israelis 120
Bosnia 62
Boycott, of South Africa 133–134
British Foreign Office 26, 28
British Raj 130–131
British Royal Commission of Enquiry on Palestine (1928) 28–29
British Royal Commission Report on Palestine (1937) 38–39
Brown vs. the Board of Education 132
Buber, Martin 58
Buddhism 24
Bulgaria 125
Burgundians 70
Buruma, Ian 181, 183–184
Byzantine Empire 71
Camp David Accords (1978) 95, 99, 123
Camp David negotiations (2000) 143, 145–146, 148
Canaan, ancient 74
Canada 16, 28, 33–34
CARE, International 120–121

Catholicism 22, 35
Celts 63, 70
Central Intelligence
Agency (CIA) 126
Chaco War (1928-1935)
61, 154
Chad 98, 120
Checkpoints, Israeli 120,
149-150
Chequers 50
China 14, 63, 67-68, 154,
164
Chinese Revolution 14
Chomsky, Noam 23-24,
48-49, 104-105, 155-157,
159, 168, 181
Churchill, Winston 60
Civil Rights Movement,
U.S. 130, 132-133
Civil War, U.S. 181-182
Clinton, Bill 61
Cohen, Aharon 49
Cohen, Morris 28
Cold War 173-174, 181
Collateral damage, in war
160-163
Collective punishment,
of Palestinians 119-120
Columbia University 155,
185
Congo (Zaire) 64
Council for Peace and
Security 135-136
Croatia 16, 62, 124
Cruise missiles 138,
180-181
Cuba 14, 19, 134
Cuban Revolution 14, 19
Curzon, Lord George 28
Czechoslovakia 174
Danes 70
Davis, Uri 149
Dayan, Gen. Moshe 103,
105, 107-108, 119-121
D-Day (1944) 156
Dead Sea 147
Death camps (Nazi) 60,
64, 152
Declaration of the

*Establishment of the State of
Israel* (1948) 30
Dekel, Michael 113
Democracy 14-15
Denmark 71
Der Judenstaat (Herzl) 41
Dershowitz, Alan 141
Double standards,
applied to Israel 181-183
Dresden, allied firebomb-
ing of 164
Drinking the Sea at Gaza
(Hass) 114
Druze 44
East Jerusalem, annexa-
tion of 105-106
East Timor 156
Egypt 42-43, 93-95, 100,
102, 123, 138, 142,
173-175, 178, 187
Eisenhower, Dwight D.
132
Elon, Amos 114-115,
189-190
English Civil War 14
English Revolution 14, 17
Ethnic cleansing 7, 46-47,
64, 128
Ethnic identity, of Jews
22-24
Ethnic identity, of
Palestinians 20-21
Ethnic nationalism 17-19,
54-55, 78, 89, 187-188
Ethnic purity 19-20
Eugenics 15
European Union
147-148, 173
Fascism 78, 105, 108
Fatah 100
Feisal, King of Saudi
Arabia 96-97, 123
Final Solution (Nazis) 67,
76-79
Finkelstein, Israel 73-74
Finkelstein, Norman 4,
38, 59, 181
Fisher, Sydney Nettleton
58

Fitleberg, Gary 185
Flemish 62
Fourteen Points 7, 13
France 14, 24-25, 29, 41,
62, 95, 122, 139, 153
French Revolution 14, 17
Gandhi, Mohandas K.
130-131, 133
Gaza 90, 93, 99, 114-115,
120-121, 127-128, 144
Gazit, Shlomo 103
Geneva Conventions 162
Genocide 89-90, 110-111,
156
Genocide, as divine com-
mandment 110-111
George, Lloyd 26, 60
Germany 15-16, 34, 62,
71-72, 76-79, 81
Ginsburg, Rabbi 112
Global Management
Consulting Group
120-121
Golan Heights 95, 105,
126
Great Britain 7, 14, 21-22,
24-25, 38, 41, 44-45, 56,
60, 71, 73, 81, 103-104,
123, 182
Great Calcutta Killing
(1946) 131
Greater Israel platform
95
Greece 67-68, 153
Greeks, ancient 71
Greeks, of Alexandria 62
Guernica, bombing of
(1937) 164
Gulf War (1990-1991) 180
Gush Emunim 108
Gypsies 16
Hadrian's Wall 83
Haganah 135-136
Hamas 177
Hamburg, allied fire-
bombing of 164
Hapsburg Empire 61
Harkabi, Maj. Gen.
Yohoshafat 90, 108-109

Harvard University 155
Hass, Amira 114
Hawk missile 173
Haycraft Commission (1921) 50
Hebrew language 22
Hebrew University 39, 111
Hebron Riots (1929) 38
Herzl, Theodore 25-26, 41, 54
Hess, Rabbi Yisrael 110
Hiroshima, nuking of 64, 164
Hirst, David 25
Historical claims to Palestine 67-76
Hitler, Adolf 49, 67, 76-79, 80, 152, 163
Hizbollah 138, 177
Hobbes, Thomas 101
Holley, David 186-187
Holocaust 190
Holocaust compensation 78-79
Holocaust Museum, U.S. 99
Home demolition, of Palestinians 118-120
Horovitz, David 99, 142
Human rights violations, by Arab states 181-184
Human Rights Watch 1, 6, 181, 183
Hussein, King of Jordan 96, 103-104, 105
Hussein, Saddam 101, 178-179
Hutus 17
Iceland 58
Immigration, Jewish to Palestine 51-54
India 17, 130-131, 182
International law 6
Intifada I (1987-1993) 99, 130
Iran 96, 177, 180-181
Iran/Iraq War (1980-1988) 96

Iraq 62, 95-96, 137, 160-161, 178-179
Irgun 56
Irish Republican Army 133
Islam 24, 64, 75, 177
Israel in the Age of Terrorism (Horovitz) 99
Israel, ancient Kingdom of 73-76
Israel, as Jewish state 24-26, 33-34
Israel, establishment of 86-89
Israel: an Apartheid State (Davis) 149
Israeli Defense Forces (IDF) 108, 113, 115, 117, 119, 130, 136, 138
Israeli Ministry of Foreign Affairs 30, 57-58
Israeli Occupation, origins of 93-94; as strategic defense, 93-101; and settler movement 103-106; as ethnic cleansing 109-118; consequences for Palestinians 119-128
Israeli settlements, 100, 102-106, 107-128, 171-173
Israeli settler ideology 110-114
Italy 12-13, 71, 79
Jabotinsky, Vladimir 121-122, 151
Jaffa Riots (1921) 37
Jamaica 35, 140
Japan 63, 88, 131, 152
Japanese, racial stereotypes of 152-153
Japanese-Americans, internment of 43
Jenin, Israeli raid on 186-187
Jerusalem Institute for Israeli Studies 146
Jerusalem Riots (1920) 38
Jewish Agency 58-59, 81
Jewish Awareness

Movement 185
Jewish Chronicle 28
Jewish National Fund 53-54, 176
Jewish people, definition of 20-22
Jewish self-defense 67, 79-85
Jewish sovereignty 36-37
Jewish Virtual Library 30
Jewish Week 111-112
Johns Hopkins University 120-121
Johnson, Lyndon B. 132
Jordan 48, 95 97, 102-105, 113, 125-126, 138, 142, 178-179
Jordanian Option, for removal of Palestinians 125-126
Judah, ancient 74
Jutes 70
Karsh, Efraim 4
Kennedy, John F. 132
Kerry, John 186
Khatib, Rutti 106
Khmer 70
Kibbutz Youth Federation 105
Kimche, Jon 102-104, 188-189
Kimmerling, Baruch 20-21, 47-48
King, Martin Luther Jr. 132-133, 134
Kivvunium 111
Klatzko, Rabbi Benzion 185
Klein, Menachem 146-147
Klepfisz, Irena 190
Kook, Rabbi Zvi Yehudah 108-109
Korean War 164
Krdlicka, Professor Josef 153
Kuwait, invasion of (1990) 101
Land claims, adjudica-

tion of 72–73
Land purchases, Jewish in Palestine 53–54
Lansing, Robert 29
Laquer, Walter 29
Law of inheritance 68–69
Lebanese Civil War 51
Lebanese Constitution 47
Lebanon 46–47, 51–52, 95, 122–123, 125, 138, 178
Leopold, King of Belgium 64
Lewis, Bernard 181, 183–184
Libya 96, 180
Likud Party 95, 112
LionPAC 185
Louis XIV, King of France 61
Luthuli, Albert 133
Magyars 70
Maimonides 75–76
Malnutrition, in Palestinian children 120–121
Mandela, Nelson 149
Mapai Party (Israel) 47
Maronites 44
Marxism 96–97
MASH 167
McGreal, Chris 118
Meir, Golda 20–21, 104, 136
Mennonites 24
Merkava tank 11
Merriam-Webster Dictionary 23–24
Messianic settler movements 108–109
Mexico 16, 23
Migdal, Joel S. 20–21, 47–48
MIT 155
MK (Umkhonto we Sizwe) 133
Modise, Joseph 149
Moedet Party 113
Moral philosophy 4
Moral theory 63–64

Moratinos, Amb. Miguel 147–148
Morocco 22, 182
Morris, Benny 4, 27, 58, 87, 99–100, 113, 122, 142
Moses 74
Moslem Brotherhood, Israeli aid to 177
Mount Lebanon Massacre (1860) 44
Mozambique 134
Nagasaki nuking of 164
Nakhal Brigade (IDF) 115
Nasser, Gamal Adel 96, 122–123, 173–175
National Conference of American Zionists (1942) 57–58
National Guard, U.S. 132
Native Americans 17, 46, 62–63, 71–72, 154
Nazism 15, 60, 64, 72, 76–79, 81, 83–84, 86, 105, 141, 152, 164, 190
Neoconservatives, U.S. 165
Netanyahu, Benjamin 186
Nigeria 120
Nisan, Mordechai 111
Nixon, Richard 179–180
Nobel Peace Prize committee 186
Non-exclusive Zionism 37–38
Non-violent resistance, as option for Palestinians 129–131
Nordau, Max 25–26
North Korea 181
Northern Ireland 124
Nuclear non-proliferation 180–181
Nuclear weapons, Israeli 94–95, 97, 137–138, 140, 180–181
Nutritional Assessment Survey of Palestinians 120–121

Occupied Territories 11, 93–98, 100–106
Oil, as motive for U.S.-Israeli alliance 178–179
Olive groves, destruction of 114, 116, 118
Organisation de l'Armée Secrète 156
Orthodox Judaism 75–76
Osiraq nuclear plant, Israeli bombing of (1981) 137
Ottoman Empire 14, 41–43, 46, 70, 71, 103–104, 122
Pakistan 138, 180–181
Palestine Revolt (1834) 42
Palestinian Liberation Organization (PLO) 143–144
Palestinian people, definition of 20–22
Palestinian People, The (Kimmerling) 20–21
Palestinian resistance 63–66, 118–120, 130–135
Palestinian Revolt (1936) 63
Palestinian self-defense 86, 100–101
Palestinian sovereignty 145–146
Paraguay 154
Partition, of Palestine 55, 62
Peters, Joan 52
Pinochet, Gen. Augusto 186
Playboy magazine 39
Pogroms, in Russia 80–81
Poland 16, 71–72
Pollution, by Israeli settlers 118
Portugal 71
Premises for a Determination of a Government in Palestine (1930) 48–49
Presbyterian Church, resolution on Israeli

Occupation 141
Prodos Institute 185
Property rights 69
Quemoy and Matsu Crisis (1955) 174
Rabbo, Yasir 147
Rabin, Yitzak 136
Race liberation 14-15
Racial destiny 108
Racial hatred 150
Racial supremacy 110-112
Racism 18-19, 34-35, 78
Reagan, Ronald 176
Red Sea 126
Refugee camps, in Gaza 114-115
Reich, Walter 99
Reverse racism 34-35
Right of conquest 7
Right of return, for Palestinians 127, 139, 145
Right to exist, Israel's 89-90
Righteous Victims (Morris) 122
Roman Empire 71
Romans, ancient 71, 118
Roosevelt, Franklin D. 153
Roth, Kenneth 181
Rothschild, Lord Walter 60
Rubinstein, Ammon 110
Rumsfeld, Donald 156
Russia 14, 16, 22, 71
Russian Revolution 14
Rwandan Genocide 17, 156
Sadat, Anwar 95, 97
Sampson Option, Israeli nuclear weapons 94-95, 97, 137-138, 140, 180-181
Saudi Arabia 96, 173, 179-180
Security buffer zone, Israeli 136-137
Segev, Tom 25, 81
Segregation, in U.S. 184
Self-defense, right of 100-101
Self-determination, right of 12-14, 15-17, 23, 35
Sennacherib 110
September 11, 2001, attacks of 169, 177
Serbia 16, 123
Shamir, Yitzak 113
Sharon, Gen. Ariel 147-148
Shatila and Sabra Massacre (1982) 125
Shiloh, Israeli settlement 115
Shin Bet 136
Silberman, Neil Asher 73-74
Sinai Peninsula 126
Sinn Fein 133
Six Day War (1967) 90, 93, 95, 100
Slave trade 182
Smithsonian Institute 153
Sobih, Kamal 117
Socialism 23-24, 40
South Africa 130, 133-135
Soweto Riots (1976) 133-134
Spain 71, 79
Spanish Civil War 153
Special Night Squads 56
Star Trek 36
State terrorism 158, 160, 163-164
Sudan 97
Sudentenland 16
Suez Canal 126, 131, 174
Supreme Allied Council 29
Supreme Court, U.S. 132
Switzerland 61
Syria 46, 95-96, 122, 125-126, 178-180, 187
Taba negotiations (2000) 143, 145, 147-148
Talmud 76
Targeting of civilians, in war 159-161
Taylor, A.J.P. 131
Tel Aviv University 73
Terror Out of Zion (Bell) 155
Terrorism 7, 98-99
Terrorism, definitions of 155-157
Terrorism, justifications for 162-167
Terrorism, morality of 159-162
Terrorism, reasons for 166-168
Third Army, Egyptian 94
Thirty Years War (1618-1648) 45
Thompson, Judith Jarvis 64-65
Tokyo, U.S. firebombing of 164
Torah 75-76, 108-110, 112
Transfer Agreement (1933) 81
Transfer policy, for Palestinians 4, 27, 44, 81, 87
Trotsky, Leon 31
Turkey 14, 17, 26, 42, 67-68, 71, 73, 122, 153
Tutu, Archbishop Desmond 149
Uganda, as potential Jewish state 79, 84-85
Unilateral withdrawal, from Occupied Territories 135-137
United Nations 6, 13, 30, 89, 137, 162, 173, 180
United Nations Charter 13
United Nations Resolution 242 106
United Nations resolutions 6-7, 106
United States 14, 16, 19, 21, 33, 36, 61, 71, 77, 90, 94-95, 126, 132-133, 139, 149, 159-160
U.S.S Cole, attack on (2000) 257

USS Liberty, Israeli attack on (1967) 176
USSR 49, 94, 95-97, 173-174, 180
Utilitarianism 5
Versailles Peace Conference (1919) 13, 47
Vietnam War 19, 154, 156, 160, 166-167
Violent resistance 46-47
Wahabism 177
Walloons 62
War crimes laws 6
War in the Air (Wells) 164
War on Terror, U.S. 155, 175
Warsaw Ghetto Uprising (1943) 156, 190
Weber, Max 31-32, 33
Weimar Republic (Germany) 34, 43
Weizmann, Chaim 26-27, 29, 47, 52, 60, 123
Wells, H.G. 164
Werhmacht 101
West Bank 90, 93, 99, 103, 114, 120-121, 127-128, 144
White nationalists 142,
White supremacism 19, 142
Wilson, Woodrow 7, 13-14, 15, 17-18, 35
World Fact Book (CIA) 126
World War One 7, 13, 35, 122, 131, 153, 164, 179
World War Two 43, 60, 64, 131, 160, 163-164, 176
World Zionist Conference (1945) 58
World Zionist Organization 111
Yariv, Aharon 135-136
Yediot Aharanot 147
Yeman 97
Yom Kippur War (1973) 93-94, 179
Young, Herbert 26
Yugoslav National Council 17
Yugoslavia 17, 51, 61
Zangwill, Israel 43-44
Ze'evi Rehav'am 113
Zionism, definition of 3, 11-12; origins of 23-30; demands for Jewish state 34-40; international support for 41-46; Nazi persecution as justification for 76-79; as Jewish self-defense 79-86
Zippori, Mordechai 113

Available from CounterPunch/AK Press

Call 1-800-840-3683 or order online from www.counterpunch.org or www.akpress.org

The Case Against Israel
by Michael Neumann

Wielding a buzzsaw of logic, Professor Neumann dismantles plank-by-plank the Zionist rationale for Israel as religious state entitled to trample upon the basic human rights of non-Jews. Along the way, Neumann also offers a passionate amicus brief for the plight of the Palestinian people.

Other Lands Have Dreams: From Baghdad to Pekin Prison
by Kathy Kelly

At a moment when so many despairing peace activists have thrown in the towel, Kathy Kelly, a witness to some of history's worst crimes, never relinquishes hope. *Other Lands Have Dreams* is literary testimony of the highest order, vividly recording the secret casualties of our era, from the hundreds of thousands of Iraqi children inhumanely denied basic medical care, clean water and food by the U.S. overlords to young mothers sealed inside the sterile dungeons of American prisons in the name of the merciless war on drugs.

Dime's Worth of Difference: Beyond the Lesser of Two Evils
Edited by Alexander Cockburn and Jeffrey St. Clair

Everything you wanted to know about one-party rule in America.

Whiteout: the CIA, Drugs and the Press
by Alexander Cockburn and Jeffrey St. Clair, Verso.

The involvement of the CIA with drug traffickers is a story that has slouched into the limelight every decade or so since the creation of the Agency. In *Whiteout*, here at last is the full saga.

Been Brown So Long It Looked Like Green to Me: The Politics of Nature
by Jeffrey St. Clair, Common Courage Press.

Covering everything from toxics to electric power plays, St. Clair draws a savage profile of how money and power determine the state of our environment, gives a vivid account of where the environment stands today and what to do about it.

Imperial Crusades: Iraq, Afghanistan and Yugoslavia
by Alexander Cockburn and Jeffrey St. Clair, Verso.

A chronicle of the lies that are now returning each and every day to haunt the deceivers in Washington and London, the secret agendas and the underreported carnage of these wars. We were right and they were wrong, and this book proves the case. Never leave home without it.

Why We Publish CounterPunch
By Alexander Cockburn and Jeffrey St. Clair

Ten years ago we felt unhappy about the state of radical journalism. It didn't have much edge. It didn't have many facts. It was politically timid. It was dull. *CounterPunch* was founded. We wanted it to be the best muckraking newsletter in the country. We wanted it to take aim at the consensus of received wisdom about what can and cannot be reported. We wanted to give our readers a political roadmap they could trust.

A decade later we stand firm on these same beliefs and hopes. We think we've restored honor to muckraking journalism in the tradition of our favorite radical pamphleteers: Edward Abbey, Peter Maurin and Ammon Hennacy, *Appeal to Reason*, Jacques René Hébert, Tom Paine and John Lilburne.

Every two weeks *CounterPunch* gives you jaw-dropping exposés on: Congress and lobbyists; the environment; labor; the National Security State.

"*CounterPunch* kicks through the floorboards of lies and gets to the foundation of what is really going on in this country", says Michael Ratner, attorney at the Center for Constitutional Rights. "At our house, we fight over who gets to read *CounterPunch* first. Each issue is like spring after a cold, dark winter."

The Politics of Anti-Semitism

Edited by Alexander Cockburn and Jeffrey St. Clair

What constitutes genuine anti-Semitism—Jew-hatred—as opposed to disingenuous, specious charges of "anti-Semitism" hurled at realistic, rational appraisals of the state of Israel's political, military and social conduct?

There's no more explosive topic in American public life today than the issue of Israel, its treatment of Palestinians and its influence on American politics.

Yet the topic is one that is so hedged with anxiety, fury and fear, that honest discussion is often impossible.

The Politics of Anti-Semitism lifts this embargo.

Powerful Essays By

Michael Neumann	Scott Handleman
Alexander Cockburn	Lenni Brenner
Uri Avnery	Linda Belanger
Bruce Jackson	Robert Fisk
Kurt Nimmo	Will Youmans
M. Shahid Alam	Norman Finkelstein
Jeffrey St. Clair	Jeffrey Blankfort
George Sunderland	Kathleen and Bill Christison
Yigal Bronner	Edward Said

Other Lands Have Dreams

From Baghdad to Pekin Prison
Kathy Kelly

At a moment when so many despairing peace activists have thrown in the towel, Kathy Kelly, a witness to some of history's worst crimes, never relinquishes hope. *Other Lands Have Dreams* is literary testimony of the highest order, vividly recording the secret casualties of our era, from the hundreds of thousands of Iraqi children inhumanely denied basic medical care, clean water and food by the US overlords to young mothers sealed inside the sterile dungeons of American prisons in the name of the merciless war on drugs.

WHAT OTHERS HAVE SAID

"She is a direct descendant of Dorothy Day, who when asked why she was making so much trouble for the authorities answered simply, 'I'm working toward a world in which it would be easier for people to behave decently.'"
Studs Terkel, author, *Hope Dies Last*

"The work of Kathleen Kelly ... represents a comprehensive approach to the problem of economic sanctions against Iraq and the devastation wrought on the population of that country, particularly the children."
American Friends Service Committee
Letter nominating Kathy Kelly for 2000 Nobel Peace Prize

AK Press

Ordering Information

AK Press
674-A 23rd Street
Oakland, CA 94612-1163
U.S.A
(510) 208-1700
www.akpress.org
akpress@akpress.org

AK Press
PO Box 12766
Edinburgh, EH8 9YE
Scotland
(0131) 555-5165
www.akuk.com
ak@akedin.demon.co.uk

The addresses above would be delighted to provide you with the latest complete AK catalog, featuring several thousand books, pamphlets, zines, audio products, video products, and stylish apparel published & distributed by AK Press. Alternatively, check out our websites for the complete catalog, latest news and updates, events, and secure ordering.

Also Available from AK Press

The first audio collection from Alexander Cockburn on compact disc.

Beating the Devil

Alexander Cockburn, ISBN: 1 902593 49 9 • CD • $14.98

In this collection of recent talks, maverick commentator Alexander Cockburn defiles subjects ranging from Colombia to the American presidency to the Missile Defense System. Whether he's skewering the fallacies of the war on drugs or illuminating the dark crevices of secret government, his erudite and extemporaneous style warms the hearts of even the stodgiest cynics of the left.

Additional Titles from AK Press

Books:

MARTHA ACKELSBERG – Free Women of Spain

KATHY ACKER – Pussycat Fever

MICHAEL ALBERT – Moving Forward: Program for a Participatory Economy

JOEL ANDREAS – Addicted to War: Why the U.S. Can't Kick Militarism

JOEL ANDREAS – Adicto a la Guerra: Por que EEUU no Puede LIbrarse del Militarismo

PAUL AVRICH – Anarchist Voices

PAUL AVRICH – The Modern School Movement: Anarchism and Education in the United States

PAUL AVRICH – Russian Anarchists

ALEXANDER BERKMAN – What is Anarchism?

ALEXANDER BERKMAN – The Blast: The Complete Collection

HAKIM BEY – Immediatism

JANET BIEHL & PETER STAUDENMAIER – Ecofascism: Lessons From The German Experience

BIOTIC BAKING BRIGADE – Pie Any Means Necessary: The Biotic Baking Brigade Cookbook

JACK BLACK – You Can't Win

MURRAY BOOKCHIN – Anarchism, Marxism, and the Future of the Left

MURRAY BOOKCHIN – Ecology of Freedom

MURRAY BOOKCHIN – Post-Scarcity Anarchism

MURRAY BOOKCHIN – Social Anarchism or Lifestyle Anarchism: An Unbridgeable Chasm

MURRAY BOOKCHIN – Spanish Anarchists: The Heroic Years 1868–1936, The

MURRAY BOOKCHIN – To Remember Spain: The Anarchist and Syndicalist Revolution of 1936

MURRAY BOOKCHIN – Which Way for the Ecology Movement?

MAURICE BRINTON – For Workers' Power

DANNY BURNS – Poll Tax Rebellion

MAT CALLAHAN – The Trouble With Music

CHRIS CARLSSON – Critical Mass: Bicycling's Defiant Celebration

JAMES CARR – Bad

NOAM CHOMSKY – At War With Asia

NOAM CHOMSKY – Chomsky on Anarchism

NOAM CHOMSKY – Language and Politics

NOAM CHOMSKY – Radical Priorities

WARD CHURCHILL – On the Justice of Roosting Chickens: Reflections on the Consequences of U.S. Imperial Arrogance and Criminality

WARD CHURCHILL – Since Predator Came

HARRY CLEAVER – Reading Capital Politically

ALEXANDER COCKBURN & JEFFREY ST. CLAIR (ed.) – Dime's Worth of Difference

ALEXANDER COCKBURN & JEFFREY ST. CLAIR (ed.) – Politics of Anti-Semitism, The

ALEXANDER COCKBURN & JEFFREY ST. CLAIR (ed.) – Serpents in the Garden

DANIEL & GABRIEL COHN-BENDIT – Obsolete Communism: The Left-Wing Alternative

EG SMITH COLLECTIVE – Animal Ingredients A–Z (3rd edition)

VOLTAIRINE de CLEYRE – Voltairine de Cleyre Reader

HOWARD EHRLICH – Reinventing Anarchy, Again

SIMON FORD – Realization and Suppression of the Situationist International: An
Annotated Bibliography 1972-1992
YVES FREMION & VOLNY – Orgasms of History: 3000 Years of Spontaneous Revolt
BERNARD GOLDSTEIN – Five Years in the Warsaw Ghetto
AGUSTIN GUILLAMON – Friends Of Durruti Group, 1937-1939, The
ANN HANSEN – Direct Action: Memoirs Of An Urban Guerilla
WILLIAM HERRICK – Jumping the Line: The Adventures and Misadventures of an
American Radical
FRED HO – Legacy to Liberation: Politics & Culture of Revolutionary Asian/Pacific
America
STEWART HOME – Neoism, Plagiarism & Praxis
STEWART HOME – Neoist Manifestos / The Art Strike Papers
STEWART HOME – No Pity
STEWART HOME – Red London
KATHY KELLY – Other Lands Have Dreams: From Baghdad to Pekin Prison
JAMES KELMAN – Some Recent Attacks: Essays Cultural And Political
KEN KNABB – Complete Cinematic Works of Guy Debord
KATYA KOMISARUK – Beat the Heat: How to Handle Encounters With Law
Enforcement
RICARDO FLORES MAGÓN – Dreams of Freedom: A Ricardo Flores Magón Reader
NESTOR MAKHNO – Struggle Against The State & Other Essays, The
G.A. MATIASZ – End Time
CHERIE MATRIX – Tales From the Clit
ALBERT MELTZER – Anarchism: Arguments For & Against
ALBERT MELTZER – I Couldn't Paint Golden Angels
RAY MURPHY – Siege Of Gresham
NORMAN NAWROCKI – Rebel Moon
HENRY NORMAL – Map of Heaven, A
HENRY NORMAL – Dream Ticket
HENRY NORMAL – Fifteenth of February
HENRY NORMAL – Third Person
FIONBARRA O'DOCHARTAIGH – Ulster's White Negroes: From Civil Rights To
Insurrection
DAN O'MAHONY – Four Letter World
CRAIG O'HARA – Philosophy Of Punk, The
ANTON PANNEKOEK – Workers' Councils
BEN REITMAN – Sister of the Road: The Autobiography of Boxcar Bertha
PENNY RIMBAUD – Diamond Signature, The
PENNY RIMBAUD – Shibboleth: My Revolting Life
RUDOLF ROCKER – Anarcho-Syndicalism
RUDOLF ROCKER – London Years, The
RON SAKOLSKY & STEPHEN DUNIFER – Seizing the Airwaves: A Free Radio
Handbook
ROY SAN FILIPPO – New World In Our Hearts: 8 Years of Writings from the Love and
Rage Revolutionary Anarchist Federation, A
ALEXANDRE SKIRDA – Facing the Enemy: A History Of Anarchist Organisation From
Proudhon To May 1968
ALEXANDRE SKIRDA – Nestor Mahkno – Anarchy's Cossack
VALERIE SOLANAS – Scum Manifesto
CJ STONE – Housing Benefit Hill & Other Places
ANTONIO TELLEZ – Sabate: Guerilla Extraordinary
MICHAEL TOBIAS – Rage and Reason

TOM VAGUE – Anarchy in the UK: The Angry Brigade
TOM VAGUE – Great British Mistake, The
TOM VAGUE – Televisionaries
JAN VALTIN – Out of the Night
RAOUL VANEIGEM – Cavalier History Of Surrealism, A
FRANCOIS EUGENE VIDOCQ – Memoirs of Vidocq: Master of Crime
MARK J WHITE – Idol Killing, An
JOHN YATES – Controlled Flight Into Terrain
JOHN YATES – September Commando
BENJAMIN ZEPHANIAH – Little Book of Vegan Poems
BENJAMIN ZEPHANIAH – School's Out
HELLO – 2/15: The Day The World Said NO To War
DARK STAR COLLECTIVE – Beneath the Paving Stones: Situationists and the Beach, May 68
DARK STAR COLLECTIVE – Quiet Rumours: An Anarcha-Feminist Reader
ANONYMOUS – Test Card F
CLASS WAR FEDERATION – Unfinished Business: The Politics of Class War

CDs

THE EX – 1936: The Spanish Revolution
MUMIA ABU JAMAL – 175 Progress Drive
MUMIA ABU JAMAL – All Things Censored Vol.1
MUMIA ABU JAMAL – Spoken Word
FREEDOM ARCHIVES – Chile: Promise of Freedom
FREEDOM ARCHIVES – Prisons on Fire: George Jackson, Attica & Black Liberation
FREEDOM ARCHIVES – Robert F. Williams: Self-defense, Self-respect & Self-determination
JUDI BARI – Who Bombed Judi Bari?
JELLO BIAFRA – Become the Media
JELLO BIAFRA – Beyond The Valley of the Gift Police
JELLO BIAFRA – High Priest of Harmful
JELLO BIAFRA – I Blow Minds For A Living
JELLO BIAFRA – If Evolution Is Outlawed
JELLO BIAFRA – Machine Gun In The Clown's Hand
JELLO BIAFRA – No More Cocoons
NOAM CHOMSKY – American Addiction, An
NOAM CHOMSKY – Case Studies in Hypocrisy
NOAM CHOMSKY – Emerging Framework of World Power
NOAM CHOMSKY – Free Market Fantasies
NOAM CHOMSKY – Imperial Presidency, The
NOAM CHOMSKY – New War On Terrorism: Fact And Fiction
NOAM CHOMSKY – Propaganda and Control of the Public Mind
NOAM CHOMSKY – Prospects for Democracy
NOAM CHOMSKY/CHUMBAWAMBA – For A Free Humanity: For Anarchy
WARD CHURCHILL – Doing Time: The Politics of Imprisonment
WARD CHURCHILL – In A Pig's Eye: Reflections on the Police State, Repression, and Native America
WARD CHURCHILL – Life in Occupied America
WARD CHURCHILL – Pacifism and Pathology in the American Left
ALEXANDER COCKBURN – Beating the Devil: The Incendiary Rants of Alexander Cockburn
ANGELA DAVIS – Prison Industrial Complex, The

NORMAN FINKELSTEIN - An Issue of Justice
JAMES KELMAN - Seven Stories
TOM LEONARD - Nora's Place and Other Poems 1965-99
CASEY NEILL - Memory Against Forgetting
CHRISTIAN PARENTI - Taking Liberties: Policing, Prisons and Surveillance in an Age of Crisis
UTAH PHILLIPS - I've Got To know
UTAH PHILLIPS - Starlight on the Rails CD box set
DAVID ROVICS - Behind the Barricades: Best of David Rovics
ARUNDHATI ROY - Come September
VARIOUS - Better Read Than Dead
VARIOUS - Less Rock, More Talk
VARIOUS - Mob Action Against the State: Collected Speeches from the Bay Area Anarchist Bookfair
VARIOUS - Monkeywrenching the New World Order
VARIOUS - Return of the Read Menace
HOWARD ZINN - Artists In A Time of War
HOWARD ZINN - Heroes and Martyrs: Emma Goldman, Sacco & Vanzetti, and the Revolutionary Struggle
HOWARD ZINN - People's History of the United States: A Lecture at Reed College, A
HOWARD ZINN - People's History Project
HOWARD ZINN - Stories Hollywood Never Tells

DVDs

NOAM CHOMSKY - Distorted Morality
ARUNDHATI ROY - Instant Mix Imperial Democracy
HOWARD ZINN - Readings from Voices of a People's History